Fine
WoodWorking
Design Book Two

Fine
WoodWorking
Design Book Two

1,150 PHOTOGRAPHS
OF THE BEST WORK IN WOOD
BY 1,000 CRAFTSMEN

SELECTED BY THE EDITORS
OF FINE WOODWORKING MAGAZINE

The Taunton Press

Cover photographs:

Neal M. Widett & Susan C. Wilson *(top left & p. 98)*
Boston, Mass.
Detail of butcher-block window-box table; photo by Ron Harrod.

Gerald C. Nash *(top right & p. 230)*
Santa Monica, Calif.
Detail of wall-hung cabinet: photo by Erik Nash.

Dean Torges & Don Warman *(bottom left & p. 69)*
Ostrander, Ohio.
Detail of glass & hickory dining table; photo by George Anderson.

Charles McDonough *(bottom center & p. 276)*
Glastonbury, Conn.
Satyr peghead for a guitar; photo by Color Teknika Inc.

Alvin & Velma Weaver *(bottom right & p. 123)*
Kansas City, Kans.
Detail of Chinese desk.

Stephen Laurence Casey *(back cover)*
Sepulveda, Calif.
Zipper; koa and cherry; 40 x 24.

First printing: September 1979
Second printing: February 1981
The Taunton Press, Inc.
52 Church Hill Road
Box 355
Newtown, Connecticut 06470

Hardcover.International Standard Book Number: 0-918804-08-6
Paperback International Standard Book Number: 0-918804-07-8
Library of Congress Catalog Card Number: 78-68950
Printed in the United States of America

CONTENTS

INTRODUCTION

Things made of wood are all around us, and have been since the beginnings of civilization. Although we think of the Stone Age as the beginning, a moment's thought will convince you that a Wooden Age must have come first, must have continued alongside as newer materials were discovered, and is still with us today. Think about your last stroll through the woods or along the beach. Did you first pick up a stone, or was a stick the handier implement—for aid in walking, for poking at something mysterious, for digging out an interesting stone. You can fashion the new tool with bare hands, tidy the bark, trim off twigs, break it to length. Then you might dig out a sharp-edged stone to help shape your new tool. A wooden implement is almost as perishable as flesh itself, and such artifacts did not survive for archaeological scrutiny. Nonetheless, most of our houses are still made of wood, most of our furniture is wooden, and much of our plastic is made to look like wood. Every window, every door is surrounded by intricately shaped bits of wood. We take for granted the skills and the technology that make wood, even today, our most convenient material.

How often do we point to a lovely construction detail in an old house and lament, "Of course, nobody does work like this anymore?" The truth is, many craftsmen still do work just "like this" and better, and they have been doing it all along. Have you ever muttered, as you trash the disintegrating remains of a cheap piece of furniture, "They sure don't make 'em like they used to?" The truth is, they never did make 'em like they used to. We are liable to assume that everything used to be better than it is today. But the contemporary craftsman working in wood, with modern tools, techniques and materials, is able to do more work, more varied work, and better work than his ancestors could have imagined.

Where this book came from
This book of 1,150 photographs is a documentary catalog of the state of the woodworker's art. All of the furniture, tools, musical instruments and accessories shown here were made since 1975—they are all contemporary pieces by contemporary woodworkers. And all of the photographs were initially chosen by the craftsmen themselves to represent their best work.

Design Book Two is the second book of photographs compiled by the editors of *Fine Woodworking* magazine. Our publishing venture began in 1975 as a slim quarterly journal dedicated to furthering the arts of design and construction in wood. As we had suspected, there are many more avid woodworkers in America than anyone had realized—today we print 150,000 copies of *Fine Woodworking* every two months. In the fall of 1976, we published an open invitation to our readers to send us photographs of their best work, for publication in book form. The result staggered us—thousands of photographs from hundreds of craftsmen—and we compiled them into *Fine Woodworking's Biennial Design Book*. It was two-thirds as thick as the volume you are holding now, and some of the photos were murky at best. But it was tangible proof that the woodworking arts were alive and well, and we sold 60,000 copies. It quickly became a standard reference among woodworkers, for both design ideas and approaches to construction.

Many people who were not woodworkers also saw that first book. Their delight made it clear that the very existence of such craftsmanship was hot news. It seemed a revelation to learn that good furniture could be made to measure or made to suit a particular taste, for about the same price as good-quality factory furniture. All you needed was a way to find the right craftsman.

So in 1978 we repeated our invitation for woodworkers to send us their photographs. More than 3,500 of them responded, with more than 12,000 pictures of things they had made. If you are a woodworker, you'll be able to imagine the incredible number of shop hours these photographs represented, the gallons of sweat and tears, as well as some blood. After we had winnowed the collection down to 1,150 photos for publication, we polled the woodworkers to find out who considered himself a professional looking for new business, and who was an amateur working wood for his own needs. The surprising result was, 80 percent of the woodworkers represented here make all or part of their livings from the craft. The index and directory (page 278) includes their business names, addresses and telephone numbers,

plus a list of the "specialties of the shop." If something shown herein catches your fancy, you can contact the maker and maybe have one made for you. You can also browse the book and the directory for nearby woodworkers, and go take a look.

The judging itself was done in February by the five staff and contributing editors of *Fine Woodworking*. We were the magazine's publisher, Paul Roman; its editor, myself; its art director, Roger Barnes; and contributing editors Tage Frid and R. Bruce Hoadley. Roman and I are amateur woodworkers but professional journalists whose field is woodworking. Barnes is an accomplished painter and sculptor with the artist's eye for line and form. Frid is a master cabinetmaker from Denmark and professor of woodworking and furniture design at Rhode Island School of Design. Hoadley is professor of wood science and technology at the University of Massachusetts, Amherst, and a sensitive wood carver.

We began by agreeing that it would be presumptuous to even try to judge woodworking from black-and-white photographic images. Rather, our task was to edit this remarkable collection into a worthwhile book. Thus the first criterion had to be photographic quality, from a publishing point of view. This included not only the composition, focus and tonal range of the image the woodworker had intended us to see, but also its surroundings. We had to reject many photographs of otherwise excellent work because they had been shot on a background of wrinkled bedsheet, the wrinkles welling up around the furniture legs or banjo bodies and made garish by shadowy flash lighting.

We wanted to look for good design, proper attention to the principles of wooden construction, artful use of wood, careful workmanship. But the rules of the competition had allowed up to four entries per craftsman. It quickly became clear that we would finish with two or three fat books. So we decided nobody should have more than one photo in the book. We broke this rule for things requiring two photos to reveal their intricacies, and for a few craftsmen whose work was so good that we could not choose.

After that, it was a culling process. Much of woodworking technique is concerned with ways to accommodate the way wood shrinks and swells in width and thickness, but not in length, as the humidity changes. We rejected whenever we could see two pieces joined cross-grain without providing for wood movement. We rejected sloppy joinery and joints with spaces in them, most often apparent at the corners of cabinets. We rejected smooth panels disfigured by planer marks, turnings with sanding scratches, miters filled with putty. Goodbye to nice cabinets disgraced by shoddy or inappropriate hardware, hinges or handles. We found easy agreement on these technical points. Finally, we rejected things a majority of us thought badly designed or just plain ugly—a much more subjective call. We often disagreed. All five of us looked at every photograph during the judging. I looked at all of them twice more while sorting the collection for page layout, and once again afterward. No doubt, craftsmen who entered the competition and did not get into the book will believe their work is better than some that did get in. Regrettably, those are the breaks. We did our best.

The antiques of tomorrow
When people speak of fine furniture, they usually mean genuine antiques or furniture made in period styles. Many of the woodworkers in this book evidently don't agree, for their work is contemporary in style and deliberately innovative. This is not the editors' bias, but rather an accurate reflection of the entries we received. I have met quite a few of these craftsmen and can offer some observations on who they are and why they work as they do. I see three important factors, all consequences of the industrial revolution and the changes it wrought: the ways people learn to be woodworkers since the collapse of the apprenticeship system; the new tools, techniques and materials; and the new living styles that have eliminated some furniture functions while creating new ones.

In the old days, an adolescent grew to be a craftsman during his seven-year apprenticeship. He got the basic skills by doing the hard work that machines do nowadays, and the basics of design by being taught the proportional systems of the master craftsman. You could not go to school for more systematic training, and there was no such thing as a woodworking hobby. You emerged as an adept, able to produce clean work quickly, but design was the least of it. You made what you had learned how to make. You can still do this in Europe, and sometimes in America. But the more common route is to go to college to study woodworking and furniture design. You can even get a master's degree in it, and you emerge with much broader knowledge although you don't yet have those hard-won ingrained skills. Of course this is not the only route. Many people are woodworkers because they have always been woodworkers, father and grandfather were woodworkers too. Many independent craftsmen pursue an informal sort of apprenticeship by working in industry, in cabinet and millwork shops, and for artisans whose work they admire, before striking out on their own. Many others begin as hobbyists and find in woodworking a rare satisfaction they cannot get in their regular careers. I suspect this satisfaction is the heady wine of making a whole thing from start to finish, struggling to retain control of every aspect, and then taking all the credit (or all the blame) when it is done. Few occupations have such tangible and enduring results as making things out of wood. These various routes have produced a new generation of young designer-craftsmen. They differ from their predecessors in that most went to college (whether or not to study woodworking) and while there got some formal training in art and design, instead of designs learned by rote.

In an 18th-century cabinet shop, trees were sawn into boards and the boards planed smooth by muscle power. The lathe, man-driven, was likely to be the only machine. The easiest way to make a finished leg for a table or chair was to turn it, and thus colonial furniture often has turned legs. Even the forms of the turnings—vase shapes, balls and beads, coves and shoulders—are the ones that fall naturally from the tools. Once a person masters the basic techniques, he will find it difficult to avoid these characteristic shapes.

Conversely, with a motorized band saw and planing machine, and with modern clamps and glues, it is almost as easy to make a curved leg or stretcher, or a whole curved panel. It's not that our ancestors didn't know how to make these things, but they chose not to, on account of the back-breaking labor involved. There's no doubt in my mind that colonial cabinetmakers would have reveled in hardwood-veneered plywood, if it had been invented. Now that it is available by the acre, it makes possible designs that could not be contemplated in solid wood.

The universe of new materials makes the craftsman see his wood in a different way. Formerly, wood was not only the material of choice, it was the only material. Whatever you were making, wood was what you used. It was difficult to be sentimental about it—it was just wood, one piece pretty much like the next. If you didn't want it to look the way it actually was, you filled the grain and mixed up stains to change it. Nowadays you could use chipboard or plastic laminate, glass or brushed chrome, instead. So if you make it out of wood you have chosen the wood over a number of attractive alternatives, and you'll probably want to retain its natural appearance.

It becomes possible not only to discriminate among pieces of this much-alike material, but also to adopt an almost reverent attitude toward a special piece of it, and even to muse poetically about the natural forces that grew it. Unusual figure or a knot or the delicate stain left by a fungus may become paramount. In this book you'll find entire cabinets made for the purpose of using and thereby putting on display a special chunk of wood. Such feelings toward wood result from the contrast with modern synthetic materials, which machines can make uniformly perfect—or uniformly bland. Surrounded by mechanical perfection, we strive to emphasize the variety of wood. Our ancestors, on the other hand, struggled mightily to achieve the appearance of perfection. They discarded "flawed" timber, or used it where it could not be seen.

Similarly, our ancestors festooned their furniture with elegant moldings and carvings, not only for decorative effect but also to conceal the joints that held it together. Contemporary craftsmen are likely to leave the joinery exposed, and rarely use moldings. The reason is that when all joints were cut by hand, there was nothing special about them. They were the untidy skeleton, best hidden behind an attractive molding, so the work would appear mysteriously perfect. Today machines routinely achieve apparent perfection without the intervention of skill. What machines cannot do is imitate the minute imperfections that give character to a hand-cut joint. Exposed joinery thus becomes the special mark of the craftsman, proudly displayed. And there goes the molding, not wanted any more.

Finally, consider furniture function. The colonial kitchen had to have a dry sink; there was no running water. Candles sat on stands, and people sat around the fire. We don't need dry sinks or candle stands today and we sit around the television. Our ancestors had never heard of coffee tables, lounge chairs, cabinetry for electronic gear or shelving for paperback books. Should the craftsman force a stereo cabinet into the Philadelphia Chippendale style, or should he approach the new problem anew? You'll find both approaches in this book. Even the highboy chest-on-chest, a pinnacle of the cabinetmaker's art, has been supplanted by built-in closets and open display shelving, usually modular.

It is easy to forget that Chippendale and Sheraton and their contemporary followers were all the modern rage, in their day. They were also as far removed—or as close, depending on how you look at it—from their predecessors as today's artisans are from theirs. The furniture of any age can only reflect its times. And who knows? The craftsmen represented in this book may well become the Chippendales of our era, their furniture the antiques of tomorrow.

—*John Kelsey, July 12, 1979.*

How to find your way around this book

The woodworking shown in this book is arranged by function in six major categories. For the sake of coherence we took some liberties—all tools and instruments, whether for woodworking, making music, keeping time, or paddling across lakes, are together. We declared that for our purposes a whole building was just a complicated cabinet, and we put beds and stools in with chairs because they all are for holding people, as opposed to holding things. The running headlines at the top of each page are a guide to what you'll find there, but one thing merges into the next and many pages are miscellanies.

The small capital letter above each photo will lead you to the words about it. In addition to the list of woods, dimensions (in inches unless otherwise noted) and description of principal techniques, the entry blank invited craftsmen to comment, if they wished, on their work and their lives in relationship to it. We edited these remarks only for grammar and length. As you will discover, these comments range from technically interesting but mundane, to poetic.

A. **David W. Cumming,** Toronto, Ont., Canada

Chairmaker's Scraper; Columbian boxwood, cocobolo, half a Stanley scraper blade, brass; 14 x 1³⁄₁₆ x ⁹⁄₁₆. Photo by Robert Petch.

"This tool was made out of my first piece of boxwood and first of cocobolo. The idea was found in Hayward's *Tools for Woodwork* but the specific design and dimensions are my own. The handles do not 'lift,' so use is restricted to stool and chair parts and frame parts. I found that long, thin boxwood was strong enough, when backed by cocobolo, to spring or bend in use without cracking. Initially I was afraid of this, but I now feel I made a lucky error. This tool is considerably more versatile and open to rough, even casual handling, than any of my 'store-bought' scrapers or spokeshaves."

B. (and previous page)
Richard W. Christie, Ridgewood, N.J.

Canoe; red cedar, mahogany, maple; 180 x 36. Steam-bent frames fastened with clinched copper nails, canvas covered.

C. **A. Lee Worman,** Springfield, Mo.

Small Wooden Plane with Fence; maple, cocobolo, birch; 5⅝ x 1¹³⁄₁₆. Photo by Karl Elder.

"This small wooden plane is fitted with a 90° detachable fence. The plane was designed for my work in dulcimer making, to be used for squaring up stock for fretboards. The fence is relatively wide, extending 1¼ in. below the sole; this offers a good bearing surface against the side of the stock, eliminating wobble, and giving a true 90°. The plane also has a 45° fence for beveling and chamfering.... The ½-in. threaded birch dowels can be screwed out of the maple plane body."

A

B

C

D. **Jerry Tow,** Ames, Iowa

Jointer Plane; maple, ebony, padauk, brass, steel; 24 x 2¾ x 9.

E. **Cary Childress,** Santa Monica, Calif.

Two Figures on a Plane; shedua; 21 x 2½ x 6.

"I did it the hard way, no power tools. The design evolved from clay models that fit my hands. It feels comfortable no matter where I hold it. I purposely tried to make it look and feel light. But I found the weight was needed for function."

F. **Jerry Tow,** Ames, Iowa

Bandsaw; maple, walnut, ebony, plywood, brass; 22 x 18 x 64

"Bandsaw is designed and constructed to work, awaiting motor and blade. Finish is boiled linseed oil."

G. **Gregg Blomberg,** Lopez, Wash.

Woodcarving Tools; yew, copper, bone, steel.

"All these tools are designed not to touch their edges when laid on a bench, and are very disinclined to roll off. The handles are of yew with copper ferrules. The set rolls up inside the sheepskin and ties tightly with a thong. For point protection I use rubber hose of various sizes. The adzes have leather sheaths, the whittling knife has a yew case."

"I make the adzes of old carpenter's hammers with the claw cut off. They are well-balanced, powerful tools for roughing, and will also produce a very smooth surface.... Crooked knives, type O-1 tool steel, deer antler handles, copper rivets. Properly designed crooked knives are not available commercially. They should be in more general use. These knives will cut on both the push and pull stroke, although used most often on the draw. Crooked knives will get into the darndest places. Very useful."

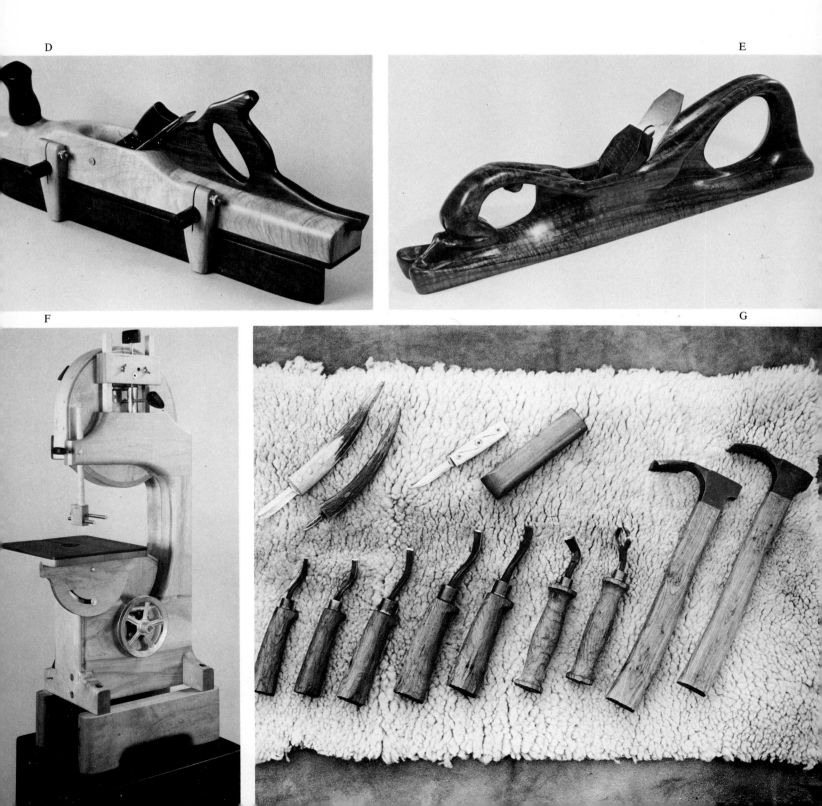

A. **Howard Jaeger,** Tucson, Ariz.

Smoothing Plane, koa with paumarfin sole, brass; 9¼ x 2½ x 4½.

"This European smoothing plane was commissioned as a functional gift for William Smith by his wife, Susan Smith. Blade width is 1¾ in.; secured by standard wedge and side-grip system."

B. **A. B. Acker,** Amherst, Mass.

Lyre Bowsaw; ash, red oak, teak, copper; 15 x 21 x 1.

"I designed and built this saw for my antique tool collection—few others are affordable or available. People seem to like it."

C. **Rick Pohlers,** Bloomington, Calif.

Hand Adz; walnut, 01 tool steel; 5 x 2 x 7½, $100.

"This tool is based on the Northwest coast 'D' adz treated in a contemporary and sculptural way. Emphasis was placed on grip feel."

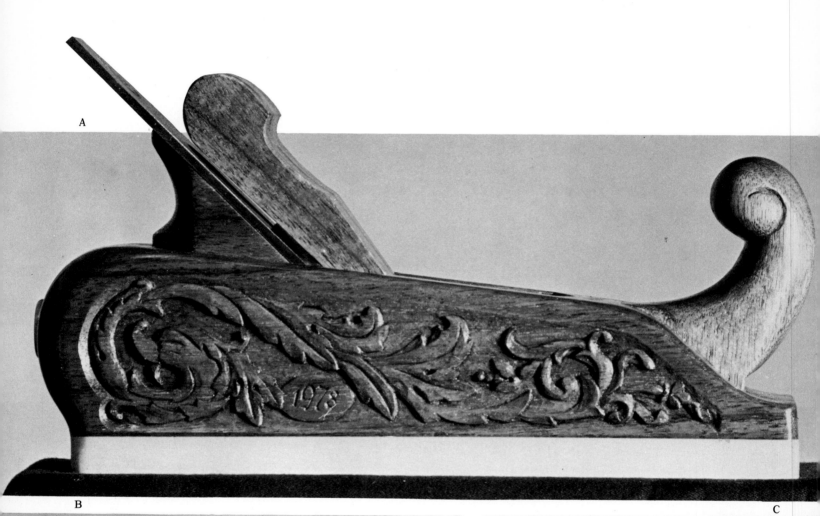

A

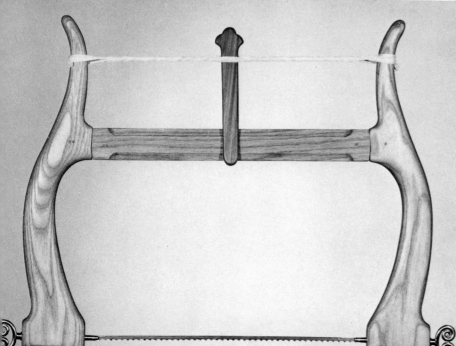

B

C

D. **David Gissen,** Concord, Mass.

Smoothing Plane, 2¼ x 8½; Handscrew clamp, 9-in. capacity; Luthier-type clamp, 3½-in. capacity; walnut, hornbeam, birch, leather.

E. **Ed J. Schweinfurth,** Larue, Ohio

Fore Plane; cherry, walnut, sugar maple, beech, burr oak, osage orange; 3½ x 8½ x 19½. Photo by Brad Secord Studios.

"Design based on early style but constructed with modern principles. Oil-finished so that grain and texture of all the woods can be felt."

F. **William J. Lavin,** Syracuse, N.Y.

Wooden Hand Plane; black cherry; 13 x 3 x 4.

"This plane is made of native cherry cut and surfaced by hand from a relative's farm. After the block was cut and made to work, I shaped it to the perfect fit for the size of my hand. A personal tool."

G. **Darwin S. Knight,** Moro, Ore.

Traditional Router Plane; maple, walnut; 9⅛ x 5 x 2⅜. Forged knife keeper from steel lag. The blades were purchased.

H. **Michael Mott,** Edmonton, Alta., Canada

Plane; lignum vitae, ebony, boxwood, steel; 5½ x 1¾ x 1½.

"This plane was made as a gift for a left-handed friend."

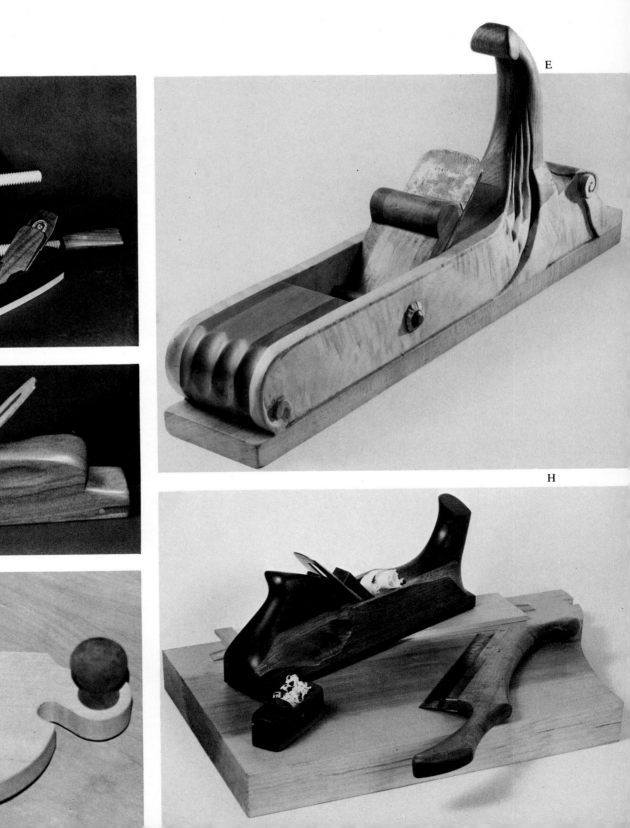

D

E

F

G

H

A. **John R. Beck,** Sycamore, Ill.

Coffee-Table Workbench; maple with walnut pegs; 36 x 18 x 18. Photo by Roger Cliffe.

"Built for the craftsman who has to be busy even when relaxing or has to work out of a closet workshop."

B. **Thomas Smith,** Woodlyn, Pa.

Grinding Bench; red oak, leather, sandstone wheel; 36 x 16 x 42.

C. **Christina Eaton,** W. Brookfield, Mass.

Molding Planes; bird's-eye maple; 9½ x 1⅝ x 3¾. Photo by Donald F. Eaton.

"Table rounds were used during the William & Mary period. They preceded the rule joint."

A

B

C

D. **Edward C. Smith,** Marshfield, Vt.

Bowsaw; ebony, brass; 25⅝ x 18. Photo by Cougar Photography.

E. **T.M. Cromwell,** Lancaster, Calif.

Plane; shedua, western red alder, ash; 15 x 2¼ x 2⅞.

F. **Colin Butler,** Layton, N.J.

Prototype from the Hand Plane Research Department Division of Space Tool Inc.; Brazilian tulipwood, rosewood, ivory, brass, powerful magnifier, fiber illuminator; 14 x 2½ x 8.

"The illumination in combination with the magnification of the fiber structure gives the viewer a clearer understanding, and at the same time, an opportunity to see how it's going."

G. **Cary Modd,** Kenton, Ohio

Smooth Plane; sugar and bird's-eye maple, black locust, osage orange; 3½ x 3 x 10½ (body). Photo by Brad Secord Studios.

"Made to fit my own hands. Blade is an old Barton cast steel double iron; wedge is held with osage cross pin instead of double key.

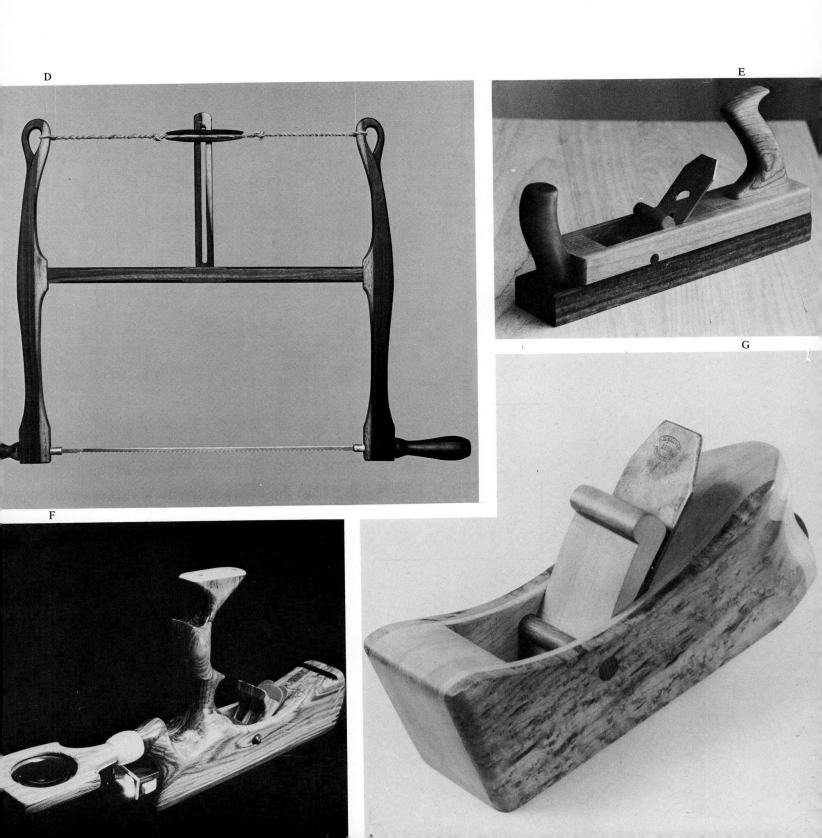

D

E

F

G

A. **Kenneth R. Fisher,** Poseyville, Ind.

Time Stops for the Artist; black cherry, black walnut, birch, sugar pine, hard maple, red oak, white oak; 48 x 96 x 144.

"The clock weighs about 350 lb. Unfortunately, it won't run by weight as designed—that would take 900 lb. on the chain. When I discovered this I didn't complete the last drive chain to the hand. I had guessed at it, and my guess was about 200 lb. The pendulum swings accurately and smoothly, however, if weight is applied to the 6-ft. gear or escapement gear."

B. **Ronni Komarow,** Durham, N.C.

Clock With Storage Compartments; cherry; 15½ x 10 x 7½.

C. **John Edwards Tyler,** La Jolla, Calif.

Case for 18th-Century Bracket Clock; walnut, brass; 6¾ x 10½ x 16.

A

B

B

C

D. **Charles H. McCain,** Pittsford, N.Y.

Tall Clock with Chime; mahogany, Carpathian elm burl, ebony; 72 high.

"The base of the clock is constructed of vertical laminates of Central American mahogany chainsawn to rough shape and taken to final shape with drawknife and spokeshave. Mortise and tenon and splined joints are used where the pieces are joined for the crook in the base. The 'lazy' ellipse clock housing is hammer-veneered mahogany over a chipboard form. The Carpathian elm burl clock face is veneered in a four-piece book and butt match pattern. The hands of Gabon ebony are driven by an eight-day mechanism which chimes hours and half hours."

E. **Dennis Lucero,** Denver, Colo.

Standing Clock; koa; 16 x 63.

F. **Rick Stoner,** Longmont, Colo.

'Wave;' cherry, glass, brass, 8-day strike movement; 18 x 18 x 4½.

"When the pendulum is swinging, the shape of the clock makes the viewer feel the entire piece is in motion. Like watching a wave."

G. **Eric Albinson,** Running Springs, Calif.

Clock; red oak, teak; 7 x 3 x 7, $86. Photo by Bill Upston.

H. **Vern Rumble,** Clinton, N.C.

Desk Clock; black walnut, bubinga, silvered acrylic; 9 x 6 x 3, $75.

D   E   F

G   H

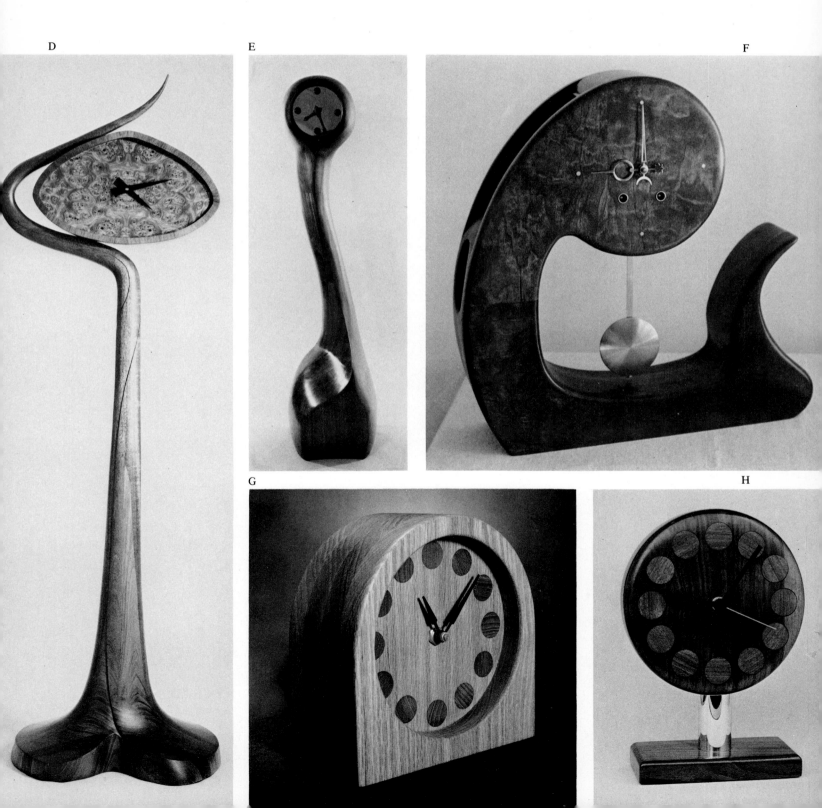

A. **Wm. & Peggy Riemer,** Ogdensburg, Wis.

Grandfather Clock; Honduras mahogany; mahogany veneers; 88 high. The design also includes a hand-engraved brass dial.

B. **Tom E. Moore,** Springfield, Va.

Clock Cases; walnut, cherry; shown finished and under construction.

C. **Peter R. Fisher,** Pittsburgh, Pa.

Clock; cherry, Carpathian elm burl, Plexiglas; 9 x 15 x 64. Photo by Joe Schaad.

D. **Phillip Adams,** Canton, Ga.

Grandfather Clock; walnut, glass, West German movement; 19¾ x 12¾ x 85, $1,000.

"The design of this clock is of no particular style. I just combined the features of several different styles that I liked."

E. **Robert Ludwig,** Lorain, Ohio

Clock Case; black walnut, glass; 18 x 12 x 78. Case finished with acrylic latex applied with a CO_2-charged spray bottle to impart a textured finish.

F. **Don Hintz,** Northbrook, Ill.

Bracket Clock; cherry, oak; 7½ x 14½ x 16½. After the style of Thomas Tompion (late 17th century).

G. **Alvin & Velma Weaver,** Kansas City, Kans.

Clock Case; American walnut, figured and crotch; 20¾ x 12½ x 89¾.

"The techniques used were learned in 49 years of full-time work in fine cabinetry and furniture making."

H. **Malcolm L. Ray,** Damariscotta, Maine

Four-Spire Clock; cherry, acrylic paints on reverse glass, urgos movement; 20 x 13 x 6½.

A B C

D E

I. **Stephen L. McAnulty,** Alexis, Ill.

Grandfather Clock; cherry, brass, spring steel; 36 x 84.

"The works are made primarily of wood with equipment found in the woodworker's shop. The scale of the mechanism is large enough to enhance the beauty of the moving gears yet small enough to fit a grandfather clock case.... The time train will give the time of day in minutes and hours, as well as seconds. The strike train will strike the proper number of times on the hour with the use of a coil gong. The mechanism will also strike once on the half-hour with a 5-in. brass bell. The calendar train will give the day of the week, date of the month, and month of the year.

"The mechanism was designed to use as many gears of the same size and count as was possible. Indexing jigs were made to hold the gears and pinions. Small pieces of old files were used to make cutter bits for the milling procedure. The mechanism was suspended, rather than supported in the case, by ¼-in. brass rods. This procedure provides adjustment nuts at the top of the case which greatly help in leveling the mechanism.... All three time-keeping shafts project from the center of the clock face. This was achieved by supporting the minute and hour shafts on wooden bearings be-

tween the front plate and the clock face. The seconds shaft projects through these two shafts without touching them. This allows friction-free rotation of the seconds shaft and room on the face for the calendar dials."

F

G

H

I

G

A. **Jerel R. Wittkopf,** Algona, Iowa

Grandfather Clock Cabinet; walnut and walnut burl, crotch, butt veneers and solids; 25 x 13 x 84, $3,200.

"Incorporated into the cabinet design are veneer inlays and solid pieces of walnut crotch, burl and butt along with various straight grains to best show the various types of grain formed in the entire walnut tree, while still maintaining a functional and pleasing design."

B. **William J. Kravarik,** Brookfield Center, Conn.

Grandfather Clock; American black walnut, 80 x 18 x 12. Photo by Gary Burdick.

"The spindles are parquet stacked, and each is constructed of more than 100 individual cubes of American black walnut. The tedious process of creating these spindles took 1½ months of my senior year of high school."

C. **Rudy Jasiak,** Ware, Mass.

Open Grandfather Clock; black walnut; 73 x 19 x 11½.

D. **Steven A. Widom,** East Northport, N.Y.

Grandfather Clock; East Indian rosewood, brass; 38 x 90 x 24. Photo by Joan C. Beder.

E. **Dennis R. Wilson,** Wynne, Ark.

Desk/Mantel Clock; white oak, cocobolo, quartz movement; 9½ x 6, $125.

F. **R. Jesse Morley,** Westwood, Mass.

Clock Movement; oak, cherry, birch, nylon, acrylic; 3 x 6 x 9½. 30-hour meter pendulum movement. Laminated and quartersawn wheels and plates. Nylon lantern pinions and bushings. Nylon pallets and acrylic escape wheel.

"The use of nylon at all friction points eliminates the need for oiling."

A

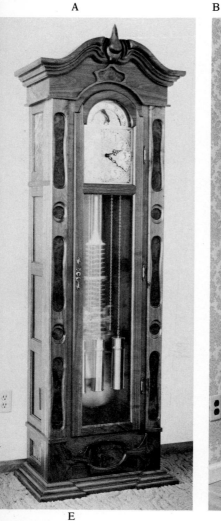

B

C

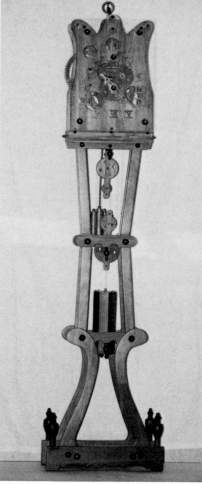

D

F

E

F

G. **Charles W. Keller, designer, James Szaforanski, maker;**
Andover, Mass.

Grandfather Clock; cherry; 70 x 10 x 14, $800.

H. **Darrell Sage,** Carbondale, Colo.

Wall Clock; zebrawood, garnet; 9 x 19.

I. **Nicholas J. Disparti,** Escondido, Calif.

Bracket Clock; avocado; 13 x 6 x 15.

J. **William Alvut,** Penfield, N.Y.

Grandfather Clock; oak; 18 x 12 x 60.

"The oak was rough-shaped and bent green. After air-curing
the handcrafting and finishing were completed."

K. **Gary D. Kroeker;** Wichita, Kans.

Clock; zebrawood; 3½ x 13¾ x 23⅛.

G

H

I

J

K

A. **Hugh Gundry,** Pasadena, Calif.

Hardwood Toys; birch, walnut, African zebrawood; 9 x 5 x 6. Custom-designed, disc sanded to shape; all edges rounded.

"My toy designs are based on absolute simplicity, to present only a basic image and to allow the imagination to fill in the rest. This allows a child to get involved with the toy and play with it, rather than simply turning a switch and watching it go. Hardwoods are used for durability and beauty with large axles and thick wheels. Six years ago I began guaranteeing my toys against breakage by children and rarely get one back to repair. Over the years I found I was selling a good third of my toys for decorative pieces to adults without children, so I began using more exotic and expensive woods."

B. **Robert J. Ostrowski,** Toledo, Ohio

Biplane; cherry, walnut, maple; 9¾ x 10 x 4, $30.

"Toys should be simple and sturdy and take advantage of the natural beauty of the wood."

C. **Jerry L. Smith,** Rogers City, Mich.

Double-Winged Airplane; pine; 12 x 13 x 6. Photo by Jeffrey Hopp.

"Although I usually work in hardwoods, I have retained the use of pine in this design because of its warmth and light weight. The design has also proven durable over the years."

D. **Bernard Maas,** Cambridge Springs, Pa.

Bulldozer; red and white oak; 18 x 8 x 8, $30. No metal fasteners, laminations only.

"Toy was designed as functional sculpture for children. Effective life is indefinite."

E. **Paul H. Stahlhuth,** Mission Viejo, Calif.

Fork-Lift Truck; maple; 7 x 3¼ x 5, $15. Band saw and radial arm saw. Cut threads on band saw; music wire helix for smooth operating nut.

"Fork lift operates, rear wheels steer."

F. **William Stockhausen,** Northville, Mich.

Traction Engine; oak, mahogany, maple, cherry, poplar, walnut, hickory, mulberry; 11 x 7 x 10.

"The use of contrasting woods for the different parts of a toy eliminates the need for painting, and thus the child also learns to appreciate the material as well as its function. In this pull toy the wheels, of course, rotate, causing the flywheels to rotate, which causes the flyballs to spin around and the cylinder and connecting rod to oscillate. The man's head will bob up and down and turn from side to side due to the off-center cams on the main shaft. Steering is accomplished either by the string or by turning the smokestack by hand."

G. **Robert Neil Winland,** Hamilton, Ohio

Biplane With Winged Boots; redwood, pine, birch dowels; 12 x 14 x 8, $65.

"The biplane is an original design with movable prop which incorporates features from many early biplanes and my own flights of fantasy. Designed with the older 'boy' in mind."

H. **Charles J. Honsik,** East Dubuque, Ill.

Pirate Ship 'Sea Ghost;' pine, birch, brass; 28 x 19 x 29.

"I built the ship for my 7-year-old grandson with the intention of withstanding everyday play. It was built to match the size of my grandson's toy soldiers and is my own design. I'm proud to say it is still in one piece after a whole year of play. The hull is formed from laminated pine board and is covered with strips of birch steamed in a jig and stained to give the appearance of weathering. I am a 72-year-old retired carpenter and spend many enjoyable hours working on various wood projects."

I. **Ted L. Jacox,** Vista, Calif.

Formula-One Race Car; walnut, maple, mahogany; 13 x 8 x 4.

J. **Kenneth C. Vliet,** Oldwick, N.J.

Toy Dump Truck; 25 different hardwoods; 5 x 7 x 18. Mostly scraps of exotic and domestic hardwoods. I used table saw, lathe, band saw, router, hand tools.

"Made as a quiz for wood arts students to identify types of hardwoods. Linseed oil finish."

A. **Lauren McDermott,** Rochester, N.Y.

Unicycle; ash, beanwood, rosewood, leather; 24 dia. x 38.

B. **Mark H. Fleitzer,** Old Greenwich, Conn.

Wooden Train; clear white pine, red oak, birch, chestnut; 16¾ x 5¼ x 7⅝, $150.

C. **William V. Chappelow,** Descanso, Calif.

Tricycle; spalted bird's-eye maple burl, $200. Initial bandsaw shaping, refined with a bank of rasps, files and rifflers.

"A laterally oriented inspection will reveal that the grain of the wood follows the lines of the frame in a natural arc which seems to enhance the fluid feel of the piece as well as its functional strength. The finish is oil and wax."

D. **Joseph T. Yanuziello,** Toronto, Ont., Canada

Sedan Delivery; pine, birch, brass, steel rod, acrylic paint; 12⅝ x 6 x 7½.

E. **Robert G. Zauke,** Normal, Ill.

Pull Wagon; yellow pine; 17 x 10½ x 13, $22.

"Wagon is constructed of ½-in. yellow pine with dovetailed sides and dadoed bottom. Wheels are turned from 5/4 yellow pine with ½-in. axles. Handle is shaped from 6/4 yellow pine and is loose-pinned to the tongue. The finish is sprayed clear lacquer. The simple design stresses longlasting construction that will withstand the loving abuse of its playmate."

F. **George W. Albritton,** Houston, Tx.

Walking Tricycle/Learning Balance; parana pine, birch; 21 x 12 x 16, $45.

"Designed to use as few pieces as possible."

G. **Stanley Dolberg,** Weston, Mass.

Rocking Giraffe; white ash; 60 high, $325. Turning.

H. **Mike Martin,** Crestline, Ohio

Wagon; birch, maple; 30 x 14 x 18. Photo by Bart Susor.

I. **Earl McNeil,** Olympia, Wash.

Child's Pump Car; red oak, walnut, padauk, teak, purpleheart, maple; 40 x 25 x 23, $350. Steam-bent wheel rims, all wood—absolutely no metal.

"Split wheel, split axle, off-center rear-drive crankshaft."

A. **John E. Allen,** Berkeley, Calif.

Rocking Horse; mahogany, oak, hair; 54 x 14 x 36. Bent laminated rockers. Handcarved laminated body.

"There are over 300 hair follicles. I try to make each horse have a happy, smiling personality and to be fun and charming."

B. **Ray Jones,** Monona, Wis.

Carousel Rocking Horse; basswood, brass pole; 41 x 8 x 30 (rockers 52 in.). Hollow body; legs, head and neck solid. Entire form is laminated of $^{13}/_{16}$-in. boards.

"Horse carved and crafted with the same techniques used by the early carousel carvers."

C. **Dan Delaney,** Sacramento, Calif.

Child's Horse; Honduras mahogany, red oak, shedua; 21 x 22. Hand-shaped.

D. **Betty Babbitt Pfouts,** Woodland Hills, Calif.

Carousel Horse; sugar pine; 50 x 11¼ x 31. Entire construction is held together with dowels—no metal used. Photo by Tynee Vidal.

E. **Frank C. Koehle,** Ludington, Mich.

Rocking Horse; poplar; 30 x 6½ x 16. Head and tail hand-carved.

F. **Jonathan Byrne,** Detroit, Mich.

Rocking Horse; basswood, maple, linen; 52 x 15 x 34.

D

E

F

A. **John Linck,** Danville, Ill.

Oak Rocking Horse; red oak and birch; 33 x 13 x 27, $50. All joints use dowels only—no metal in toy.

"This horse's simple design allows a low price and at the same time will support several hundred pounds and last for generations."

B. **Peter W. Waxter,** New Hope, Pa.

Chess Set; walnut, holly, felt, velvet, lead; 23 x 23 x 18. Turned and carved men, 2 to 3¾ in. tall. All weighted with lead. Felt on bottoms for protection; dovetailed drawers lined with velvet. Photo by R. Chesterton.

C. **Tamma Boze,** Houston, Tex.

Domino Set; walnut, birch. Dovetailed corners, wooden hinge and catch.

"I am an 11th-grade student at Jersey Village High School, Houston, Tex."

D. **Leo Doyle,** San Bernardino, Calif.

Chess Set; cherry; 18 dia. x 12. Turned.

"Inlaid playing surface is on bottom of lid, which when removed is the top."

A

B

C

D

E. **Michael P. McDunn, Jr.,** Simpsonville, S.C.

Backgammon Set; maple, walnut; 25 x 18¼ x 2⅛, $250. Photo by Ken Howie.

"Original design based on right-angle emphasis by Doug Grange."

F. **Randy Bader,** Huntington Beach, Calif.

Backgammon Board; koa, oak, walnut, padauk, rosewood, birch; 9 x 22 x 3, $225. Wooden hinge as center bar and sliding lock on handle.

G. **Stephen T. Wilson,** Birmingham, Mich.

Windrose Chess Game; red oak, poplar; 17 x 14½ x 5 including playing pieces. Laminated and routed board. Photo by Roe Green.

H. **Wally Parker,** Honolulu, Hawaii

Backgammon Board or Table; koa, South African rosewood, zebrawood, leather; 36 x 32 x 30 with legs, $850. Photo by Pete Jensen.

"I sculptured the bordering koa with a smooth-flowing free-form effect; yet it is symmetrical at its center. The points have been tooled, as well as the floral designs separating each quadrant on a solid oak leather playing surface. The leather is then dyed and finished. The dark chips are South African rosewood, the light chips are zebrawood; the doubling cube is porcelain. Each playing surface is 11½ in. x 21¼ in.

"The koa was sculptured with a half-round Surform and an awful lot of hand-sanding! The places holding the dice, doubling cube and chips were routed, sometimes with the base of the router removed, using the router as an electric chisel. The places that hold the chips were done that way to shape a half-round so the chips fit in perfectly.

"The wood is very natural looking but very durable and waterproof (as is the leather)."

I. **Lewis O'Hara,** Cape May Court House, N.J.

The Queen; mahogany, walnut, red oak; 27 x 18 x 1¼.

"Construction was long and educating; the design just happened."

E

F

G

H

I

A. **Gary W. Cook,** Eugene, Ore.

La Grandeur—Finest in Foosball Tables; vermilion, Central American walnut, holly, red oak; 73 x 51 x 36.

"The area inside the playing field protecting the wood is ⅛-in. thick clear plastic, which provides a much faster playing surface than the standard table. To ensure that the table would withstand many years of use, every joint was joined in more than one way: the box joints in the corners of the main body are also doweled, etc. Eight levels (designed by me) embedded into the playing surface indicates the table's levelness—a feature no other foosball table has. The turn of a dial at the bottom makes leveling far easier than the standard table, and 100 lb. of added weight gives stability and eliminates sliding. I took special care in selecting and combining different colored woods."

B. **Ken Wilke,** San Jose, Calif.

Backgammon Board; vermilion, walnut, maple, rosewood, ebony, oak; 16½ x 27½.

C. **Paul Bernero,** Elizabeth, N.J.

Chess Set; walnut, maple; 20 x 20 x 11.

D. **Paul Darnell & Grady Watkins,** Phoenix, Ariz.

Backgammon/Chess Game Set; goncalo alves, zebrawood, bubinga, walnut, oak, koa, onyx pieces; 24 x 24 x 4. The backgammon side was accented with additional inlays as well as the points; the dice-cups were made by laminating thin exotic woods and drilled out to form the striped effect; the chess side was made by routing techniques.

"Design intention: To produce a functional piece of furniture linked to the past but crafted by modern techniques. As James Krenov has put it, 'to come up with the new without borrowing too much of the old.'"

A

B

C

D

E. **Allen Townsend,** Dahlgren, Va.

Bread; mahogany, walnut, porcelain; 14 x 14 x 8. Stacked and carved mahogany.

"This piece functions as a smile-getter. The fabric wrapper opens to reveal a mahogany loaf of bread. Within the loaf, bakers are hard at work."

F. **Jim & Judy Williamson,** Asheville, N.C.

'Saturday Morning Special'—Toy Gun; birch plywood, rosewood; 8¼ x 4, $9.

G. **Jim Montgomery,** Little Rock, Ark.

'Bop-Shoe-Bop;' red oak, walnut, East Indian rosewood, bubinga, silver, copper penny, gold-filled wire; 11 x 15 x 24. Fingers pivot on silver pins, the second finger and thumb 'snap' when crank is turned. Photo by Fred Wilson.

"The crank moves two interlocking cogs inside the base, one of which operates the back-and-forth lever action of the thumb, and the other raises the second finger by pulling a wire running above the pivot points of the finger. The se-

quence is as follows: (1) second finger rises, (2) thumb moves under second finger, which then (3) drops onto top of thumb. (4) Thumb moves out of the way allowing, (5) finger to drop or snap on the base of the thumb. Action repeats for each revolution of the crank."

H. **Gunther Keil,** Rexville, N.Y.

Octopuzzle; maple; 11 x 1½ x 4½, $12. Photo by Les Mertz. Eight interlocking pieces.

A. **Mark Davis,** Rhinelander, Wis.

Tree House; cedar, birch; 13 x 15 x 13.

"A tree house always seemed to be the ultimate plaything. This is a model of what an adult mind thinks a tree house should be. Have fun!"

B. **Richard Ogren,** Downers Grove, Ill.

Piggy Bank; butternut.

"Money is removed through the nose."

C. **James Parker,** Livermore, Calif.

Flying Saucers—Mother Ship and Scout; maple, walnut, Lucite; 10 dia.. Turning.

"The polished Lucite dome has a flange—inserted from bottom. It is non-removable (by child or anyone else). Portholes are walnut plugs."

D. **Cymantha Patterson,** Newburgh, N.Y.

Sycamore, rosewood, black walnut, ebony, mahogany; 12 x 7 x 5.

"This piece is kinetic. There are two buttons, one on each side, which when pushed make the eyes and tongue move from side to side."

E. **Joel Hogan,** Memphis, Tenn.

Multi-Animal Puzzle; ash; 10 x 5½. Cut from a single block of wood.

"This dinosaur is an ecosystem unto itself, carrying a bird perched on a bear's back and a whale in the bear's belly."

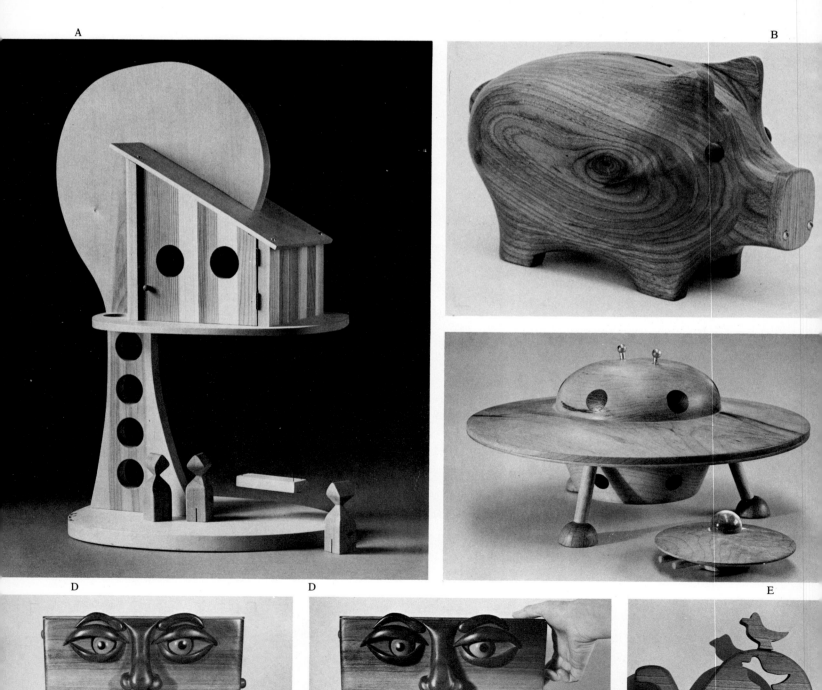

A   B

D   D   E

F. **Carolyn Wagner,** Canoga Park, Calif.

Jacks; maple; 12 x 18.

G. **Dennis Dorogi,** Brocton, N.Y.

A-Model Lap Dulcimer; walnut, cedar, ebony, ivory; 37 x 9 x 3, $450.

"The asymmetrical design enables a greater sounding area on the bass side of the instrument, resulting in a rich, full and balanced bass sound. The peghead design retains the traditional scroll, and the asymmetrical peg arrangement is functional in that the musician does not have to reach all the way around the peghead to reach the pegs. Scalloped fingerboard and relieved tailpiece help to give the instrument a rich, balanced tone quality with more than ample volume."

H. **Laurence R. Van Meter,** Vershire Center, Vt.

Crayon Holder; Mexican rosewood; 12 x 2 dia.

I. **George Bieri,** Yellow Springs, Ohio

Child's Workbench; hard maple, mahogany, red birch; 20 x 10 x 8½.

"The bench was made for my four-year-old daughter in order to entice her into something besides dolls and dramatic play. She has spent hours playing with it and has increased her manual skills and mechanical knowledge considerably."

J. **Bill Walker,** Elkhorn, Ky.

Four String Dulcimer; Brazilian rosewood, wormy chestnut, holly, ebony; 38 x 7½ x 3, $300.

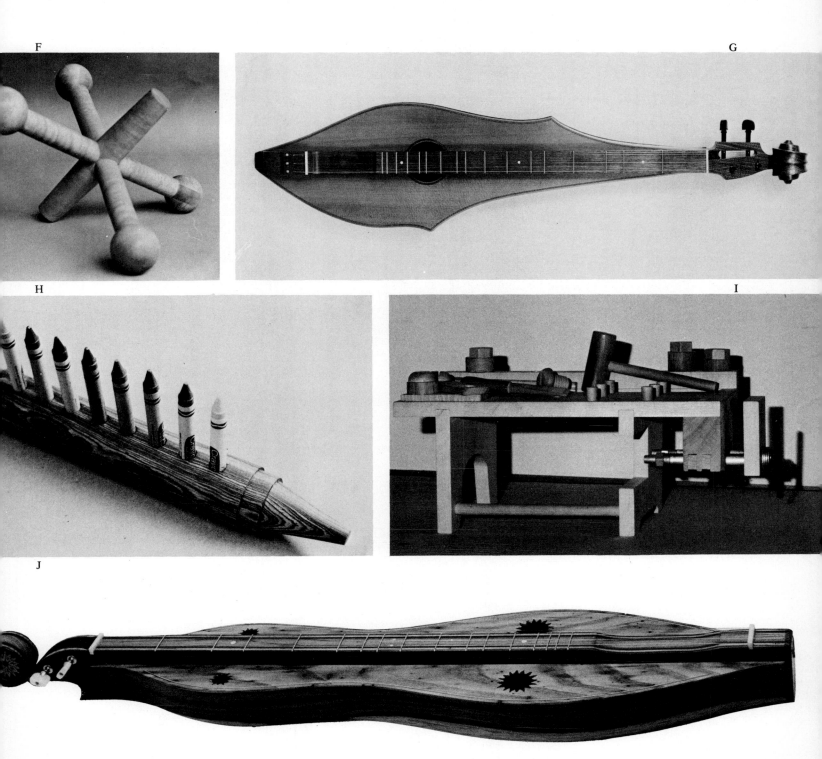

A. **Ken Riportella,** East Calais, Vt.

Metamorphis II (An American Dulcimer); cherry, Honduras mahogany, walnut, rosewood, Sitka spruce; 27 x 12 x 4, $4,200.

"Metamorphis II is a fairy-tale instrument with magical qualities. It is free-formed and hand-hewn creating a unique sculptural experience that exists within a three-dimensional world of visual and audial imagery: the human, the animal, the esoteric. A pot-bellied dragon stretching out of the canvas; a sparrow whisping through eternity. One form grows from the other. The work is experimental in nature, yet logically calculated acoustical gymnastics control various sound phenomena fabricating a tone that is rich, sweet, and yet, captivatingly innocent. The fingerboard is extremely short for a dulcimer, 19½ in. A soprano."

B. **Tony Ascrizzi,** Newton Centre, Mass.

Dulcimer; East Indian rosewood, Sitka spruce, Honduras mahogany, ebony, Brazilian rosewood inlay, maple/ebony purfling, mother-of-pearl; 45 x 13 x 2½, $500.

"The design and construction of this instrument centered around two points; to create an instrument that was visually exciting and to have an instrument with a full tonal range that would enable it to be played either solo or as backup. In order to achieve these goals I employed treatments usually not used on dulcimers: gradation and bracing of the soundboard, increasing soundbox volume, changing fretboard design, and utilizing three double-course strings tuned in octaves. I started with the traditional hourglass shape and combined it with the heart motif usually associated with dulcimers into a double heart body shape."

C. **Jeff Whitaker,** Grand Rapids, Mich.

Mountain Dulcimer; tulip, poplar, zebrawood, maple; 42 x 9 x 5.

D. **James Marsh,** Stockton, Calif.

Plucked Dulcimer; maple, spruce, rosewood, red & green abalone, mother-of-pearl, holly, ivory, celluloid, ebony; 39 x 7¼ x 4, $400. Photo by Jim Bartz.

A

B

C

D   D   D

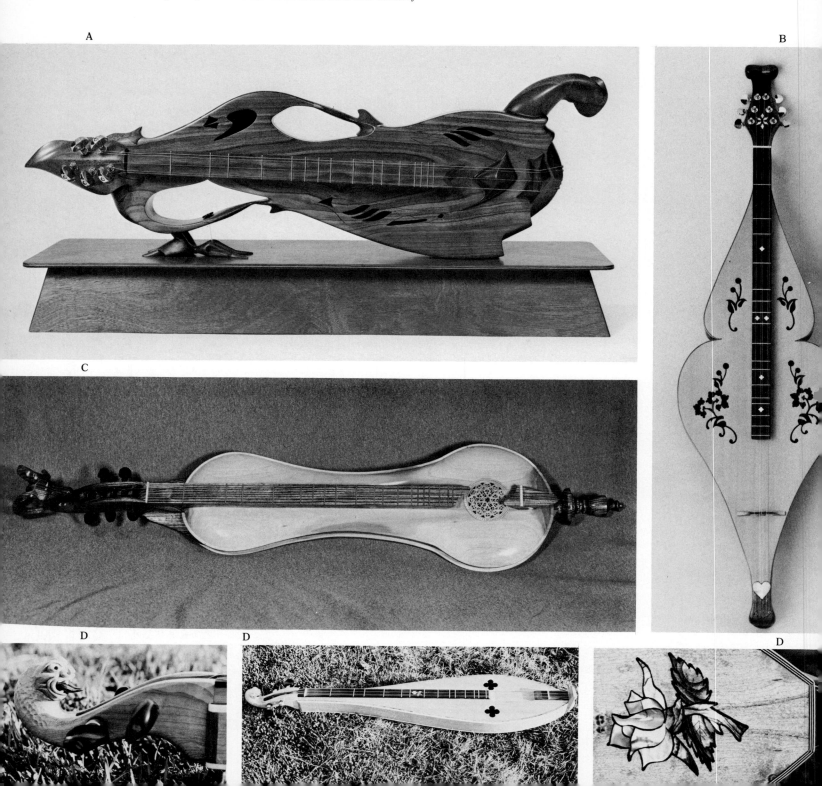

E. **Gregory S. Kindig,** Harrington, Del.

Mountain Dulcimer; rosewood, bird's-eye maple, bone, nickel fret-wire, strings; 37 x 9⅝ x 3.

"This is the eighth dulcimer I have built. It is the second with yin and yang sound holes. I try to incorporate this Eastern philosophy of balance into my designs."

F. **Geoff Eacker,** Middletown, Ohio

Dulcimer; cherry, spruce, ebony, mother-of-pearl; 36 x 8, $145.

"The headstock is made from six separate pieces of wood, which facilitates the use of a strengthening and stiffening member, running under the headstock and between tuning keys. The heat-bent sides are glued into the head and tail; then back and top, with fretboard attached, are glued. The finished instrument is finished with meticulous sanding, tung oil and paste wax."

G. **Ray Popelka,** Santa Cruz, Calif.

Dulcimer; koa, rosewood, Sitka spruce; 34½ x 7 x 2⅞. Photo by Adams Photography.

H. **Richard Marks,** Carbondale, Colo.

Dulcimer with Case; walnut, ebony, leather, macrame; 39 x 7 x 4. All joints in case are different—one spline joint, three tongue-and-groove and two rabbet dado joints.

"Made for a special person whose astrological sign is Pisces so I interpreted fish into soundholes. Music box in case."

I. **Earl Bushey,** Monterey, Calif.

Dulcimer and Case; redwood, narra, spruce; 9.4 x 25 x 18 cm.

"Redwood was from abandoned sand processing plant, stained black from minerals in the sand."

A. **J. Robert & Anne Willcutt,** Lexington, Ky.

Dulcimer; curly maple, bird's-eye maple, Indian rosewood, ivory, abalone inlay; 37½ x 8 x 3. Bentwood sides, hollowed neck, original design bracing including special air chambers in the neck, kerfed on the inside. The wood used for the head-stock was chosen so that the direction of the curls in the maple would be those of the girl's hair. Also a small dark knot on the left side of the head was integrated into the design and carved to look like a rose. The rosewood long-stem roses for the tuning keys carry out this theme. The abalone in-lay in the neck echoes the pattern of the soundholes.

"Instrument-making, a union of music and art, incorporates the practices of good construction techniques with the end result a beautiful object producing a pleasing sound."

B. **R.J. Regier,** Freeport, Maine

Fortepiano, Vienna, c. 1785-1800; spruce, cherry, ebony, bone; 86 x 40 x 35, $9,125. Photo by Pieter van Slyck.

"The case is wood, exclusively. A cast-iron frame is unnecessary, due to light stringing and a five octave (63-note) compass. Total string tension is about 1½ tons (in contrast to a modern concert grand's 88 keys and 15 to 20-ton tension). This early step in the evolution of the fortepiano was the type of instrument known to Mozart, Haydn, Beethoven and their contemporaries."

C. **Steven W. Sorli,** Carlisle, Mass.

Flemish Double-Manual Harpsichord; basswood, Sitka spruce, pearwood, ebony; 103 x 38 x 10, $9,000.

"Made entirely from scratch using solid wood construction and dovetail joints. Curved parts steam-bent. 1,200 man hours."

A

B

A

C

D. **James G. Mackie,** Minneapolis, Minn.

Ten-course Renaissance Lute, (Concert Model); curly maple, spruce, ebony, pearwood, poplar; 77.4 x 32 x 16 cm.

"While the design is my own, all the design parameters conform with those of surviving Renaissance lutes. My goal is to capture the spirit of the master luthiers of the Renaissance without resorting to copies of specific instruments."

E. **Rolfe Gerhardt,** San Antonio, Tex.

Unicorn Mandolin; fiddlebackmaple, fir, ebony; 30 long. Finish is potassium permanganate-shaded stain sealed with lacquer. All metal is gold-plated. Top and back are arched (carved).

"This mandolin is #100, made for my personal keepsake. I put my best into it and just wish you could personally examine it."

F. **Keven P. Rodel,** Topsham, Maine

Fiddle Case; teak, ebony, ash, brass; 31½ x 9½ x 5.

G. **John Montgomery,** Salt Lake City, Utah

Hurdy-Gurdy in Lute Form, 19th-Century French; maple, spruce, ebony, basswood, ivory, bone; 69 cm long, $1,000.

"Design is my own in the direction of making an instrument of folk music that is capable of playing outdoors with bagpipes or other wind instruments. Result: a clear, powerful and well-rounded sound."

D

D

E

F

G

A. Tom Pixton, Boston, Mass.

Replica of 1642 Flemish Harpsichord; northern white bass-wood, Sitka spruce, beech, bone, ebony, maple; 88 x 31 x 10, $6,500. Photo by Peter Vanderwarker.

"The instrument is painted in two tones on the exterior with a shellac finish. The turned stand, as well as the moldings, are stained and finished with shellac. The interior of the instrument, as was customary with 17th-century Flemish harpsichords, is decorated with block-printed papers that were executed in our shop. The soundboard is adorned with typical motifs found on early 17th-century Flemish harpsichords—flowers, birds, fruit and shrimp—that were executed in egg tempera by my wife, Barbara Pixton."

B. John Rocus, Ann Arbor, Mich.

Harmonograph; walnut, brass; 96 x 30 dia., $2,000.

"The harmonograph is a drawing instrument. It takes many forms but this one consists of a weighted drawing board suspended from the ceiling by means of a gimbal joint. Free-form drawings are made by starting the drawing surface in motion with a random push and then dropping a counter-balanced pen onto the paper. The character of the drawing is influenced by the motion of a secondary weight suspended below the drawing board."

A

B

C. **John Watson,** Cary, N.C.

Italian (17th-century style) Harpsichord; basswood, ebony, boxwood, spruce, walnut; 78 x 31½ x 8½, $3,500. The rose hole design is carved from three layers of sheepskin parchment in a gothic style. Photo by Gary Forbes.

B

C

B

C

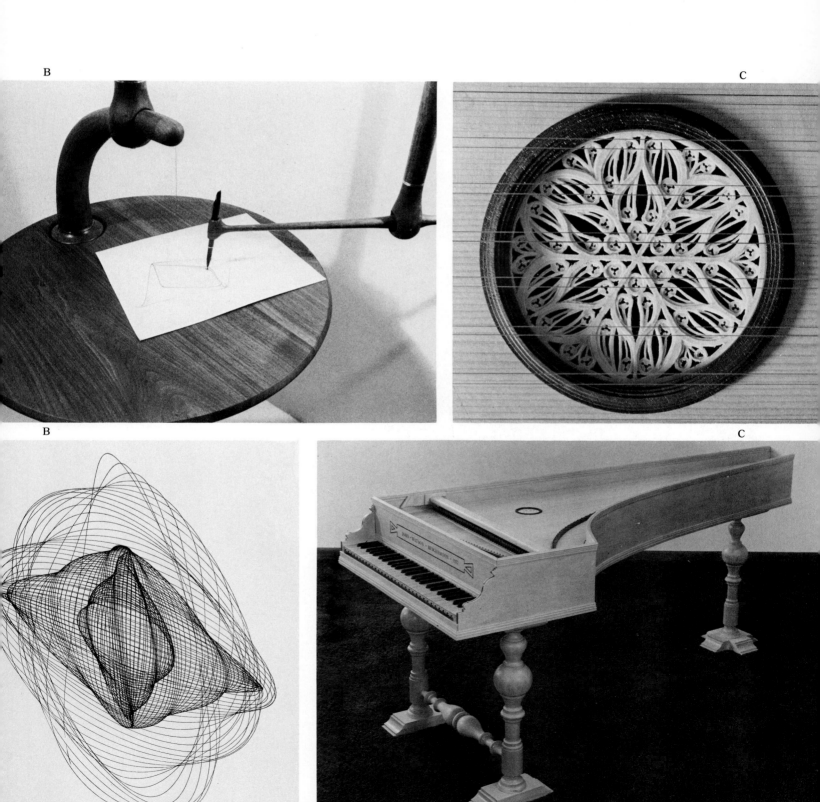

A. **Robert Brooke,** Rockville, Md.

Italian Virginal, (17th century); apple, basswood, Thai box-wood, Italian cypress, ebony, holly, maple, red oak, Swiss pear, Sitka spruce, walnut, virgin wool, Delrin plastic; 66 x 22 x 8, $3,500.

"The Italian cypress of the case is not amenable to planing. It can be thicknessed on a planer, but not to finish thickness. The grain is so irregular that tearing out is unavoidable, even with the sharpest tools. This particular instrument was constructed of cypress thicknessed $\frac{1}{16}$ in. oversize and the finish thickness arrived at with an industrial drum sander. Previous instruments have been constructed with the finish thickness achieved by dint of hand-scraping—a time-consuming and laborious process.

"This instrument is based on no existing antique. The string length and plucking points were taken from a set of measurements by Frank Hubbard. The case dimensions approximate an average of a number of instruments, either measured by me at the Smithsonian Institution or whose dimensions were made available to me from other sources. The design is otherwise original. The instrument compasses four octaves, C to c'''. It is tuned to a'=415 (a half step below modern pitch) but has a transposing keyboard that allows it to be played at a'=440 without retuning. The case walls are ⅛ in. thick. This lightness of construction allows the overall weight (not including stand) to remain below forty pounds."

B. **William K. Webster,** Detroit, Mich.

Dulcimer, mansonia, spruce, maple, redwood; 44 x 17 x 4, $450.

"Played with bamboo hammers that strike the strings, has a range of four octaves. Can be played in more than twelve keys. I use it at square dances."

C. **George Denninger,** Sugar Loaf, N.Y.

Piano; Brazilian mahogany; 71 x 30 x 54.

"This piano has a Mason & Hamlin works. Construction took about a year. The acoustical properties were improved significantly through basic speaker cabinet techniques. Object was to design a piano that visually and tactilely exemplifies the music it produces. Next year I will begin work on a 7-ft. Steinway grand. Experimenting with redesigned hammers and mechanism as well as cabinet."

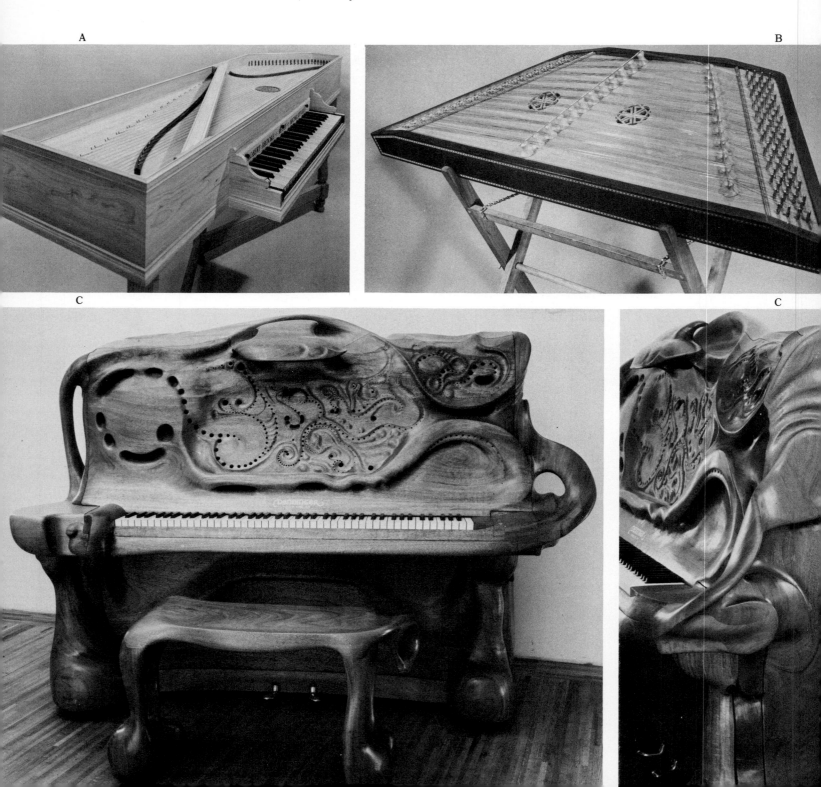

A

B

C

C

D. **Christopher F. Bannister,** Hopewell, N.J.

Concert Double Harpsichord; plain Honduras mahogany case-work; 260 cm, $11,700.

"Custom-built in 1978 for Philadelphia Orchestra; case and inner framework design emphasis on laminated construction to maximize seasonal dimensional stability; 63-note compass, F_1-g^3; 2 x 8 ft., 1 x 4-ft. choirs of strings with buff stop, manual coupler and lute registers, pedal-controlled stops and registers."

E. **Paul Y. Irvin,** Glenview, Ill.

Bentside Spinet Harpsichord; paldoa, Honduras mahogany, spruce, walnut, northern maple, poplar; 66½ x 31 x 8 (excluding legs).

"I wanted a harpsichord to use in a space-precious apartment. The efficient spinet configuration was the obvious choice, but there were several things about the standard, somewhat underdeveloped design which bothered me musically and mechanically, so I set about designing my own."

"I chose to use a single row of jacks guided by holes cut directly through the soundboard and corresponding mortises cut through a batten supported somewhat below. The lower batten can be adjusted for seasonal shifts. Cutting directly through the soundboard allows a clean visual sweep across the soundboard uninterrupted by the usual strip of wood crossing it. It's a nice touch, and one which I enjoy, although I doubt I would go through the trouble again.

"Since I had the lower batten to adjust for shifts, what the single row of jacks permitted me to do was to easily give the instrument another musical voice by the addition of a buff stop. This is a thin wood batten lying along the nut with pieces of felt on its top arranged so that when the batten is slid to the left each piece of felt lightly touches a string, resulting in a sound somewhat like that of a lute. This is much more complicated to arrange on the typical spinet with its jacks facing in opposite directions and is rarely found on them."

F. **Anden Houben,** Tuscaloosa, Ala.

Fretted Clavichord, (late 17th-century Italian); walnut, box-wood, maple, spruce, $850.

D   D

E   F

A. **Francis M. Kosheleff,** Los Gatos, Calif.

Balalaika; rosewood, walnut, spruce; 26 x 18, $400.

"The balalaika is a traditional Russian musical instrument. The carving and woodburning on the two instruments presented are of my own design and not traditional."

B. **Phillip J. Petillo,** Ocean, N.J.

Cutaway Steel String Guitar; Brazilian rosewood, spruce, ebony, Austrian curly maple, Nigerian ebony, mother-of-pearl inlay, German silver spruce; 42¾ x 16 x 4⅞, $3,000. Photo by Photographic Associates.

C. **Steve L. Hunter,** Rome, Ga.

Banjo (#2), Five String; curly maple, hard maple for internal parts, ebony, brass, mother-of-pearl, ivory; 26¼ fingerboard scale. Photo by Sue Wolf.

"Solid curly resonator back rabbeted to multi-plies of hard maple resonater rim, lathe-contoured and trued. Maple veneer added to resonator side for carving. Rim and shell made of multi-plies of hard maple, lathe-turned and hand-fitted. I could not bring myself to put the traditional purfling rings in the exceptionally fine curly maple resonator back."

D. **Edward Dick,** Peterboro, Ont., Canada

Mandolaser (electric mandolin); padauk, ebony, maple; 30 x x10 x 2, $600.

"The mandolaser arose out of a musician's very specific need. Although 'Mr. Blue' played electric guitar, he was more familiar with the mandolin and violin fingerboard. These instruments are tuned so that the strings are equal fifths apart, making it easier to transpose keys. It also facilitates a greater range of pitch within one hand position. Yet he wanted something that sounded like an electric guitar. The shape was to be unusual—he wanted something that looked 'space-agey, exotic and aggressive.' His only other demands were that he have access to the entire fingerboard and that it have a place to pivot his right elbow while playing. Mr. Blue was overjoyed with the result."

A

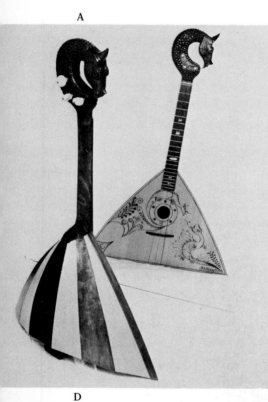

B

C

D

C

E. **Cabell J. Fearn**, Robinson Barracks, APO N.Y.

Banjo; teak, maple, ebony, rosewood, ash, silver, ivory, brass, steel; 38 x 12 x 3, $1,000.

"About two years ago I decided to build a couple of banjos for my brother and myself after pricing some at the music stores. It took me a year to find all the information I needed as I wanted this project to be a truly professional job. Comments from musicians who have played it indicate that this banjo sounds as good as the best instruments available today."

"One interesting innovation is the use of a ⅝ in. square solid steel bar embedded the length of the neck as opposed to the usual adjustable rod originally patented by Gibson. This idea came about from a number of things; first is the Martin guitar, which uses a hollow square tube, probably the strongest way you can do it; secondly Les Paul's experiments with guitars, which showed that a high mass would increase the amount of energy that goes to make sound as opposed to vibrating various parts of the instrument not directly connected with making sound. . . . I feel that the extra three or four pounds is worth living with in order to get a better sound."

F. **Jim Bartz**, Birds Landing, Calif.

Fiddle (5-string electric); maple, spruce, ebony (with rosewood pegs, walnut and abalone inlays); 23 x 7½ x 3¼.

"My dog, Raggy, chases the rabbit around the fiddle. The rabbit ducks into the soundhole and goes under the bridge. Raggy loses him and goes over the bridge. The rabbit runs into the thicket where he can sit and scratch. The dog plays with a note and then howls at the moon."

G. **M. E. McAtee**, Savannah, Ga.

Violin; curly and bird's-eye maple, spruce, ebony, willow.

"This violin is based on the work of Antonio Stradivari. It is not a copy of a particular model but work based on several years' study of information that is available on his work. The varnish used was made myself from material and methods that were known to be used for varnish in his day."

H. **Kim C. Walker**, Nashville, Tenn.

Guitar.

A. **David A. Dietrick,** Westport, Conn.

Frailing Banjo; cherry, rosewood, black walnut, padauk, maple, poplar, lacewood, mother-of-pearl, mahogany; 11 x 36. Photo by Mark Aalfs.

B. **Timothy L. Olsen,** Tacoma, Wash.

Flattop Bass; Sitka spruce, eastern hard maple, ebony, amaranth, basswood, boxwood, ivory, mother-of-pearl, brass; 130 x 52.5 x 15 cm.

"Such an instrument as this is often mistakenly called a bass guitar. There is such a beast as a bass guitar; the Mariachi bass or guitaronne. This instrument, on the other hand, is an acoustic version of the electric bass, which is in turn an electric version of the bass viol. So the name 'bass guitar' is inappropriate for two reasons. (1) The name is already taken. (2) This instrument is, by its tuning and music, more closely related to the bass viol than to the guitar. As with all my instruments, this flattop bass was designed to fit the hands and music of the client. I make no standard models, and do not begin an instrument until I have received a commission."

C. **James S. Gershey,** Lake Ariel, Pa.

Musical Instrument; cherry, cork, copper; 25 high.

"This instrument is based on the Renaissance krumhorn. The reed is enclosed by the removable mouthpiece and does not come in contact with the lips. The drill used to bore it was made to special order by a machinist."

D. **Jerry Womacks & Paula Snow Womacks,** Yellow Springs, Oh.

Baroque Viola da Gamba; maple, spruce; 46 long, $1,200. Photo by Bill McCuddy, Jr.

A A B

C

C

E. **Barklie Henry,** Big Sur, Calif.

Bass Talking Drum; redwood, monkeypod, madrone, manzanita, muleskin, bronze, lignum vitae, birch, oak; 48 x 36 x 21. Main barrel is a lamination of rings cut out of clear, straight 2-in. x 22-in. redwood. With a finished thickness averaging about ¾ in., the barrel is light and adequately strong.

"This is a two-pedal bass talking drum. It is mounted and ridden, so the musician's feet are available for pedal work. The left pedal alters the tension of the head and enables the musician to vary the head note significantly. The right pedal 'chokes' the bottom hole, which slightly varies the pitch of the low-bottom note (approx. C below low-bass E), sort of a bending effect in the low-bass range. Also this pedal enables the musician to vary the relationship between head note and barrel low-note when the instrument is double-miked for electrically amplified work."

F. **Bruce R. BecVar,** Cotati, Calif.

Six-String Electric Guitar; maple, purpleheart, bone; 41 x 16 x 1 ⁷/₁₀.

G. **Richard Schneider,** Kalamazoo, Mich.

Concert Classical Guitar; spruce, Indian rosewood, Honduras mahogany; 103 cm long, $5,000. Photo by Dennis Crawford.

"This instrument is designed acoustically to the concepts of Dr. Michael Kasha of Florida State University, whom I have been collaborating with for the past eleven years. The profile of the bridge is such for acoustical reasons and has led to an artistic expression much more modern than most traditional classical guitars. Esthetically the instrument has become very modern also. The rosette concept is no longer the fine mosaic hardly visible to the audience but an entirely new concept in dyed and natural woods that presents itself one way up close and then another from a distance. It is in fact quite visible from a distance. The bindings on my instruments utilize a great deal of color rather than the usual rosewood or dyed black bindings. The purfling colors vary with the rosewood used for particular instruments. This instrument is based on the colors green (main color) with purple, blue and white accenting. Every instrument I make is different in art, wood color and rosette design."

D

E

F

G

G

A. **Rick Duszynski,** Winlock, Wash.

'I Did It On Porpoise' One-Tongue Drum; African wenge, bamboo; 12 x 8 x 5.

B. **Terry Moore,** Newport, N.H.

Steel-String Guitar; rosewood, cedar, ebony, mahogany; 39¾ x 14¾ x 4½, $700.

"Instead of the traditional way of bending the guitar sides on a pipe, I made up a bending jig to the exact shape of the side. I traced my pattern of the side curve onto a plywood block. Then using the bandsaw, I cut ½ in. inside the original pattern line. Over the top of this now shaped block, I put ¼-in. aluminum plate with an old broiler unit from an electric stove running between the aluminum and the mold blank. The mold blank was overlaid with asbestos."

C. **John C. Maddocks,** Asheboro, N.C.

Drum; birch plywood, walnut veneer and trim, aluminum; 8 x 16 x 32. Butt-jointed plywood, veneered. Top sawn and brushed, mounted on rubber bushing with brass screws.

"Design is an adaptation of the Aztec talking drum. The ¼ in. aluminum top was tuned by sawing various lengths and then filing the back to produce tones at the first, third, fourth, fifth, seventh and octave intervals. The volume and depth of the resonating chamber were selected to maximize fundamental rather than harmonic pitches."

D. **Danyel Clouse,** Prescott, Ariz.

Quetzal Drum; bird's-eye maple; 12 x 6 x 6, $65. Photo by Lewallen.

". . . of Aztec orgin and contemporary design, the drum is inspired by the Quetzal bird, national symbol of Guatemala. It is a highly playable instrument for all ages and musical capabilities."

A

B

C

D

E. **Bruce E. Shull,** Charleston, W.V.

Chapel Pipe Organ; case: poplar, cedar, walnut; windchest: white oak, sugar pine, western red cedar, mahogany; bellows: yellow pine, white oak, sheep leather; key action: sugar pine, hickory, aluminum; faced with boxwood naturals, ebony sharps; pipes, alloy of tin and lead (17% tin); 112½ x 59 x 18, $22,000.

"The instrument took some 2,300 hours to complete. Suffice it to say that the instrument employs time-tested mechanical (tracker) action similar to that found in European organs dating from the 15th to the 17th centuries, using electricity only to power the blower that provides the air for the pipes. Given the simplicity of the overall design (no electrial parts to go bad or become obsolete and few moving parts as well) the instrument should easily last more than 100 years."

F. **Charles M. Ruggles,** Cleveland Heights, Ohio

Chamber Organ; cabinet: black walnut, western red cedar; bass pipes: ash, walnut; pedal keys: white oak; manual keys: cow bone, grenadilla; stop labels: engraved bone; stopknobs: Gabon ebony; windchests, bellows: Honduras mahogany, sugar pine, poplar, hard maple, beech; brass, steel, aluminum. Pipe alloy: 84% lead, 16% tin; 58½ x 38 x 102, $30,000.

"The instrument functions as a practice organ, teaching organ and a chamber-music instrument for use with other musical instruments. Its tuning and general sound is based on 18th-century Dutch chamber organs. The organ consists of eight ranks of pipes, or a total of 410 pipes."

G. **Richard G. Brown,** Sandpoint, Idaho

Fireplace Bellows; walnut, maple, brass, leather; 20 long.

E

F

G

A. **Thomas Landon Davies,** Narberth, Pa.

Camera Obscura; mahogany, rosewood, lignum vitae, glass, brass; 13 x 8½ x 6½.

"Original design, based on photograph of c. 1810 camera obscura. Focusing is accomplished by sliding front in or out of back. The scene is focused on a pane of glass over which is placed a sheet of tracing paper. A pencil tracing is then made."

B. **M.U. Zakariya,** Arlington, Va.

Cross Staff; wavy grain maple, brass; 35 x 20, $1,100. Hand-tooling techniques with many special jigs and features.

"This 16th to 18th-century European style navigation instrument is used for taking the angular observed altitude of a celestial body from a ship. It was very popular before the invention of the back staff, octant and sextant."

C. **Thomas F. Higby,** Fowlerville, Mich.

Spinning Wheel; cherry, rosewood, maple, vermilion; 22½ wheel.

D. **Francis Palermo,** Kapaau, Hawaii

Lithographic Printing Press; white & red oak, lignum vitae bearings and bearing housings, teak and cocobolo for accent, metal strap, channel and bearings, hydraulic pump and cylinders, drive chain, sprockets and caster wheels. 90 x 36 x 52, 525 lbs.

"The object of the press is to apply pressure (about 2,000-2,000 psi) to a lithographic stone while cranking the bed through the press to get a print, and to my amazement it really works."

A

B

B

C

D

E. **Jack Edwards & Jim Tilford,** El Rito, N. Mex.

Weaving Loom; cherry, walnut, brass, copper; 60 x 70 x 70, $4,500.

"This is a four-harness countermarche loom. It is done primarily in cherry with walnut and ebony accents. Ratchets are sand-cast brass and hand-finished by the artists. Construction is with classical woodworking joinery, including mortise and tenon, and hand-cut dovetails. The loom can be disassembled; the side frames are rigid, the cross struts have through tenons with cross wedges, and the castle assembly is mounted with four 1¼-in. wooden screws."

F. **Paul R. Kersten,** Greensburg, Pa.

Camera Stock.

"Various types of wood were glued together, cut out with band saw and sanded to form."

G. **Angelo Daluisio, maker;**
Lester Fader, designer; Honolulu, Hawaii

4 x 5 View Camera; koa, brass, ground glass; 12 x 7½ x 9.

H. **F. Stewart Roberts,** Jacksonville, Fla.

Niddy Noddy—A Yarn Skeiner; black cherry; 13 x 13 x 17.

"Unique release tab is not found in traditional models. Carved shape is also unique."

I. **William McCarthy,** Riegelsville, Pa.

Pennsylvania Long Rifle; tiger maple, brass, silver, gold; 60 x 8, $1,900. Relief and incised rococo carving and engraved precious metal inlay—after the golden age of Pennsylvania German gunmakers, 1790-1820.

"This piece is not a kit or copy but a new work using original designs in the carving and stock architecture. I make all my own inlays and cast the brass parts (butt plate and trigger guard) in the finest tradition of the craft."

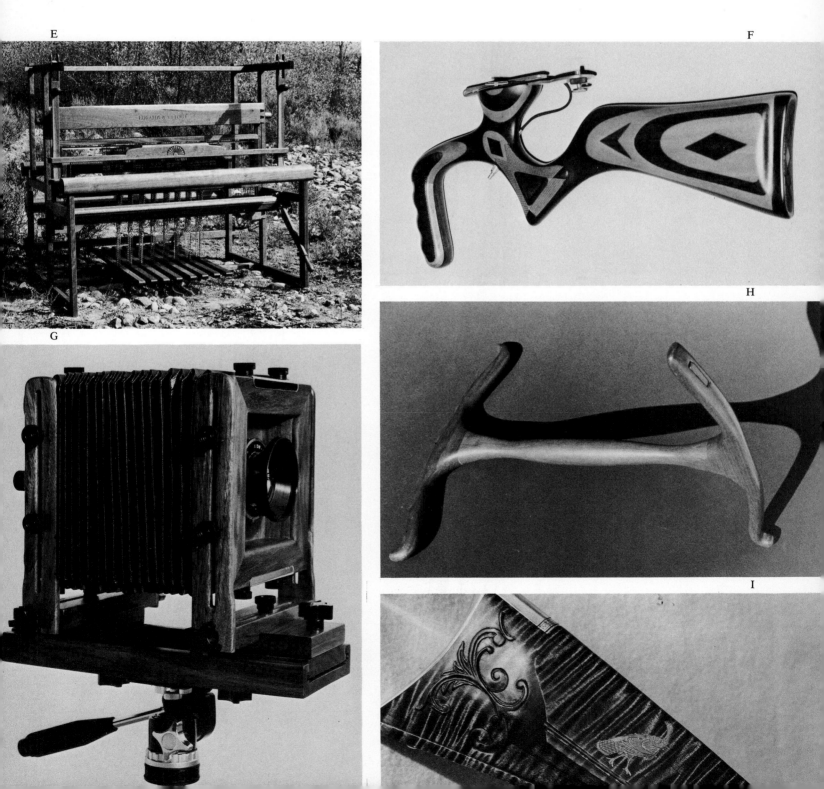

E
F
G
H
I

A. **D. Kim Lindaberry,** Kansas City, Mo.

Potter's Treadle Wheel; mahogany, pecan, steel, leather; 33 x 33 x 36. Can be disassembled for moving or transporting.

B. **Lew McMillan,** Sylvan Lake, Alta., Canada

Spinning Wheel and Stool; eastern maple, black walnut; wheel, 24 dia. Photo by Dallas Harris.

"The wheel is an original design, built with the proportion and symmetry of several museum pieces and the feature of an enlarged orifice/flier assembly, preferred by spinners today."

C. **Wm. S. Coperthwaite,** Bucks Harbor, Maine

Canoe Paddle; cherry. Shaped with ax, knife, sandpaper and finished with tung oil.

D. **Gerald Crawford,** Sedona, Ariz.

Handweaving Loom; maple, birch, oak; 59 x 41 x 37, $2,200. Photo by Peter L. Bloomer.

E. **George B. Kelley,** Hyannis, Mass.

Canoe; fir, cedar, oak, elm; 162 x 26.

"Lightweight canoe after style of J. Henry Rushton, noted boatbuilder of upstate New York in late part of last century."

A

B

D

C

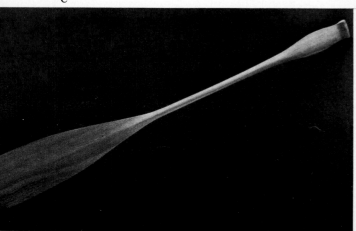

F. **William Charles Houston,** New Market, Tenn.

Painting Easel; walnut, red oak, bird's-eye maple; 80 x 42 x 32.

"Many design features are traditional but many personal innovations were introduced to allow the easel to be more useful and to fit it into a symbolic relationship of the paintings made on it."

G. **Craig Marks,** Altadena, Calif.

Spinning Wheel; walnut with brass fittings; 19 x 19 x 36. Photo by Leonard Thomas.

"This was an effort to express a very old and practical instrument in a contemporary statement. Sharp angles and straight lines are replaced with curved joints and abstract shapes. Whenever possible, simple hand tools were used for making the brass fittings and orifice. Wood grain was carefully matched and enhanced with an oil finish. The design thrust was to give an airy and inviting appearance to the usual cumbersome design of the traditional spinning wheel."

H. **Garry Kvistad,** W. Hurley, N.Y.

Nurse Ratchet; mahogany, maple, padauk, cherry, oak, rosewood, oak veneer, brass hardware; 17 x 16 x 43.

"This bass ratchet was originally built for Charles Amirkanian's 'Duet for Ratchets' performed by the Blackearth Percussion Group (of which I am a member) and is dedicated to the memory of composer/instrument builder, Harry Dartch. Nurse Ratchet does only one thing: make noise."

I. **Arthur Weitzenfeld,** Fair Haven, Vt.

Hand Loom; hard maple, steel, aluminum; 48¾ x 42 x 41½. Photo by Johan Severtsen.

"Bolt construction is the best method for looms, provides rigidity and resilience. I have been building looms for eight years. This loom is in production in a two-man shop."

E

G

H

F

F

I

A. **Nat Ayer,** Johnston, Vt.

Cradle; butternut, walnut, mansonia, mahogany, purpleheart; 38 x 22 x 62. All joints, shapes and contours cut with hand tools. Photo by Don Hanson.

"The height of the stand gives the cradle a very gentle swing, proven soporific. The cradle uprights hang and swing from the crosspiece. Can be disassembled. The purpleheart inlay on the headboard was to give the baby something to look for when she starts to raise her head upon awakening."

B. (and previous page)
Nathan Rome, Cambridge, Mass.

Child's High Chair/Rocker; Baltic birch plywood; 19 x 21 x 35. The legs of the high chair are splayed out at the seat level by using a shouldered scarf joint in each side. The sides were cut with a router using a hardboard template. All joints are mortise and tenon.

"The high chair is designed to be used in three different positions. In its normal upright position it can be used with its adjustable tray; or the adjustable tray may be removed and the chair can be pulled up to a table. Lying on its backside, the chair becomes a rocker. Lying on its front side, it is a low table and seat for eating, drawing or play."

C. **Mark R. Anderson,** Portland, Ore.

Cradle for Carrie; cherry; 40 x 32 x 23.

"The hooks that suspend the cradle slide into a T-shaped slot in the uprights. This allows easy removal from the supports."

D. **Tom Van Dette,** North Adams, Mass.

Cradle; white oak; 36 x 20 x 29.

E. **Anthony Giachetti,** East Boothbay, Maine

Cradle on Stand; black walnut; 43 x 28 x 43. Cradle: panel and frame sides, solid matched ends, slot-dovetailed joinery. Stand: through mortise and tenon joinery. Photo by Stephen Rubicam.

"Cradle rocks in stand. Rosewood thumbscrews stop cradle."

F. **Alexandra Sladky,** Pinole, Calif.

Cradle; walnut, cherry; 39 x 23 x 15. Photo by John Kassay.

"There is a special arrangement of the slats to give comfort to the baby. They break away from the bottom curve and flatten out, and as the slats get closer to the bottom they get closer together. The outer slats were shaped to conform to the shapes of the endboards. The curve of the endboards creates a natural rock so that additional rocking equipment is not needed.... This is my first attempt at fine woodworking."

G. **Robert Calcagni,** Williston, Vt.

Crib; walnut, butternut, maple; 55 x 30 x 40, $1,800.

"Crib sides and mattress frame slide on walnut corner spindles. Unit disassembles for storage."

H. **Robert H. Toombs, Jr.,** Cincinnati, Ohio

Cradle; Baltic birch plywood, plastic laminate; 36 x 24 x 22.

I. **J.M. Sears,** Sebastopol, Calif.

Thrice Cat; white and yellow pine; 60 x 30 x 56¼. Spline joints, dowels and screws were used so that this piece can be taken apart for portability. Eight pieces.

"Drawers go completely through for maximum storage. This piece was created by observation of my son, as an interpretation of his being after nine months here on earth."

F   G

H   I

A. **Christopher A. Hauth,** Salem, Ore.

Cradle; Oregon ash, cocobolo; 45 x 22 x 46, $2,200. Steambent and laminated. Photo by Haugen Photography.

"The base can be disassembled and the basket may be hung from a ceiling beam."

B. **John C. Huntington,** Worthington, Ohio

Crib with Portable Bed; oak, birch, Masonite; 20 x 29 x 48.

"Uses no metal. Portable crib with rack can be carried around so child will have familiar place."

C. **Ted McLachlan,** Winnipeg, Man., Canada

Cradle for Ian Morrish; black walnut, birch inlay, copper; 42 x 24 x 40.

"Cradle swings from two machined bearings set into the uprights. Swing is such that the cradle can be placed against a wall, yet will not touch the wall while rocking."

D. **Yvonne M. David Long,** Houston, Tex.

Cradle; walnut, cane and spline; 42 x 24 x 41.

"I chose walnut wood because I thought its darkness would make a beautiful contrast against the natural finish of the cane. I also thought that a hand-rubbed oil finish would be best because working with the wet cane could damage any other finish. After many months of trial and error, patient guidance by my woodshop teachers and miles of sandpaper, my dream of making an heirloom for the future became a reality."

E. **Gregory W. Tyler,** New Braintree, Mass.

Cradle; cherry; 36 x 22 x 22. Bottom is shiplapped and rabbeted in.

F. **Roy Dewey Duerock,** Seattle, Wash.

Cradle/Dresser; red oak, black walnut; 38 x 20 x 43.

"The cradle was built so that it can be removed from the uprights. After the child has grown to the need of a larger dresser, a larger three-drawer unit will be built and put into

A

B

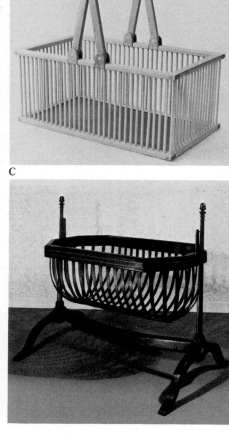

B

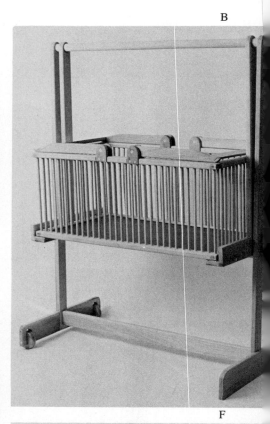

C

D

E

F

place between the uprights. I built this piece as a gift to my sister's first child."

G. **Ron & Helen Vellucci,** Houston, Tex.

Weinerwald Bed; white oak, red oak, Honduras mahogany, basswood, walnut, ¾-in. birch plywood; 86 x 72 x 54.

"Headboard and footboard cores are solid hardwood with 3-in. by 3-in. shaped oak frames joined to them. Mattress pedestal is red oak with a ¾-in. birch plywood deck; it was built in two sections that bolt together to make the pedestal rigid. For access to bolts, as well as the carriage bolts that attach the headboard and footboard, removable 4-in. wide strips of ¾-in. plywood are at the head and foot of each section. Each pedestal half has two storage drawers built into it."

H. **By Design Inc., Tara & Feely,** Wiscasset, Maine

Bunk Beds (demountable); red oak; 80 x 40 x 72 (as bunks).

I. **Alan M. Arkles,** Richboro, Pa.

Night Forest Bed; Amazon mahogany on red oak; 80 x 78 x 50.

"One of the nicer features of this bed is that each branch on the headboard can be used as a stand to hold a clock, candle or ashtray....Also, the moon over the left-hand side of the tree functions as a night light. It is composed of a stained-glass panel lit with a small light bulb."

J. **Richard Marko,** New Haven, Conn.

Bed; red oak. Photo by Al Ventresca.

G

H

I

H

J

A. **Stephen Nutting,** Rockport, Mass.

Queen-Size Bed; maple; 78 x 60 x 42.

B. **Art Heinkel,** Eugene, Ore.

Bed and Side Tables; Central American oak; overall 60 x 80, headboard, 36 high; footboard, 24 high.

"Your basic Chinese Greene and Greene."

C. **Stephen Heckeroth,** Albion, Calif.

Birthing Bed; madrone; 84 x 48 x 48, $1,600.

"The birthing bed was commissioned by the Obstetrics Department of the Mendocino Coast Hospital. Their desire was to get away from the cold plastic and metal hospital beds and provide a warmer, more inviting place for labor and birth."

"The old system was to move the mother during the hardest part of labor from a labor bed to a gurney and then to a surgery table. I designed the bed so that the lower portion of the bed could slide in like a drawer and a backrest would fold up at the head. This arrangement allows the mother to stay in one place the whole time. The bed is big enough to hold both mother and father during labor so the father can give back rubs and encouragement. As the moment of birth nears, the backrest can be lifted up to a comfortable position. Then the cushion lifts off the bottom of the bed and the footrests slide into one of three positions, depending on the mother's height. After the birth, the cushion can be replaced and the bed can be a place for the baby to get its first nourishment and rest with its mother. At the time the pictures were taken, the bed had been in the hospital for five months and had been the site of over 100 births."

D. **Craig A. Peterman,** Denver, Colo.

Bed; American black walnut, cherry, cocobolo; 88 x 65 x 65. Photo by Mark Archer.

"The headboard is a flat layered design. Each thickness is ¾ in. thick. It is 3½ in. thick at its center."

A

B

C

C

D

E. **Tim Armstrong,** Portland, Ore.

Queen-Size Bed; eastern red oak; 62 x 82 x 45. Mortise and tenon joints, hand-shaped posts; side rails fastened with metal detachable hooks.

F. **Russ Hare & Carol Gable-Hare,** New Baltimore, Mich.

Four-Poster Bed; quartersawn and flatsawn red oak; 78 x 64 x 90, $1,600. Seashell is integral, not attached. The center section of the bed is triple-laminated with the middle crossgrained to prevent checking through carving. Glued-up 8/4 red oak posts were turned in one section 85½ in. long. Extensive use of hand tools. All turnings one at a time—no duplicators. Carving and design original, not a copy. In the style of Goddard and Hepplewhite.

"Our bed is often judged to be an antique due to design, choice of wood grains and woodworking techniques."

G. **Steven Schlossman,** Vashon Island, Wash.

Jeff & Shari's Bed; red oak; overall, 60 x 80; footboard, 22 high; headboard, 48 high. Headboard and footboard laminated of ⅜-in. thick red oak to a core of 1½-in. thick red oak.

"The piece is meant to use the various recurrent grain patterns within oak to form patterns and joinery within the form of the bed. It is a very deliberate piece. The mismatched right footboard post breaks the compulsion."

H. **Douglas E. Sigler,** Rochester, N.Y.

The Bed; cherry, fabric, suede, mirrors; 110 x 65 x 72, $5,000. Knocks down to 22 parts.

"The client wanted a canopy, curtains to block out the sun from a skylight, a backrest for reading and lots of storage area. The backrests are suede. The lights are controlled separately and are on a dimmer so one can read or sleep. The mirror in the back is at an angle so that both parties can see each other having sex instead of just one getting a good view. The four drawers are very large and have sliding trays. The console has three switches for the lights and music, an alarm clock, telephone."

E

F

G

H

A. **Larry Davis,** Salem, Ohio

Sculptural Bed; pine, poplar; interior, 72 x 60; exterior, 96 x 84 x 60, $4,000. Laminated wood curved with a Craftsman 7-in. grinder and sanded with a Rockwell block sander.

"The construction took place over the period of one year. The design is similar to the curved, organic type of sculptures that I have been building. The lamination process of sculpture is an additive process, as opposed to the subtractive process of chipping away at a piece of stone or wood. In the end, however, both processes are used, since grinding the wood is subtractive."

B **Judy Kensley McKie,** Cambridge, Mass.

Couch with Dogs; poplar; 80 x 35 x 24. Carved.

A

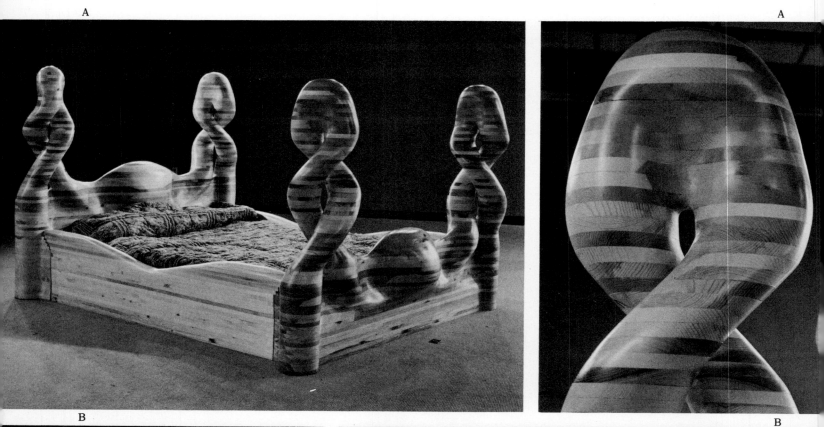

A

B

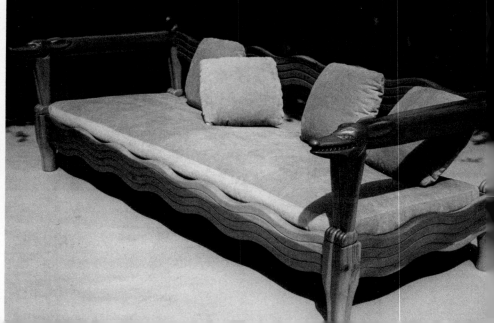

B

C. **Donald H. Pecora,** Alstead, N.H.

Four-Poster Bed; Oak rails, fir posts, tile inlay and covers; 82 x 65, $350.

"Done by practicing woodworker these past four years."

D. **James Thielman,** Richland, Wash.

King-Sized Relief-Carved Headboard; oak; 72 x 44. Posts are ¾-in. stock laminated to 2¼ in.

"This was the piece that led me into cabinetry, for I was commissioned to do the rest of the bedroom set. I do less carving now but recommend it highly....One becomes intimate with wood's secrets."

E. **John Tinkler,** Winnipeg, Man., Canada

Knock-Down Couch; red oak, handwoven wool tweed; 92 x 33½ x 26½, $1,500. Side panels were doweled, glued and clamped. Photo by Len Schlichting.

"The couch can be completely assembled and detatched without any tools; slip joints used throughout. Commissioned by Design Manitoba."

F. **Steve Drenth,** Dowling, Mich.

Bed; oak; 84 x 64 x 56. Laminated, bent headboard carved with drawknife and Surform tools.

A. **Martin J.V. Fischer,** Ottawa, Ont., Canada

Child's Stool; oak; 15½ x 10½ x 10¼.

"I wanted to make something for my little brother Rolf that he could use now and when he was older.... I used oak because it's strong enough to take a child's abuse, and yet has pleasing grain and color. I made the stool after work at the shop where I am now into my fourth year of apprenticeship. I had cut and laminated the pieces, when my boss showed me, with great pride, how dovetails like these were made by hand in the old country, Austria, where he earned his master's license. I had started carefully marking off the dovetails with a sliding T-bevel when he crossed it out, turned the top end-for-end, and told me to do it by eye. So I did it by eye, and it gives the dovetails character and personality, instead of cold, machined uniformity. My little brother, after finally receiving it this summer, carried it into the bathroom and into his bedroom, the living room for TV, and the kitchen to see what's cooking."

B. **Jonathan L. Knight,** Seattle, Wash.

Oak and Fabric Couch; oak, elastic strapping, wool; 80 x 33 x 26. Blind mortise and tenon joints in frame. Horizontal supports triple-laminated for strength because of the long span between sides.

"Designed as a companion piece to a chair, but a bit deeper to encourage the occupant to stretch out. The back is low so that one may put one's arm over the back. Meant to be freestanding in a room to enjoy the repetitive vertical of the back supports."

C. **John D. Wright,** Bay City, Mich.

Low Stool; walnut; 15 x 12¼ x 16.

D. **Karlin Wong,** Los Angeles, Calif.

Love Seat; pine and sisal rope; 56 x 31 x 39. Two-inch lumber laminate sides, mortise and tenon cross members.

"Shown without cushions."

A

B

B

C

D

E. **John Bellingham,** Lansing, Mich.

Stool; white ash; 14 x 14 x 25¼, $250. Photo by Dorothy Potter Barnett.

"There were several major issues involved for me in the construction of these stools: design, duplication, laminated ring, joints and finish. In the design phase, experiments with three and four legs, different leg shapes and slopes, various shaped seats and different edge treatments were tried out on paper and with cardboard. Given the decision to laminate the ring, structural design considerations (such as strength of legs and joints) were determined. Esthetic issues such as continuity between seat and ring, gradual taper upward, and light, 'airy' feeling yet sense of solidness and security also influenced several experimental variations. . . . Although relatively uncomplicated, I found the project a real learning experience. I have just seen the stools again after eight months in order to get the photograph and they seem to be performing well."

F. **Peter Resnik,** Vergennes, Vt.

Bench; cherry; 60 x 20 x 30, $1,000. Dovetailed ends.

G. **Archa Vaughan III,** Richmond, Va.

Stool; ash; seat, 12¾; legs, 16¾ dia. Hub was stacked, then carved; legs are steambent laminations.

H. **Howard Werner,** Mt. Tremper, N.Y.

Love Seat; poplar burl; 66 x 42 x 42. Carved.

E

F

G

H

A. **Robert Lovejoy,** Santa Barbara, Calif.

Love Seat; cherry, cane; 60 x 30 x 35. Spline and tenons.

"Designed with a stool. Love seat shown without cushion."

B. **Sheldon Smith,** Salt Lake City, Utah

Bench; solid oak; 25 x 26 x 37, $3,200. Laminated strips of oak with a reinforced form of metal rods.

"Bench is accentuated by a boldly carved face. Two blank textured panels balance the design."

C. **Joel Forbes,** New Canaan, Conn.

Work Stool; ash, oak; 18 x 14 x 32.

D. **Tom Hurley,** Toronto, Ont., Canada

Bench; black walnut, teak; 48 x 17 x 26. Storage box under seat joined with canted dovetails.

"Raised seat rests flat against back of bench."

A

B

C

D

E. **Glenn Gordon,** Chicago, Ill.

Low Bench; cherry, maple, ebony, cocobolo. 66 x 14½ x 15, $1,000. Surfaces, curves and chamfers planed and spoke-shaved. Cracks lightly carved to emphasize textures. Photo by Don Marshall.

"Made from a single flawed but beautiful 2 in. plank of cherry. Stretcher is maple, doubled wedges are ebony. The butterflies restraining the crack are of cocobolo and maple."

F. **Meg Rodgers,** Philadelphia, Pa.

Swing; teak with brass marine bolts; 72 long, $1,200. Laminated with resorcinol glue.

G. **Dave Anderson,** St. Helens, Ore.

Bent-Leg Stool; Oregon white oak, claro walnut, maple, Pacific yew; 24 high, $325. Photo by R. Neil Haugen.

"This stool uses the common technique of laminating steam-bent parts to maintain strict control of the curve of a bent component. The legs cant at 5° to the vertical so each one has a different shape. They are 1 in. thick (four ¼-in. layers) and taper from 2 in. wide at the top to 1 in. at the bottom. The layers of each leg are cut from the same 2-in. stock, and the orientation is maintained. This makes the hue of the wood consistent across the laminations....All of the stock for this stool was logged and air-dried by my father or myself. I gain much pride in following the wood from the standing tree to the finished product."

H. **Ike Mallula,** Rochester, N.Y.

Bar Stool; cherry, maple; 30 high; from a set of four.

A. **Gordon Keller,** Williamstown, Mass.
   Rocking Stool; brown ash; 18 x 16 x 26.

B. **Timothy Philbrick,** Narragansett, R.I.
   Love Seat; Swedish pearwood, wool; 55 x 24 x 38. Frame carved, shaped and French-polished.

C. **Charles Becker,** Philadelphia, Pa.
   Cobra Stool; laminated cherry.

A

B

C

D. **Sam Caldwell,** Madison, Wis.

Rocking Stool; walnut; 23 x 17 x 17½.

E. **Gary Rogowski,** Milwaukie, Ore.

Stool; red oak, walnut wedges; 16 x 16 x 24. Photo by Harold Wood.

F. **D.H. Meiklem,** Yantic, Conn.

Stool; Honduras mahogany; 25 x 18; made for jewelry store.

"Legs to left and right of front are angled for side-to-side stability. Front and back are at 90° angle. This creates optical illusion. Rear leg comes through seat and is wedged in place."

D

E

F

A. **Stephen Fay,** Pleasantville, N.Y.
   Stool; cherry; 30 high.

B. **Mark R. Habicht,** Baltimore, Md.
   Chair; zebrawood, walnut; 30 x 21 x 33, $860.

C. **Kurt Holsapple,** Germantown, N.Y.
   Stool; walnut; 22 x 13 x 17.

A

B

C

D. **Dean Torges & Don Warman,** Ostrander, Ohio

Set of Ten Chairs; Hickory, leather, canvas; 17 x 16 x 30¼. Photo by George Anderson.

"The chairs weigh five pounds, yet because of design and construction are strong beyond appearance. All the hickory is straight-grained, and every joint except the crest rail and the leg strut at the side seat rails is wedged. Furthermore, the wood was air-dried and the chairs assembled at exactly the right moisture content as the mortises have shrunk slightly around the tenons without pulling away at the shoulders. The backs are steamed and bent in concentric radii and are shouldered inside the back leg posts. The back post is thickest where the seat rails join in, and tapers around and up to distribute flex evenly when people lean back. All the tenons were turned from squared stock and are of different dimensions, depending on their location in the chair. All the members are shaped by hand, primarily with rasps and rattails, as each joint is sculpted at its junction. The seat is of leather reinforced underneath with a light but strong canvas, principally used in convertible car tops. It keeps the leather from sagging and wraps around the seat rails. It and the leather are bonded together and then hand-stitched with waxed linen thread."

E. **Richard Bronk,** Glenbeulah, Wis.

Chair; oak, leather; 34½ high, $290.

F. **Tom F. Urban,** Eugene, Ore.

Bipper; walnut, aluminum.

"You may sit in it, but it is low."

D

E

D

F

A. **Ron Dubreuil,** North Adams, Mass.

Highback Dining Chair; ash, ebony, leather; 22 x 20 x 57. Top is bent laminates, 20 layers of ash veneer. Leather bonded to canvas backing and stretched. Finished with tung oil.

"A study in black and white. All joints mortise and tenon or through wedged tenons. Wedges are ebony; ebony on slats is surface-mounted and bookmatched."

B. **David Van Nostrand,** Atlanta, Ga.

Chair; spalted beech; 17 x 20 x 39. Chain-saw carved from log.

"This chair was designed around the curved form of the tree section to provide a balance between the heartwood and spalted sapwood."

C. **Lee A. Schuette,** Durham, N.H.

'Rake Back' Lawn Chair; white oak, bamboo, grass; 36 x 17 x 21½. Joined, turned, fitted, pinned and planted.

D. **Amy A. Lothrop,** North Adams, Mass.

Highback Chair; cherry, birch ply, paint; 19 x 16 x 57, $600. Traditional seat construction, slats hand-carved, circle laminated and painted.

E. **Fred W. Forrester,** Santa Barbara, Calif.

Norwegian Chair; painted spruce, rush seat; 40 high.

"Chairs of this period (1675) were made in rural home workshops. They were painted in bright colors to add life and color to the homes."

A   B   C

D   E

F. **Paul Nicles,** Longmont, Colo.
   Galley Chair; ash; $225.

G. **Peter Superti,** Boston, Mass.
   Chair; mahogany, padauk, velvet. Laminated, hand-shaped.

F

F

G

A. **Martin Stan Buchner,** Florham Park, N.J.

Child's High Chair; walnut; 22 x 16 x 43. Oil finish.

"Tray moves in/out and locks at 'in' position by dropping on-to the wood detents. Chair is moved by grasping knobs at top and tilting slightly rearward. This positions recessed wheels, at rear of base, against floor."

B. **Maurice Fraser,** New York, N.Y.

Musician's Chair; cherry, walnut, leather; 45 x 17 x 14½, $575.

"Piano/harpsichord chair: A high, contoured back provides support for the performer's back, welcome in relaxed chamber-music setting and continuo accompanying sessions. The curvature of the chair back, in profile, was derived from x-ray photos of a human spine in a posture of repose. The relatively shallow front-to-back seat depth allows the player free leg movement for pedal or knee-lever manipulation without the backs of the knees fouling the seat front—and without perching uncomfortably on the edge of the seat."

"The walnut back slats (ovoid in cross section) are tongued into the back members, but remain unglued to allow for the slats' seasonal contraction/expansion. A housing in the lower edge of the head rest permits the uppermost slat to enter when the slats are in an expanded state and to recede back without a gap when contracted. The slats are grooved in tightly enough not to rattle but loosely enough to be finger-pried back into close proximity when dry and contracted. Mortise and tenon construction throughout."

A   B

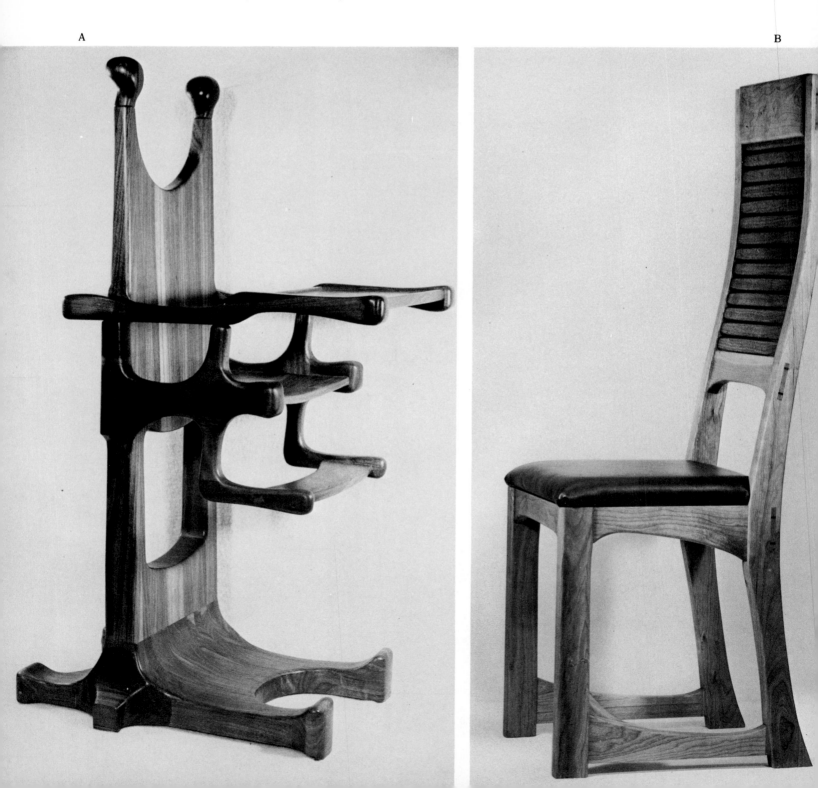

C. **R. Alcusky,** Boston, Mass.

Chair; hickory. Steambent and laminated.

D. **Robert T. Tedrowe, Jr.,** Providence, R.I.

Love Seat; red oak; 48 x 24 x 48.

"Each unit was designed to give the appearance of four floating forms—back, arm, seat, center leg—connected by dowels. They can be used separately or together."

E. **Leslie R. Wells,** Providence, R.I.

Dining Chairs; walnut, Naugahyde over cotton; 19 x 18 x 30, $200 each. Shaper jig production, router jigs, special jigs created for joints.

F. **William Parsons,** Richmond, Va.

Formula-I Chair; cherry, leather; 96 x 48 x 48. Compound bent strip-laminations, stacking, carving.

"Completed May, 1978 for MFA thesis exhibition in wood-working and furniture design at Virginia Commonwealth University."

C
D

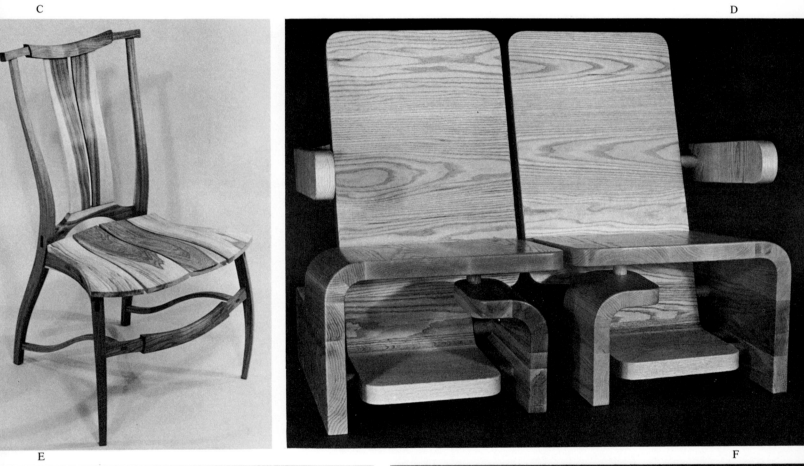

E
F

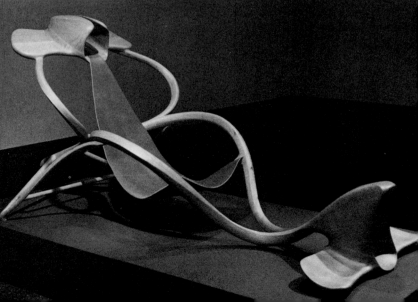

A. **David Wessel,** Durham, N.H.

Chair; cherry, cane; 17 x 18 x 34. Photo by Gary Samson.

B. **Gerald Curry,** Auburn, Maine

Settee; Queen Anne, Philadelphia style; walnut; 40 x 52. Photo by M.A. Bonenfant.

C. **John Michael Pierson,** San Diego, Calif.

Wall Chair; fir plywood, fiberglass; 29 tall, $250.

"This chair mounts directly to the wall using a bracket mortised into the back. The chair is easily removed by lifting up and out, leaving a small plate on the wall. Designed primarily for use in public buildings . . . constructed of stack-laminated fir ply, shaped with a body grinder, finished with a single layer of 6-oz. fiberglass.".

D. **John A. Murray,** Houston, Tex.

Lounge Chair; birch, canvas, steel ring pins; 39 x 22 x 42.

"Lightweight nomadic lounge chair, knockdown."

E. **Jeffrey B. Fabe,** Cincinnati, Ohio

Hall Tree; cherry, walnut; 75 x 32.

"The hall tree is my expression of furniture as a 'living art.' J.R.R. Tolkien's *Lord of the Rings* and in particular the Ent named Treebeard is the fantasy I hoped to catch as a piece of furniture."

F. **Ron Bray,** Santa Ana, Calif.

The Throne; solid oak, leather, china, solid brass; 80 x 22 x 28, $1,300.

"Design work by Al Lamback and Ron Bray; constructed by Heads Up, Inc."

A

B

C

D

E

F

G. **Arthur Medore, Jr.,** Hemet, Calif.

Ejection Reading Lounge; red oak; leather, found object; 42 x 32 x 46, $2,600. Photo by James L. Thomas.

"Hand-carved laminated wood cradle, rebuilt and restored F-86 fighter jet ejection seat, oil and wax finish on wood, green metallic paint on seat."

"Chair is adjustable up and down, magazine storage under seat. Reading lights located on each side of headrest are activated by the ejection levers on each armrest. Compartments for books and tobacco are on each side of seat."

H. **Kirk D. Wonner,** Cardiff-By-The-Sea, Calif.

Sculptchair; Finnish birch plywood (¾ in.); 25½ x 26½ x 30½, $1,500.

"I set out to make a comfortable, elegant yet simple and sturdy chair of wood which would be sculptural, practical and beautiful. But mostly, I was concerned that it be an original design."

I. **Bradford Rankin de Graf,** Alexandria, Va.

Rocker; ash, leather.

J. **Huff Wesler,** Madison, Wis.

Split Tube Chair; cherry; 28 x 28 x 26. Lathe-turned tubes on solid frame.

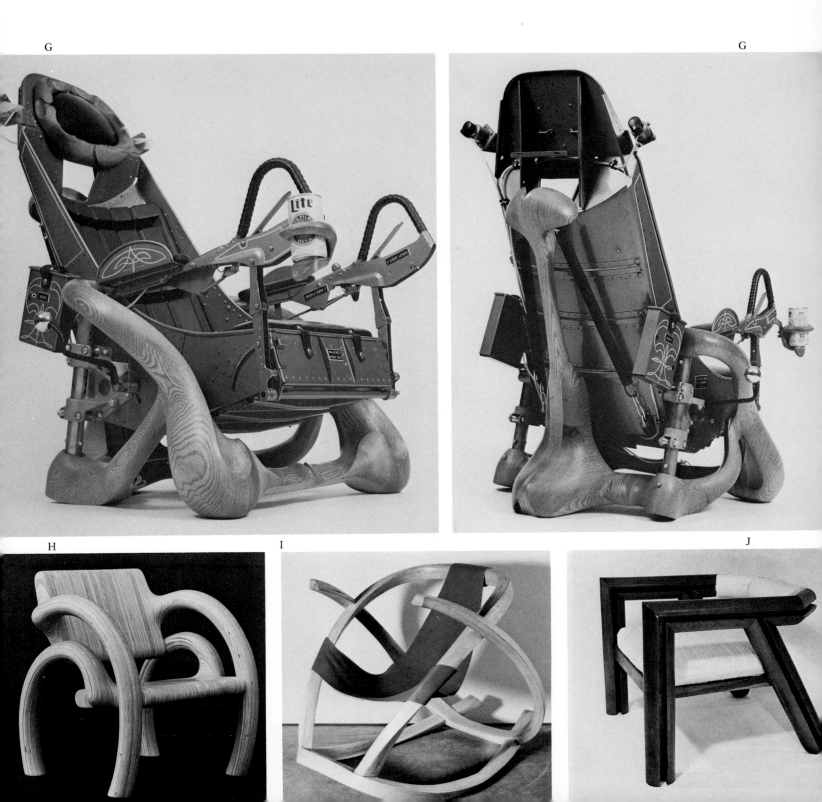

G G

H I J

A. **William A. Keyser,** Honeoye Falls, N.Y.

Altar Chair for St. John the Evangelist Roman Catholic Church (Rochester, N.Y.); red oak. Coopered and hand-shaped.

B. **Bruce Beeken,** Burlington, Vt.

Easy Chair; Andaman padauk. Fabric designed and made by Sandy Weisman, Westboro, Mass.

C. **Michael R. O'Connor,** Milwaukee, Wis.

Chair Throne; red oak, ¼-in. mirror; 80 x 27 x 24. Glass etched by William Krupinski. Photo by Sara McEneany.

"I have been doing woodworking for about four years and now I'm 26 years old. I am proud of this piece and what I'm trying to find in wood. This has evolved from a lot of sources, machines, shop, wood, skills, feelings. I know my direction is positive and I know it will happen. I would love to spend the rest of my life, living wood, learning wood, and someday showing other people this beautiful treasure we all have."

D. **Clark Pearce,** Ann Arbor, Mich.

'Sack Back' Windsor Armchair; maple, ash, pine, green paint.

"Americans in the 18th and 19th centuries took the Windsor form to a very high level of sophistication. The forms are simple, light and strong. Yet, when one tries to make one, it becomes clear how complex and ingeniously thought out they really are. I want people to look at the form of my Windsors, so I paint them, as did all the 18th and 19th-century Windsor chairmakers. There are so many different woods employed in the making of a Windsor chair that without the unification of the paint, the chair would look like a hodge-podge of colors and textures, thereby dissolving the exquisite form."

E. **Dale Broholm,** Hingham, Mass.

Whale's Tales Chair; white oak; 51 x 36 x 24.

"It was my first piece, completed for a design project at college. The arms are continuous laminations of oak, ⅛ in. thick, bent on a metal form. The wood was bent three times, leaving the back twisting 90° to make the turn and then bending down to join the seat."

F. **Bob Ingram,** Youngstown, Ohio

Child's Chair; bird's-eye maple, mahogany; 11 high.

G. **Jeannot Belanger,** St. Foy, Que., Canada

Windsor Chair; white ash.

H. **James D. Conger,** Richmond, Va.

Chair; oak; 26 x 37 x 31.

I. **Pete Greenwood,** Farmington, Conn.

Norwegian Chair; American black walnut; 48 high. Turned and carved; tung oil finish.

"I finished this chair on my 18th birthday last January, in time to sit in it at the head of the table and eat a roast-beef dinner. I have about 300 hours in it. All of the chair parts except the turnings were done at home in my workshop. Every joint is perfect and nothing has moved in a year's time."

J. **Lee J. Weitzman,** Chicago, Ill.

Three-Legged Low-Backed Rocker; mahogany, cherry, aluminum; steel; 35 x 22 x 33, $900. Stacking, bent lamination. Photo by James Riegel.

"The center laminate in both rocker bottoms is 20-ga. aluminum. The two chair backs are cherry wood laminated to a solid steel core that has been forged to a taper and polished. The backs are fastened to the chair side-piece with a pinned mortise and tenon joint."

G

H   I

J

A. **Jeffrey S. Warshafsky,** North Adams, Mass.

Side Chair; red oak, black walnut inlay, brown corduroy seat; 36 x 21½ x 20.

"Back splats were cut from the solid to achieve the curve needed and to get the grain pattern."

B. **Christopher Sabin,** Greenfield, Mass.

Armchair; African bloodwood, cane; 19 x 22 x 34.

"The chair was inspired by the Ming dynasty Chinese armchairs of so-called Lohan type made during the 14th through 17th centuries. My intent was to distill the original design down to its basic components, redesign these and add my own ideas, to try and come up with a chair that would not be connected with any particular period. The Chinese joint used in making the circular armrest is referred to as a cogged scarf joint."

C. **Timothy B. Phillips,** Port Arthur, Tex.

Philadelphia Chippendale Armchair; mahogany, ash; 30 x 23½ x 40.

"The chair was designed after examples attributed to Eliphalet Chapin, although the arms and front legs are unique to the style."

A

B

B

C

D. **Dave Wermuth,** North Adams, Mass.

Highback Chair; cherry, velvet; 22 x 18 x 58.

E. **Ellis B. Walentine,** Coopersburg, Pa.

Dining Chair; ash, Indian rosewood, ivory, upholstery; 18 x 22 x 40. Laminated using wedges to achieve flare at bottom and top. Photo by Ellis Walentine.

"Ivory rosebud is my patented trademark. Back panel of chair is designed to provide support in the center of the user's back and to relieve pressure on the shoulder blades."

F. **Thomas Flemming,** North Adams, Mass.

High Back Chair; cherry, leather seat; 58 high.

G. **Mark Van Dette,** Williamstown, Mass.

Knock-Down Dining Chair; black walnut, cane, wool, foam; 54 x 22 x 25.

"Chair knocks down and assembles in less than two minutes. All fittings remain in place and work with a twist of a screwdriver."

H. **Steve Smyres,** North Adams, Mass.

Highback Dining Chair; cherry, ebony, leather; 57 x 23 x 24.

"Designed as a chair whose appearance and presence are not lost with a person seated in it."

A. **Ross M. Colquhoun,** East Toronto, Ont., Canada

Chable; maple, birch ply, Arborite; 40 x 40 x 29½. All articulations of bolted maple slats, legs self-locking.

"This table-chair seats four very comfortably for meals and folds into a chair of the most comfortable proportions with the addition of feather-stuffed cushions. These cushions are of one piece of corduroy and fold to become a hassock when chable is in table configuration."

B. **Alan Marks,** Pacific Grove, Calif.

Asilomar Easy Chair; white oak, leather; 30 x 32 x 36. Doweled, leg in rear double-splined to rails.

"I tried to create a chair of outstanding comfort for the person of average height. My construction drawing includes dimensions for making it to suit the comfort requirements of very short individuals and six-footers."

C. **Allen Miesner,** Oakland, Calif.

Chair & Ottoman; koa, leather; 21 x 25 x 36.

"The back of the chair was designed to give an open-air feeling. As the chair was built for myself and around my dimensions, it gives excellent support despite what one would imagine from visual examination."

A

A

B

C

D. **Dave Egan,** Kaukauna, Wis.

Lounge Chair; white ash, mahogany veneer, painted birch plywood, cotton denim, foam; 31 x 36 x 39½.

"This chair was designed for limited production runs utilizing knock-down fittings and commercially available fabric design."

E. **John J. Dunnigan, Jr.,** Saunderstown, R.I.

Upholstered Armchair; walnut, cotton fabric; 24 x 24 x 36.

"I used native wood cut near my shop and steambent members before they were fully seasoned. Then I air-dried the stuff for a few months before gluing up the laminates. Next I cut the joints, assembled the chair and finished it. Finally I upholstered it."

F. **Porter E. Littlefield,** East Brunswick, N.J.

Armchair; ash, plywood, foam; 20 x 24 x 34.

G. **Margaret E. Bigelow,** Victoria, B.C., Canada

Triangular Wall Chair; fir, Plexiglas, vinyl; 72 x 1½ x 72.

"The structure of the chair is 1½-in. fir dowels with clear Plexiglas panels slotted in on either side. The sling seat is flexible vinyl. The chair hangs on the wall using a dovetail slot/strip and is held in place by molded Plexiglas clips. The chair is essentially a two-dimensional object until it hangs on the wall, where it takes on the third dimension. It is intended as a functional sculpture: a throne that makes one feel important."

D   E

F   G   G

A. **Warren S. Fenzi,** Phoenix, Ariz.

Library Chair; laminated beech, leather.

"Four principal molds were used, one for each of three sections and one to combine the three into one finished frame. One other mold was used for the seat frame (interior)."

B. **Robert Freeman,** Newton Center, Mass.

Side Chair; ash, mahogany, upholstery; 20 x 38 x 21.

C. **John W. McNaughton,** Evansville, Ind.

The McNaughton Chair; fir plywood; 34 x 24 x 30, $500. Cut from one 4-ft. by 8-ft. sheet of ¾-in. plywood.

D. **Jerry Konicek,** Madison, Wis.

Adjustable Recliner; oak, Naugahyde; 60 x 29 x 52, $750.

"All wooden members are shaped in a triangular motif. The chair is adjustable from an upright position to a fully reclined position by sliding within the base."

A   B   C

D

D

E. **Peter Danko,** Alexandria, Va.

*Hands & Feet Chair; cherry, leather; 32 x 26 x 26, $900 +
fabric. Laminated, carved.*

F. **Brandon J. Santos,** Dixon, N. Mex.

*#1:2-25-78; fir plywood, French oak, leather; 36 x 24 x 40, $500.
Photo by Brother Martinus, C.S.C.*

"Plywood is my favorite. The raucous striping counterpoints
the smooth, soft contour of the chair's shape."

G. **Donald C. Bjorkman,** Los Osos, Calif.

Spring Rocker; white oak; 42 x 30 x 41.

H. **Carolyn & John Grew-Sheridan,** San Francisco, Calif.

Recliner & Ottoman; Honduras mahogany; 52 x 24 x 38, $925.

"The chair has three positions and the ottoman two. Each of
the slats in the seats and the back is individually adjustable—it is not a tambour."

E   F

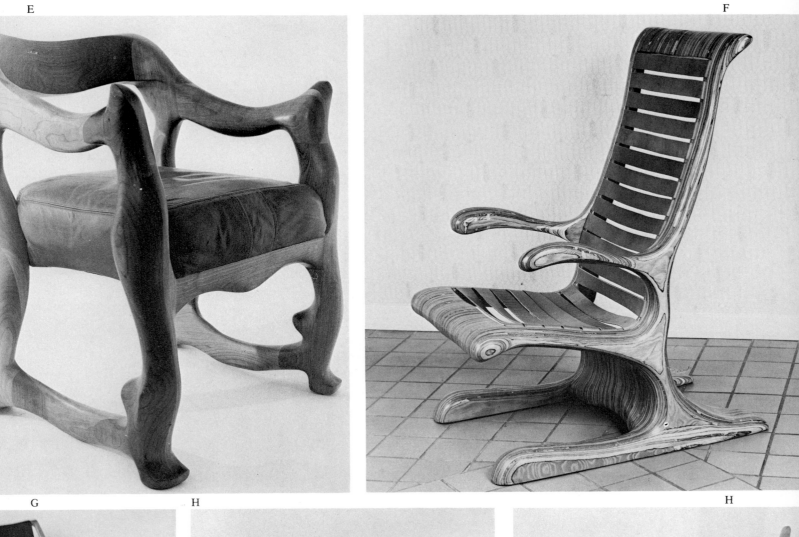

G   H   H

A. **Edward Zucca,** Putnam, Conn.

Office-Chair-Throne; cherry, black leather, gold leaf; 20 x 26 x 61. Chair built on existing office-chair base— swivels, tilts and rolls.

"The design is very derivative of ancient Egyptian styles. The lion is a conglomerate of royal dynasty sculptures. The traditional sun disc over the head is gold leaf. On either side is the owner's name, rendered in hieroglyphics relief-carved with gold leaf background behind the characters. Stripes of maple veneer are inlaid on the sides of the arms to accentuate the effect of a padded fabric draped up and over each arm."

B. **Gordon Kyle,** Waterford, Conn.

Convertible Armchair; maple, birch plywood, fabric, polyester fiber; 33 x 27 x 37, $189. Photo by Thomas Hahn.

"Chair is held together by 'nuts and struts' which allow for complete disassembly without any tools. Design is U.S. Patent Pending. The chair can be converted from the armchair to the rocker by a simple manipulation of the free-floating seat section. The design employs a design concept I call 'conspicuous construction' where the mechanics of the construction are made obvious."

C. **Roger Bartman,** Keaau, Hawaii

Dining Chair; koa; 22 x 23¾ x 48.

D. **John Kevin Barth,** Portland, Ore.

Chair; maple, hickory; 24 x 24 x 34. Rear legs laminated, other parts bandsawn and hand-shaped. Photo by Victor H. Wandtke.

A

A

B

C

D

E. **John A. Kapel,** Woodside, Calif.

Chair; laminated oak; 20 x 20 x 34. Molded on pressed wood forms.

"I design and make prototypes for industry. This chair is now produced by Kosuga Furniture Co. of Japan. The chair pictured is the original prototype made by me."

F. **Stephen B. Crump,** Memphis, Tenn.

Rocker; white oak; 37 x 25 x 45.

E

F

F

A. **Charles R. Parenteau,** Freehold, N.J.

Rocking Chair; black walnut; 28 x 16 x 47.

"The design is completely my own for the purpose of fitting my wife perfectly. It was finished on Christmas Eve of 1978 and was given to her as a gift."

B. **Mitchell Ackerman,** Providence, R.I.

Reclining Chair Which Folds Flat; maple, birch dowels, ¼ steel rod; 36 x 2 x 24, flat.

"This chair consists of two intersecting dowel panels. These panels support the seat and back separately. When one sits back in the chair it reclines, without any special hardware. By disengaging the bottom member, the chair folds completely flat. Patent Pending."

C. **Steven A. Foley,** Lake Oswego, Ore.

Rocker; walnut; 35 x 17 x 30, $1,500.

"The cage ornament, as with the rest of the chair, is of bentwood construction, achieving great strength with diminutive proportions."

D. **F.L. Wall & John Ruthwell,** Herndon, Va.

Rocking Chair; Honduras mahogany; 36 x 24 x 44.

E. **E. Allen McLane,** Eugene, Ore.

Child's Rocking Chair; walnut, leather saddle skirting; 15 x 15 x 30.

"I am 69 years old and retired. On moving to Eugene, I purchased a home, and on the property stood an old stump about 6 ft. high and 10 in. in diameter. I decided to remove the stump and on doing so found it to be walnut. Although it was much weathered and damaged by insects I decided to see what I could do with it. The chair in the picture is the end result. Designed and built as a present to my first grandson on his first birthday."

A   B   B   C   D   E

F. **Alan Greenberg & Denise Eagleson-Greenberg,**
Yellow Springs, Ohio

Shaker-Inspired Rocking Chair; cherry with bird's-eye maple slats; 42 x 23 x 20. All pieces hand-turned, back legs and slats steam-bent.

"We have been collaborating for two years to make comfortable, graceful rocking chairs. This cherry rocker is our latest and best effort. At one point, we produced an edition of eight rocking chairs and found that, though it made more sense economically, we lost sight of each chair as a singular entity. We now work on one chair at a time. This allows us to pay close attention to each aspect of construction as well as matching grain patterns to their best advantage."

G. **Bruce Kranzberg,** Steamboat Village, Colo.

Rocking Chair; oak; 34 x 27 x 31, $350.

H. **Randall L. Overdorff,** Blairsville, Pa.

Harp Rocker; red oak; 21 x 22 x 44

"The design is a resolution of a concept that required the building of several chairs. My object is to build three-dimensional chairs, esthetically pleasing, comfortable chairs that are a pleasure to live with—for years and years."

F

G

H

A. **Carl Simring,** New York, N.Y.

Rocker; birch plywood. Photo by Eric Kroll.

B. **Stephen Schaefer,** Providence, R.I.

Rocker; cherry. Back legs steamed and laminated with headrest, remaining pieces all solid wood; upholstered seat.

C. **Leon Manoukian,** Watertown, Mass.

Rocking Chair; black walnut, aluminum, leather; 36 x 22 x 42.

"The aluminum is used structurally to support the seat, which is cantilevered off the arms."

D. **Randall J. Calvert,** Santa Ana, Calif.

Bentwood Rocking Chair; Philippine mahogany; standard dimensions.

"This original-design bentwood rocker took first prize at the 1978 Orange County Fair in the professional furniture making competition. The free-flowing design is not only esthetically pleasing but allows for a maximum in comfort. The chair is constructed of eight layers of 1/10-in. lauan (Philippine mahogany) and took approximately 250 hours to complete."

E. **Michael Daigle,** Mississauga, Ont., Canada

Rocker; white oak, rattan; 22½ x 20½ x 46. All the pieces are laminated from one 6/4 board. Pinned and plain fox-wedged tenon construction.

"I made the chair for watching the hockey playoffs. Each game I put on about five miles."

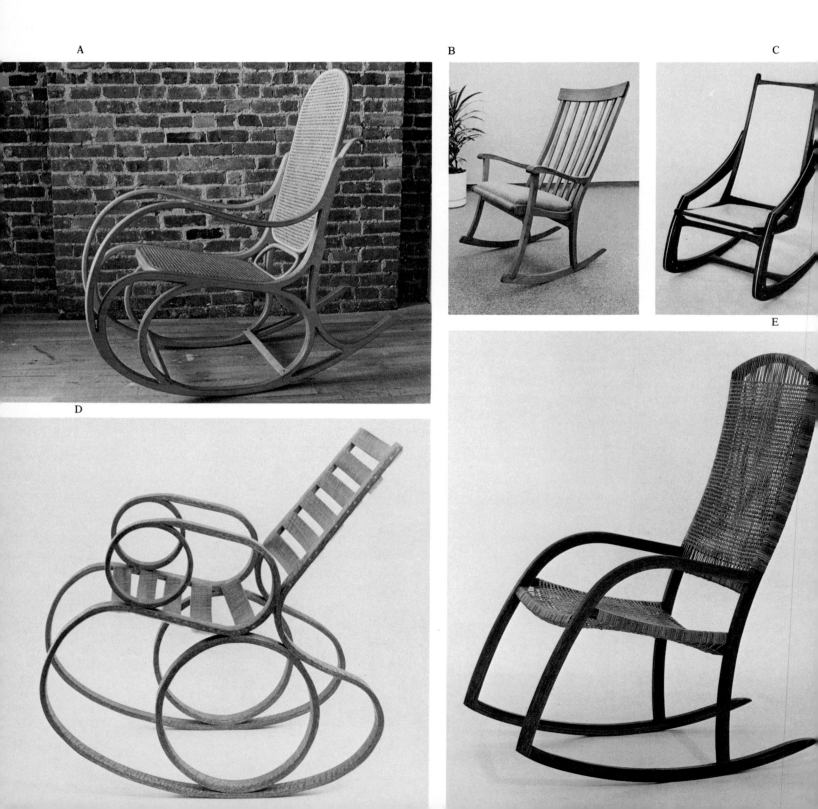

A

B

C

D

E

F. **Scott Dickerson,** Brooksville, Maine

Rocker 1; walnut, cane; 40 x 20 x 40.

"A comfortable chair for an unusually wide range of human physiques due to a supportively profiled back and resilient cane seating."

G. **C.R. Johnson,** Stoughton, Wis.

Safety Rocker #2; walnut, leather; 42 x 22 x 52, $950.

H. **Ellen Swartz,** Rochester, N.Y.

Rocking Chair; Baltic birch plywood, upholstery; 36 x 21 x 30.

"This piece was designed for multiple production. It incorporates my regular use of plywood lamination with a construction compatible with limited or mass-production techniques."

F   G

H

A. (and previous page)
Chuck Masters, San Diego, Calif.

Coffee Table; white oak, black walnut; 60 x 30 x 18, $480

"The top on each table is a uniform 1 in. thick. The imposed warp and gap were carved by hand from sections 2 in. thick. The legs are connected to the top by a three-way open slot mortise."

B. **Richard Sands,** Chapel Hill, N.C.

Game Table; bird's-eye maple, southern maple; 38 x 29½.

"To form the base, 2-in. maple was laminated together. From this piece horizontal sections of the base were bandsawn. These pieces were laminated vertically, then shaped with rasps and files. The joint was fitted, and the top screwed to the supports."

C. **Jeff Kellar & Judy Labrasca,** Portland, Maine

Dining Table; walnut; 42 dia. x 30, $425. Mortise and tenon and dowel joints. Top is attached with wooden buttons.

D. **Salvatore Abbate,** Ledyard, Conn.

Glass-Top Dining Table for Six; red oak, Philippine mahogany, glass; 62 x 38 x 30½.

"The top rails are halved joints, double dowels in each joint. Rail, uprights and feet are mortised and tenoned to each other."

A

B

C

D

E. **M. F. Doll** Milwaukee, Wis.

Power In Curves; birch, cane, glass; 18 x 50 x 18. Laminated and steam-bent. Photo by Scott Witte.

F. **Robert B. Lewis,** Onaway, Mich.

Dining Table; oak; 42 x 30.

"The top was made by cutting the individual pieces for the parquet pattern and gluing them to a base. The outer oak pieces were then added and the top cut round. A groove was then routed around the top on the underside and the face board was set into it. This board was made flexible by hundreds of relief cuts on the inside, which were filled with pieces of wood after it was glued in place. The base was glued up from eight pieces of oak and turned on a lathe. The legs were glued from three pieces of oak, bandsawn and shaped by hand."

G. **Clifford Wagner,** Churchville, Pa.

Glass-Top Grid-Work Dining Table; black walnut, maple, glass; 62 x 42 x 29, $2,000.

"The grid is all half-lap joints, cut on the table saw using a sliding plywood jig."

H. **Mark Daley, Woodsong,** West Los Angeles, Calif.

Freeform Breakfast Table, red oak, glass; 42 x 29.

"Rough shape doweled and glued, then hand-sculpted with band saw, router and hand tools. Bringing back the curves and asymmetry the wood originates from was the goal of this design."

E

F

G

H

A. Eric Hoag, Madison, Conn.

Dining Table & Chairs; cherry, glass; table, 51½ x 35½ x 29¾; chairs, 17½ x 17½ x 18.
Photo by William K. Sacco.

"With this minimal leg design, much work goes into making it structurally sound, and I decided to use a glass top on this one to show structural details."

B. Patrick Warner, Escondido, Calif.

Dinner Table with Bench; cherry; 72 x 36 x 31, $950.

"Feet are glued up from five pieces and hand-shaped. Beams 3½ in. thick prevent warping. Benchtop rests on ⅜-in. rabbet and floats, also is removable to allow cleaning of slot."

C. John M. Westgate, Everson, Wash.

Trestle Table; eastern birch, black walnut; 80 x 33 x 29.
Photo by Jean Regal Westgate.

"One of my design concerns was for great stability in a table that is easily disassembled by hand by the removal of the four friction pegs and two friction wedges. I was successful in accomplishing this by allowing for large bearing surfaces where the trestle meets the legs (mortise and tenon joints) and where the legs meet the tabletop cross-pieces."

D. Dick Cross, Crosscuts Woodworking, Creswell, Ore.

Dining Table, Trestle Style; Oregon white oak; 96 x 40 x 29, $1,300. All edge joints glued and splined; trestle hardware—blind bolts behind turned medallions.

E. **Robert Beiswinger,** Millstone, N.J.

Breakfast Table; red oak, white oak; 52 x 34 x 30.

"Jim Krenov's meticulous subtlety inspired me to do this table. Legs are about ¼ in. smaller at top than bottom. The taper is curved, not straight. I've attempted to choose wood whose grain follows the curves I've imposed. The front and back rails are planed to a slight upward and outward bow, which is accentuated by the similar curve of the wood grain. Tabletop edges have been rounded with a plane. The shimmering facets on these edges are touchable, mellow and worth the effort. The drawer has an identical front and back, a central partition, and can be opened from either side."

F. **Dennis Soden, Eclectic Woodworks,** Kansas City, Mo.

Bar & Bar Stools; red oak; bar, 60 x 22; stools, 3l x 15.

"The stools have a built-in hidden swivel—they rotate 360°."

G. **Stephen Swift,** Nantucket Island, Mass.

Sherin Table; black cherry, walnut; 60 dia., $850.

E

E

F

G

A. **Steven Altman,** Brooklyn, N.Y.

Dining Table; ash; 60 x 34 x 30.

"Trying to relate oriental esthetic to contemporary style."

B. **Ken Willis,** Glen Allen, Va.

Coffee Table; walnut, glass; 36 x 20 x 16, $750. Laminated stretcher, mortise and tenon construction.

"This table is a variation of a design I first produced as a series in 1973. A separate block is inlet into the joint at the legs and stretchers to achieve the curve without having feathered edges that occur when a piece is glued on.'"

C. **Zvi H. Weinman and Tui Weinman,** Allentown, Pa.

Dining Table; spalted ash, rosewood; 84 x 40½ x 29¾, $800.

Trestle base uprights are fastened with wedged dowels, after the method of construction of old barns in this area."

D. **Donald Lloyd McKinley,** Mississauga, Ont., Canada

Triple Position/Use Table with Shelf; Tasmanian blackwood; Game Table: 74 x l06½ cm square, Hall Table: 74 x l06½ x 38 cm, Cocktail Table: 38 x l06½ x 74 cm. $1,000.

"Through tenon pairs are double wedged; brass and steel pivot machined to my specifications. Table has pivot top and single drop-leaf; turned glides for cocktail table position."

E. **Ivan Hass,** Logan, Utah

Dining Table; maple, birch ply, black walnut; 84 x 36 x 30.

" A dining table to seat six, legs and stretcher allow for seating and foot room, top screwed to cross piece, easily broken down to two leg units, top, stretcher, and keys for moving."

F. **Mary A. Kennedy,** Rochester, N.Y.

Dining-Room Table; maple, curly maple veneer, Baltic birch; 48 x 48 x 29, with leaf 72, $1,500.

"The top surface is a reverse diamond match pattern created by the veneer; the grain radiates from the center. The extra leaf in the table is located on a pivot below the surfae of the table. When the two half-circle leaves are pulled to the sides, the center leaf can swing up into place. It is located by pins."

D

D

D

E

F

A. Amil St. Augustine, Novato, Calif.

Roll-Top Desk; oak, vermilion; 58 x 50 x 34.

"Utilizes both plain and quartersawn white oak, providing grain and color contrasts as well as helping to minimize expansion-construction problems in lower back. Highly varied storage spaces are provided by size, shape, depth and height of various drawers and inner storage arrangement (higher spaces are consecutively shallower). The middle drawer on each side is designed for use as file drawer accessible from seated position (four file bins in all); the file drawer opens fully without dropping.

"Drawer-front construction is angled sections laminated to match curve, carefully color and grain-matched to appear as single piece, lined on inside with thicker slab to strengthen and also allow desired thickness for finger hole pull. All drawers are lockable via pins inside."

B. Neal M. Widett & Susan C. Wilson, Boston, Mass.

Butcher-Block Window-Box Table; white oak base and top, pine carving with leather shoes, linen apron and pants, rubber chicken stuffed with shavings. 84 x 36 x 30. Photo by Ron Harrod.

"This is our contribution to the currently fashionable style of furniture. Dinner at (or with) this table is a unique experience."

C. F. W. Foess, F. W. Foess & Son Furniture Makers, Federal Way, Wash.

Extension Table; red oak; 42 dia. x 30 high, extends to 90, $900. Leg/stretcher assembly: blind mortise and tenon. Top: doweled and edge-glued boards (max. 5 in. wide).

"The design of this table base was the result of the client's requirement for a pedestal-type table without the instability usually associated with pedestal construction. When fully closed the base forms a uniform square figure. When extended, it forms a triangular figure supporting each end of the table.

A

B

C

D. **Jeffrey R. Lehrbaum,** Philadelphia, Pa.

Trestle Dining Table with Marquetry Top; black walnut; 63 x 35 x 30, $1,200. Photo by George Faraghan Studio.

"There are four leaf-support extensions, which pull out from beneath the tabletop on either end. With the supports in place, the seating capacity is increased from six people to ten. The tabletop is a free-form marquetry pattern consisting of ten veneers and an inlay border. The marquetry pattern increases the table's value by making it an artform as well as a functional dining-room table."

E. **Barbara N. Miller,** Watchung, N.J.

Table; cherry, glass; 112 x 44 x 30.

"Base is stack-laminated with vertical members tenoned into the bottoms and finger-lapped with top horizontal members. The top hinge and supporting bracket hinge are wood with brass pins. The table seats six comfortably with the leaves down and ten with both leaves up. In the center is a ¼-in. thick piece of glass that sits flush with the top."

F. **Steve & Vange Mueller,** Woodinville, Wash.

Spanish Dining Set; American walnut; 86 x 50 x 30½ open, $3,000.

"For the sunburst design we sliced 2-in. stock on the band saw into ³⁄₁₆-in. thick strips. The strips were then numbered in order to obtain a continual grain-pattern sequence. With a jig, the strips were cut into wedges and glued and clamped to the underlayment. Although the octagon is not authentically of Spanish design, the hand-carved, low-relief motifs are a version of the rosette. The table is opened by our own walnut sliders to accommodate two 18-in. wide leaves, exposing the finished inside of the split pedestal."

D

E

F

A. **John Kriegshauser,** Kansas City, Mo.

Dining Table; red oak veneer; 48 dia. x 30, $500.

"The base is air-pressure-laminated veneers. The top is veneer with oak edging. The top opens for one leaf."

B. **Ron Berger,** Saint Paris, Ohio

Dining Table; red oak, walnut; 48 x 48 x 30.

"Table extends to 12 ft. Center leg within hollow pedestal is attached to center slide sections, which provides support when opened. Ball casters recessed into legs."

C. **Terry Miller,** Jaffrey, N.H.

Communion Table; walnut; 36 x 18 x 30 closed, 62 open.

D. **Allen Spalt,** Pittsboro, N.C.

Walnut Dining Table; Tennessee black walnut; 48 dia. x 30. Doweled and edge-glued top, 1¾ in. thick; pegged mortise and tenon base, 2¼-in. thick sections. Pedestal divides with top to accept leaves. Photo by Markatos Photography.

E. **Emmett E. Day,** Seattle, Wash.

Table & Chairs; teak; table, 96 x 36.

"Chairs have contoured, not sawn, backs, solid teak screwed and glued construction with buttons to hide screws."

F. **Sandy Brenner,** West Henrietta, N.Y.

Dining-Room Table; red oak; 48 x 84 x 30.

"The drop-leaves are supported underneath by a sliding bar."

G. **Andrew J. Willner,** Thompson, Pa.

Nursery Rhymes End Table; cherry, red oak; 27 x 27.

H. **Charles Tedesco,** Grayslake, Ill.

Queen Anne End Table; Honduras mahogany, red oak; 20 x 24 x 22½.

"Legs are carved from a single block of wood. (Only the 'ears' are glued on.) Joinery is mortise and tenon. Although end tables did not exist in 18th-century America, this piece is offered as an adaptation appropriate in design, wood and construction."

I. **Chris Peterson,** Eugene, Ore.

Dining Table; white oak; 78 x 36 x 33. Photo by David Bayles.

"This is an arched-trestle design. The arch is laminated from ¼-in. pieces. The hinges are leather straps."

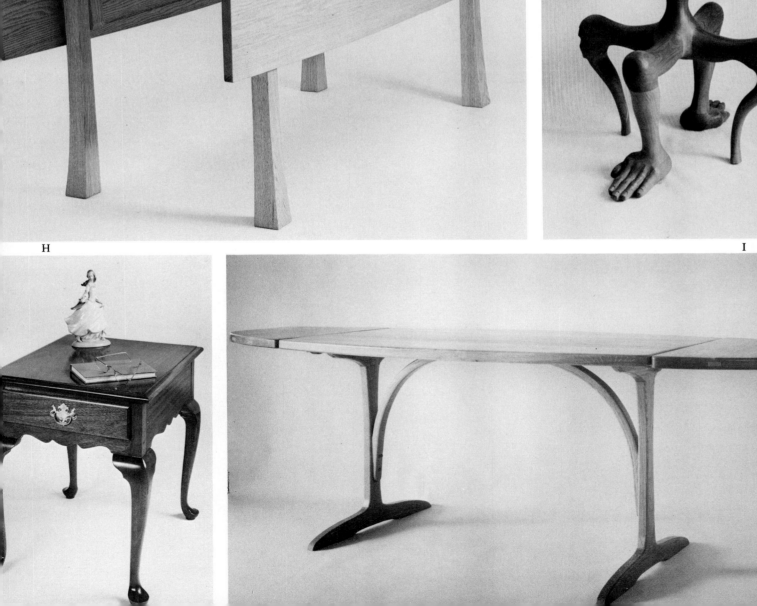

A. **James D. Sedwick,** Williamsville, N.Y.

Dining Table; cherry; 48 x 48 x 29 ½, $700.

"Four buttons, which pass through side rails, restrain top and also hold slides (two on each end), which may be pulled out to support leaves (stored separately). All parts hand-planed and spokeshaved to shape."

B. **John P. Stephenson,** Canton, N.C.

Dining-Room Extension Table; walnut, steel rod; 72 x 40 x 30, $900.

"The major feature of this table is the finger-type hinges by which the leaves are attached to the main top. Each hinge pivots on a rod of ¼-in. steel that runs the inside length of the leaf, about 36 in. The ends of the rods are concealed by walnut plugs.

"Top and leaves are made of pieces about 3½ in. wide, which are half rounded with a ½-in. rounding-over bit in a router. Those pieces which will hold the rod are then drilled with a $^{17}/_{64}$-in. drill bit that has been reground to a brad point, a size not commercially available in brad points so I had to grind my own. I drilled the holes using a chuck

mounted on the outside arbor of a radial arm saw. The feet are each made up of six strips of walnut that have been dimensioned with the use of a planer mold, which leaves the strips thicker at the ends than at the middle. This same shape could have been achieved by simply gluing up stock and then bandsawing out the shape; but I didn't want a glue line on the face of the foot. The laminations are glued up in a two-piece mold using plastic resin glue. All joinery is mortise and tenon except leaf hinge mechanism, and the main top is slip-screwed to battens underneath. The stretchers are triple-tenoned to the legs for added glue surface."

C. **J. Christopher Hecht,** Sagle, Idaho

Three-Leg Side Table; oak, bronze, glass; 24 dia. x 24. Splines of oak.

D. **David Krouse,** New York, N.Y.

End Table; white oak, suede; 19 x 19 x 17.

E. **Lynn L. Shirk**, Wenatchee, Wash.

End Table; birch, black walnut; 26 x 18 x 23, $700. Bent wood and block laminations.

F. **Tom D'Onofrio,** Bolinas, Calif.

Dragon Table; rosewood, California walnut, angico, vermilion, glass, elk antler; Top, 60 x 84 x 24, Base, 114 x 16 x 12, $15,000. Photo by Lewis Watts.

"Dished-out wings on tabletop and scaled tail serve as seats. By unscrewing two warts on side of head, the tongue slides out to reveal a secret box with a silver-cast dragon inside. Entire body is scaled and gnarled in true dragon fashion. Entire base is laminated and hand-carved."

G. **Tim Donahue,** Wilton, Conn.

Coffee Table; cherry; 48 x 24 x 16. Compound dovetails, spline miters.

E   F

G   F

A. **John M. Bogert, Jr.,** Wardsboro, Vt.

Night Tables for Four-Poster Bed; butternut, black walnut; 20 x 17 x 22, $850/pair. Compound curves of sides are staves bandsawn to vertical curve before assembly. Photo by Jurgen Schultz.

"These tables were designed to complement a black walnut four-poster bed and are part of a set that includes a butternut bureau in the same style."

B. **Michael Schuetz,** Kansas City, Mo.

Curvilinear Table; fir plywood, ash veneer; 32 x 22 x 16, $400.

"Composed of two surfaces and one undulating edge, the table can approximate the seat height or the arm height of most sofas by turning it on its side. Rotating it presents fronts of differing characters."

C. **Peter Jackson Zander,** Pound Ridge, N.Y.

Bent Laminate Coffee Table; walnut, glass; 44 x 17 x 18, $900. Bent laminates, splined 45°, glass sits in dado unattached.

D. **James T. Duncan,** Berkeley, Calif.

Pedestal Table; Claro walnut; 19 cube.

"This table was designed to serve as a pedestal for a large ceramic jar, which I especially prize. The four pieces of the top surface are tongue and grooved. All the other joints are just plain butt-glued."

A   B

C   D

E. **Steve Parks,** Tucson, Ariz.

Omega Coffee Table; American black walnut; 60 x 22 x 18.

"Top and shelves are butt-glued. Legs joined and shelves joined to legs with splines and yellow glue. 'Anti-warp' boards attached to undersides of top and shelves only, with screws countersunk from both sides to help allow for movement."

F. **David Holzapfel,** Marlboro, Vt.

Coffee Table; spalted elm, spalted American beech; 39 x 39 x 17. Photo by W. Allan Gill.

"Unlike the traditional designer who creates a design in mind and/or on paper, then joins the boards necessary to achieve the design, I (and those who use this type of wood) begin with the board. The shape, grain pattern and natural defects (checks, bark seams, etc.) of the wood influence and suggest the design of the finished piece. The top is a single board sawn out with a chain-saw mill. The base was cut into a cube freehand with a chain saw."

G. **Jeffrey Harris,** Sarasota, Fla.

Coffee Table; red oak, black walnut, padauk.

Each inlaid piece is ½ in. thick. After cutting it to fit, all pieces are numbered and removed and then beveled to approximately 45°, then glued into place. The resulting dimensional effect has become a trademark of my work."

H. **Claude Mauffette,** Montreal, Que., Canada

Coffee Table; red oak, bury, glass; 25 x 25 x 14, $90.

E

F   G

H

A. **William D. Cherkin,** Rochester, N.Y.

'Together' Coffee Table; African mahogany, glass; 44 x 30 x 16. Stacked laminations. Photo by Michael Dobranski.

"'Together' reflects upon one of the many beauties in being human."

B. **Mitchell D. Landy,** North Miami, Fla.

Coffee Table; walnut; 62 x 27 x 17.

"I'd been saving these bookmatched flitches for three years, and left a space between to emphasize the pairing."

C. **James B. Eaton,** Houston, Tex.

Coffee Table; red oak, white oak; 52 x 12 x 19.

A

B

C

D. **Randall D. Lee,** Boulder, Colo.

Coffee Table; walnut; 50 x 20 x 16. Photo by Sundance Photographics.

"Joints are mortise and tenon. Curved members were shaped by hand with drawknife and spokeshave."

E. **John Packard,** Sea Cliff, N.Y.

Tilt-Top Chair Table; cherry; 34 x 34 x 19.

"Functions beautifully as coffee table. Space behind drawer is secretly accessible. Top tilts up on turned pins."

D

D

E

E

A. **Rick Wrigley,** Arlington, Va.

Coffee Table; walnut; 35 x 21 x 17.

B. **Roy M. Tidwell,** Sunnyvale, Calif.

Coffee Table; walnut, ceramic tile; 60 x 23 x 16, $1,500.
Laminated, held together with threaded rods and glue.

C. **Morris J. Sheppard,** Santa Monica, Calif.

Helix; koa, glass, gesso; 60 x 36 x 18.

"The helix in this form is expanding at an ever-increasing
rate according to a mathematical ratio know as the Fibo-
nacci series. The whole was designed and the angles calculated on paper, cut out on the band saw, assembled and then
shaped. In order to achieve the desired forms, all the wood
was 16/4, some pieces 10 in. wide."

A

B

C

D. **Peter E. Hart,** Menlo Park, Calif.

Coffee Table; white oak, glass; 44 x 24 x 15. Photo by Nils J. Nilsson.

"Large dovetails join legs to 'floating' central core."

E. **Craig Nutt,** Tuscaloosa, Ala.

Feline Table, Egyptian New Kingdom style; black walnut, deer antler, satinwood; 36 x 18 x 20. Carved legs, claws inlaid deer antler. Photo by Janice Hathaway.

F. **Richard P. Ornsteen,** Gladwyne, Pa.

Coffee Table; teak, poplar, plywood; 45 x 22 x 15.

"The top was made by gluing sections of teak flooring offset with diagonal strips of teak to plywood. This was framed with teak, the corners rounded and the edges routed."

G. **Douglas Hale,** Providence, R.I.

Coffee Table; lacquered maple, rosewood veneer; 54 x 18 x 16.

H. **Phillip Tennant,** Indianapolis, Ind.

Coffee Table; walnut, bubinga veneer; 32 x 32 x 16.

D

E

F

G

H

A. **Michael Ciardelli,** Milford, N.H.

Display Coffee Table; teak, leather, glass; 36 x 36 x 18.

"This piece was designed to display a collection of medallions. The carved portion in the center and the top of each leg is an attempt to break up the geometry of the piece with organic forms."

B. **Dennis Olivera,** Oakland, Calif.

Coffee Table; teak, black walnut, ceramic tile; 50 x 18 x 22.

"Ceramic tile was inlaid and bordered with black walnut to enhance the color and design of the tile. Through and wedged mortises were used, top is attached with handmade, movable clips."

C. **Robert L. Grun,** Lenox, Mass.

Coffee Table; oak; 51 x 21 x 15.

A

B

C

D. **John M. Barrow,** Glen Echo, Md.

Coffee Table; walnut, padauk; 48 x 18 x 15.

"Butterfly joint on surface, splines joining legs."

E. **Dana Hatheway,** Dalton, Ga.

Oval Game Table; black walnut; 28 x 36 x 28.

"Each leg is made of three parts, and each leg is splined into a center post. The inside contour is gouged out by hand after pedestal is assembled. Top is a geometrically constructed ellipse."

F. **Paul Foster,** Wichita, Kans.

Coffee Table; white oak, Solan Cool glass, brass, copper; 50⅛ x 18 x 18. Tambour handles made with brass rod bent with copper tube in middle.

"A sculptural design intended to be easily mass-produced. The Solan Cool glass acts as a mirror until tambour is opened. The visibility to the inside then helps in getting things in and out. Magnetic catches hold the tambours shut."

G. **Steve Loar,** La Grange, Ill.

Game Table; red oak, padauk, mixed hardwoods; 36 x 30 x 32. Carved lamination with veneered board inset into frame. Photos by T.C. Eckersley.

"'Indiana—you never had such a good view' from my 'Smokie Mountain Memories' series."

D

E

F

G

A. **Ali Baudoin,** Dallas, Tex.

Coffee Table, mahogany; 62 x 23 x 18. Low-relief carving.

"I designed the table after the Tilngit ceremonial box."

B. **C. Edward Moore,** Bowie, Md.

Coffee Table; ash, ash burl veneer; 42 x 42 x 16, $750. Doweled construction with panels of veneer on Baltic birch plywood set into the ash.

"The box-on-box is really a shell suspended on a box. The unusual ash burl veneer finished beautifully, but its many defects required painstaking patchwork. The butterfly inlays at each joint were cut from the dark area of other pieces of the veneer."

C. **Peter R. Jensen,** Vergennes, Vt.

Chess Table; butternut, pine; 20 x 23 x 29¾.

D. **Sholl & Sons,** North Babylon, N.Y.

Chess Cabinet and Matching Gaming Table; afromosia, teak plywood, oak, poplar, ceramic tile; table, 30 x 30 x 17¾; chess cabinet, 25 x 25 x 7, $6,800. Limited edition of 80 units.

"The design reflects the period of time when castles and cathedrals were at their height—the Middle Ages. Obviously, the chess cabinet with its four towers, gunwhale parapets, buttresses and moat doors depicts a scaled-down model of a medieval castle. We feel that no other period of design could best complement the most highly revered game of all time—chess."

A

B

C

D

E. **Jack Ferguson,** Surrey, B.C., Canada

Chess Table; alder, oak, cherry, teak, rosewood, bronze mirror, ash, Nicaraguan walnut; 36 x 36 x 27, $1,400. Photo by Julian Gardiner.

"The men are hand-turned from ash and walnut, the base is laminated alder, 5½ in. thick, and the pedestal is laminated oak turned to a dimension of 6¼ in. The playing surface is sand-blasted bronze mirror, removable for cleaning."

F. **N. W. Harbertson,** Ogden, Utah

Chess Table; rosewood, oak, maple, Formica; 20 x 20 x 22, $1,000. 12th-century Chinese style handmade drawer pull. Photo by Dan Harbertson.

G. **Tom Ruwitch,** Eldorado Springs, Colo.

Backgammon Table; teak, needlepoint; 24 x 18 x 18, $500.

H. **Vincent R. Clarke,** Wilmington, Del.

Backgammon Coffee Table; Chinese-Chippendale style; black walnut; 42 x 24 x 17¾. Mortise and tenon legs, square tenon pins, game board marquetry mounted on ¾-in. solid-core birch ply.

E

F

G

H

A. **Donald C. Pollock,** Rancho Palos Verdes, Calif.

Hepplewhite Card Table; Honduras mahogany, rosewood, holly, ebony; 36 x 18 x 30. Serpentine front and side rails built up from white pine, both rear legs move out on wood hinges, top folds over to rest on legs. Rear rail dovetailed into side rails.

B. **Phil Hawkey,** Celina, Ohio

Altar, Immaculate Conception Church; white pine, maple, basswood; 90 x 34 x 40.

"This altar faces the priest toward the congregation in accordance with the new liturgy of the Roman Catholic Church, and was made to match the style of the other three altars. The small decorative panels were doweled together and the large members were mortised and tenoned (some with concealed drawbolts, some through-tenoned and wedged). The whole thing was painted, carvings gilded and columns painted with a feather to simulate marble."

C. **Richard B. Crowell,** Alexandria, La.

Pembroke Table (American); Honduras mahogany; 20½ x 31½ x 27½, open 38½.

"The inlay border around the skirt is English boxwood and South American tulipwood, and the white border around the curved drawer front is English boxwood."

D. **Debbie Blakeslee,** Lafayette, Colo.

Drop-Leaf Typing Table; cherry, brass rod; 46 x 22 x 29. Photo by Filip Sokol.

"The apron at the front correlates to the curve of the top and angles back so that its thickness (8/4) is not apparent—there is no apron in back so that one may sit comfortably to type. The brass tube rod through the hinges has a solid rod within it so that metal moves against metal."

A

B

C

D

E. **John Gonczar,** Pearl City, Hawaii
   Fern Stand; Hawaiian koa; 29 x 10. Photo by Steven Day.

F. **L.F. Marsh,** Gormley, Ont., Canada
   Hall Table; 42 x 19¾ x 32. After the style of Hepplewhite and Sheraton.

E

F

F

A. **James Adair & James Fairly,** Columbus, Ohio

Butcher Block; partridgewood, padauk, walnut, maple; 24 x 25 x 30.

"All long grain-joinery; colors flow up, across and down opposite side."

B. **Dirk Odhner,** Bryn Athyn, Pa.

Occasional Table; maple, East Indian rosewood; 19 x 15 x 23. Photo by Norwin N. Synnestvedt.

"Legs and stretchers mortise and tenoned. Top shaped by cutting away excess wood with a table saw, then planing and sanding to shape. Top is cut from 8/4 stock to achieve bookmatch. The butterflies are functional."

C. **James Lakin,** Iowa City, Iowa

Nested Tables; birch, plywood; 16 x 25½ x 22, open, 38 in.

D. **Howard Werner,** Mt. Tremper, N.Y.

Dining Table; walnut; 120 x 48. Carved lamination.

"Three separate tables: The two end tables can be pulled away and put against the wall."

A

B

C

D

E. **Arno Schadt,** High Point, N.C.

Console Table; pecan, marble; 30 high. Wood carving with marble top, wood covered with gold leaf.

F. **Alasdair G.B. Wallace,** Lakefield, Ont., Canada

Nestling; red oak; 24 x 14 x 18.

"So many nests of tables don't nestle. I wished to emphasize the three dimensions—the nestling—by accentuating perspective. Hence the diminished spindle design and the progressive recession of the inner tables. One looks *into* the nest."

G. **Harry Hoefener,** Providence, R.I.

Nest of Tables; crotch mahogany, maple, rosewood; 12 x 21 x 31, $600.

"Intended for writing or to prevent company from rising from their seats when taking refreshments."

H. **Joseph Kleinhans,** Madison, Wis.

Combination Pedestal and End Table; plywood, ⅜-in. steel rod, cherry veneer; 18 x 20 x 34. Stacked lamination reinforced with bolted rod which runs through the arms and main body.

"This piece was designed as one-half of a pair of stereo speaker stands. The other pedestal is as yet uncompleted."

E

F

G

G

H

A. **Larry Dern,** Eureka, Calif.

Sofa Table; black walnut; 62 x 18 x 27. Photo by Jim Kalb.

"Stacking on legs produces flowing elliptical shapes, long center rail turned in two pieces and lap-jointed (stacked and joined before turning), holes drilled for short rails in legs and for long rail in short rails and plugged before turning, stretcher rail mortises in top of legs on short sides done before turning."

B. **Mark Turnowski,** New York, N.Y.

Cabriole-Leg Hall Table; teak, Brazilian rosewood; 24 x 19 x 25.

"All work done by hand. Legs cut and shaped with spokeshave and chisels. Balls of legs shaped with files and sandpaper. The legs were made first and then mortised and tenoned to the apron. Drawer was then fitted to the table and the knob hand-sculpted. Top was then joined and hand-planed to finish."

C. **Peter Zimmer,** Port Hood, N.S., Canada

Folding (Card) Table; ash, cherry; 35 x 32 x 30, $500.

"This table evolved from an 18th-century French folding table. I was dubious of the original design—the dowels on the top of the legs fit into sockets in the bottom of the panel. I moved the pins to breadboard ends for more stability during moisture changes. The tops of the legs are round tenons. The joints are mortise and tenon, and the pivots are ⅝-in. dowel."

A

B

C

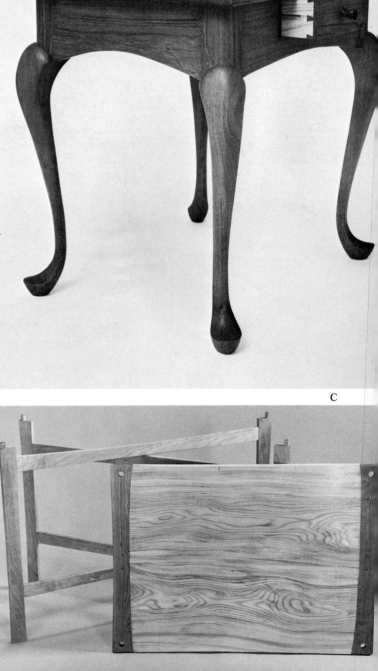

C

D. **Tom Moyer,** Belvidere, Ill.

Tea Cart; walnut; 26 x 17 x 29. Mortise and tenon construction, turned legs and wheel parts.

"The tray slides on tracks and drops down slightly when in place to avoid end movement. Tray and bottom shelf are each one board, resawn and bookmatched. Leaves are 10 in. wide and are held up by slides, which pull out from top rails."

E. **Joseph P. Lally,** Scituate, Mass.

Octagonal Table with Revolving Top; Honduras mahogany; 28 dia. x 30. Thomas Jefferson style. Spindle around which table revolves set into 'bird cage.' Photo by Rudolph Mitchell.

F. **John T. Heinrich,** Santa Rosa, Calif.

Entry-Hall Table; koa, glass; 28 x 15 x 34.

"After bandsawing, almost all the shaping was done with an adjustable-slot spokeshave. The joints are all doweled, with $7/16$-in. or $1/2$-in. dowels—16 in the center joint, 3 in each hip."

D

E

F

A. **Allan D. Smith,** Pennington, N.J.

Letter-Writing Desk; cherry; 48 x 24 x 33, $750.

"The vertical-grain side pieces adjacent to the writing surface are not structural components of the desk. The case holding the drawers is a separate unit, to which the side pieces (and the back) are fastened by means of screws from inside the case. The screw holes in the case are slot-shaped to allow for expansion and contraction of the side pieces."

B. **Lester Smiejan,** Barnegat, N.J.

Occasional Table #1; walnut, ash, aspen, ebony, 11 veneers; 19 x 19 x 18. Dowel frame construction. Top overlaid on marine-grade mahogany ply.

C. **Ebbe Borregaard,** Bolinas, Calif.

Tall Tilt-Top Writing Table; white oak, Finnply; 36 x 60 x 48.

"Genesis: Lawyer in a hurry with a bad back needs a standup work table, specifies surface size, height and light color, which he associates with functional, informal furniture. Table to be transportable home to office and back again. Simplicity becomes the theme."

D. **Curtis Erpelding,** Seattle, Wash.

Knock-Down Drawing/Writing Table; birch ply, walnut, hemlock; 60 x 30 x 30. Legs and arms fasten to frame with lag screws, which tighten into dowel nuts in frame. Edge of frame and dado in arms and legs have matching taper, allowing unit to tighten as screw draws them together.

"The drawing/writing table was built originally for my own use. I had just finished a drafting course at a local community college and had collected along the way all the tools and paraphernalia necessary for drawing except a table."

A

B

C

D

E. **John H. Longmaid,** Ellsworth, Maine

Sideboard; golden ebony, cherry, Honduras mahogany; 42 x 21 x 37, $750.

"The drawer fronts are back-beveled so that no drawer pulls are necessary. The drawers are opened by hooking your fingers around the exposed edges of the drawer. I used sliding dovetails extensively to yield a piece of furniture which, unglued, would have strength and stability. When glued, the joints resist fracture and dislocation. The result is a piece that will withstand the ravages of time and give its owner a lifetime of service."

F. **Scott Chipman,** San Diego, Calif.

Illustrator's Desk; white oak, plastic laminate; 48 x 24 x 30, $450.

"The desk was designed specifically for an illustrator working with pen and ink. The stationary portion of the top provides a flat surface for tools and inks. A drawer is located under the stationary top and paper storage is located under the adjustable top."

G. **Ronald H. Jackson,** Overland Park, Kans.

Chippendale Piecrust Tilt-Top Tea-Table; Pennsylvania cherry; 31¼ x 27. Photo by Mark Yeokum.

"Center of top was removed with a router jig, then rim was carved. Legs are tenoned rather than dovetailed for strength. Table was designed small to complement a window in my home."

H. **Jan Zaitlin,** Berkeley, Calif.

Drafting Table; birch; 54 x 38 (surface), $2,000. Photo by Lynda Koolish.

"Knock-down construction using wooden nuts and bolts. Adjusts in height and angle of table. All parts are made of wood—no metal in entire desk."

A. **Stephen Appel,** Charleston, S.C.

End Table; teak, rosewood; 21 x 20 x 15, $450.

B. **William E. Crawford,** Bethlehem, Pa.

Dining Table; red oak; 84 x 46 x 30.

"Top is butted and glued-up stock. Stringers and trestles are made up and assembled with mechanical fasteners to accommodate seasonal expansion and shrinkage.

C. **Eric Hoag,** Madison, Conn.

Coffee Table; mahogany, burl; 46 x 32 x 14; Photo by William K. Sacco.

"Each of the burl pieces that make up the top is ¼ in. thick and glued to a plywood backing, which is let into the leg structure."

D. **Janice Goldfrank,** Austerlitze, N.Y.

Chinese Desk, Ming Dynasty; native cherry; 84 x 30 x 30.

"Commissioned by a fabric designer who wanted to combine the functions of writing desk, file cabinet and drawing easel. Both the style and the details of construction are my own adaptations of traditional Chinese furniture from the Ming dynasty period (16th century especially). The classic three-way miter joint in each corner of the desk is actually comprised of seven individual joints. First there is a vertical French dovetail at the back of each miter, then there are two tenons rising above the leg into mortises made in the corners of the frame that supports the desk top; and finally, a rounded brace at the inside corner of each leg laps the inside corner of the frame and rail assembly.

"A ratchet carved into the dust panel under the easel allows for 10 different height adjustments and a pair of tiny brass bolts slip into escutcheons at the back end of each side of the easel to lock it in place when closed."

E. **JAWAR (James Rannefeld),** Taos, N. Mex.

Inspiration Bench; oak, vermilion; 42 x 12 x 17. Laminated construction and joinery, then carving.

F. **Christopher J. Campbell,** Richmond, Va.

Octagonal Table; Philippine mahogany; 36 x 30 x 30. Chip carving, cut surface, stained with polished finish.

G. **Alvin & Velma Weaver,** Kansas City, Kans.

Chinese Desk; American walnut, African mahogany; 63½ x 25¼ x 29½.

"The techniques used were learned in 49 years of full-time work in fine cabinetry and furnituremaking."

H. **Giles Gilson,** Schenectady, N.Y.

Chess Table Sculpture Vassal; Baltic birch, padauk, walnut, maple, Plexiglas, wire; 20 x 25 x 34, $1,000. Stacking, chain-saw carving.

"The top (the checkered part) is made with two layers of Plexiglas, and the effect is black squares on a black mirrored background. The tabletop itself is held under tension by four wires, which act as a structural device and as a shock absorber in case of accident. This design was proven when 12 Masonite doors fell over on this table and instead of a smashed table, we had a perfect table with stretched wires."

I. **Nick Hampson,** San Francisco, Calif.

Table; myrtle, burl root, spalted driftwood; 20 x 16 x 18, $600.

"Two years ago I started training myself in woodworking. After trying every tool and technique I heard of, I'm now very happy with a few electric grinders and sanders, but my best working hours are spent with hand tools, carving. I also prefer sanding by hand when it is practical.

"I'm interested in recycling discarded wood. All of the wood I use has been found on beaches, constructions sites or garbage dumps."

F

G

H

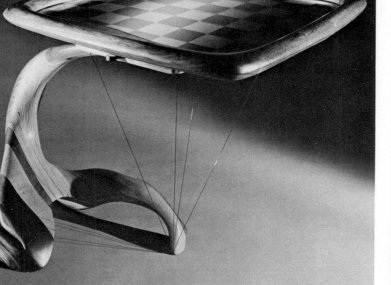

I

A. **Wallace M. Kunkel,** Chester, N.J.

Architect's Lowboy; Queen Anne style; walnut, poplar interior; 41 x 22 x 35. Photo by Jeff Kunkel.

"Adjusts from horizontal to vertical (12 positions) through three levels. Book ledge folds under for drafting. Lowboy design from Lester Margon's drawings."

B. **Norman R. Doll,** Slinger, Wis.

Desk; birch, walnut; 42 x 17 x 67. All handles hand-carved from black walnut, drawers mounted on dovetail tracks. A 28-in. box slides out 7 in. and tilts back and forth, with two 24-in. fluorescent fixtures supplying the light. Finished with Watco Danish oil.

"I enjoy modern design, but for a desk I felt I needed to combine modern and traditional to create a warm working atmosphere, hence the raised panel and divided light doors. I like things made entirely of wood; therefore I provided wooden hardware, except for the hidden mortised door hinges."

C. **David H. Bretschneider,** Shoreham, Vt.

Slant-Top Desk; American Chippendale style; Honduras mahogany, brass; 36 x 20 x 42.

"Carcase hand-dovetailed (double-lapped dovetailed top to sides) with hand-planed moldings. Cock beads surround larger drawers and fall supports."

A

C

B

D. **R. Dan Burke**, Vineland, N.J.

Walnut Burl Secretary; black walnut, black walnut burl; 23 x 40 x 83. Bookmatched walnut burl veneer. Photo by Rocky Rossi.

"The overall design of the piece is after the style of early 1700 William and Mary secretary desks. It has 32 obvious drawers, 10 hidden drawers, 28 obvious storage compartments and cubby holes, 8 hidden compartments and 2 pull-out candle rests. Pieces of this type were commissioned by the wealthy and often used to hide important papers and valuable small possessions."

E. **Ibsen Nelsen**, Seattle, Wash.

Secretary; walnut, ceramic tiles, cowhide, $1,500. Constructed by Mickey McCoy, O.B. Williams Co., Seattle, Wash.

"This secretary was designed for Mrs. Hanawalt, a retired lady in her mid-80s. The design recalls an Early American breakfront that had been in her family since it was made in Kentucky in about 1820, but which was too large to move into her retirement-home apartment. The designer believes that earlier design forms can and should be adapted and in-cluded in contemporary furniture. In this case the outward sloping unmolded cornice and the fillip at the top of the glass doors are nearly identical to the 19th-century break-front. The piece is solid walnut throughout with the exception of drawer sides and bottoms, which are Douglas fir. The inset tiles were specially made for the secretary as an ornamental feature by a local potter. The center tile has a knob, which is used to open the sloping desk front. The writing surface is top-grade cowhide; all of the hardware is solid brass."

F. **Gary D. Anderson**, Minneapolis, Minn.

Drop-Front Desk; white oak; 36 x 18 x 42.

"Top and dust panels are joined to sides with slip dovetails. Drop front has two pins spaced 6 in. apart on each side, which run in a ¼-in. groove routed into each end."

G. **Ronald W. Starnes**, Odessa, Del.

Secretary; black walnut; 42 x 22 x 82. 18th-century joinery. After the style of Newport Chippendale.

D D E

F F G

A. **Ken Strickland,** Purchase, N.Y.

Secretary; ash; 17 x 17 x 66. Steam-laminated.

B. **John C. Starinovich,** Windsor Locks, Conn.

Desk; cherry; 30 x 15 x 42. Mortise and tenon, dovetail tongue and groove, hand dovetails. Photo by Rich Baldinger.

"Lid support system made entirely of wood. When lid is pulled down, under-supports slide out automatically. If need be, entire mechanism may be disassembled by removing a few wooden pins."

C **Gerald Dwileski,** Rensselaer, N.Y.

Desk; cherry, brass hardware; 32¼ x 16¼ x 39. Hand-carved fan and feet, hand dovetails. Automatic slide supports for fold-down front, finished with Watco Danish oil.

D. **Leonard Beuving,** Kalamazoo, Mich.

Bureau Desk; tiger maple, cherry, brass; 38 x 22 x 42. Panels and borders joined with tongue and groove.

"While the bureau desk fundamentally has Chippendale lines, the uncluttered surfaces with their cherry borders accentuate the beauty of the tiger maple. Because the cherry will continue to darken, this framing effect will change and become even more dramatic over the years."

A

A

B

B

E. **Peter Pennypacker,** North Sullivan, Maine

Desk; walnut, koa, narra, birch dowel, tung oil finish; 48 x 30 x 48.

"The desk body is held between the two side supports by three bolts on each side, capped with birch plugs. The bolt holes are not round but more a slot shape with 'washers' to allow movement of wood.

"The desk body and the side supports touch only where the bolts in slotted holes and capped by birch dowels connect the two. The intended effect was a floating/suspended quality. The mortise and tenon and bolts also allow the desk to be broken down for moving, shipping or storing. The koa shelves and organizing slots slide out as a unit. The back of the desk consists of numerous vertical ¼-in. walnut slats, lapped but not glued together, pinned at top and bottom, a clever idea, the credit for which must go to Michael Bock in California."

F. **Larry E. Jones,** Merced, Calif.

Writing Desk; red oak; 30 x 16 x 40.

"Front is concave to match slight curve of sides. It folds down to produce writing surface level with inside surface with only a small gap between the two. The drawer joints are lap and dowel.

G. **Tom Deady,** Maple Valley, Wash.

Desk; white oak; 17 x 29 x 41, $700. Wood-covered steel hinge stop.

"Sides made in one piece for leg strength."

C

D

E

F

G

A. **Michael Pearce,** San Francisco, Calif.

Roll-Top Desk; walnut, shedua, koa, rosewood, teak, padauk; 26 x 43 x 46, $3,000. Side panels fit in grooves like stained glass, some carving, hidden drawer in front. Joinery: spline and mortise and tenon.

B. **Robert March,** Worcester, Mass.

Roll-Top Desk and Chair; vermilion; desk, 58 x 26 x 46; chair, 30 x 24 x 48. Mortise and tenon, floating splines, Chinese splice joints, tambour concave and curved back behind canvas, tambour slats tapered in center.

"The idea for this piece came from a Ming dynasty cabinet that was frame and panel, but all the panels were slats and not solid. Grain in the chair back and seat is controlled to follow shape in chair.

A   A

B   B

C. **JAWAR (James Rannefeld),** Taos, N. Mex.

'Avanti I' Roll-Top Desk; walnut, birch, maple; 48 x 30 x 42. Floating solid wood top.

D. **Robert Domlesky,** Shelburne Falls, Mass.

Tamboured Desk; black walnut; 60 x 34 x 35, $1,800. Photo by Robert E. Barrett.

"Tambour slides around a four-compartment file section placed horizontally in the rear of the desk top."

E. **Phyllis Bankier,** Milwaukee, Wis.

Roll-Top Desk; red oak, brass; 52 x 30 x 44. Photo by George R. Johnson.

"It is a contemporary-style desk with a trestle base. The center was built as a separate unit. It is equally balanced with three vertical spaces on one side, three horizontal spaces on the other side and six drawers in the center. All the drawers are recessed slightly. All edges are rounded. The sides are laminated and 1½ in. thick."

C

D

C

E

A. Chester Stephen Volz, Jr., Knoxville, Tenn.

Roll-Top Desk; local American walnut; 57 x 45 x 29. Photo by C.C. Overton.

"Many hours of labor went into this piece that I built during the winter 1977/1978. The wood I purchased at local saw-mills, roughsawn, and the pride of accomplishment when I completed the desk cannot be measured. It has always fas-cinated me to be able to take an old roughsawn board and turn it into something so pleasing to the eye. The wood cost me $.20 per board foot approximately eight years ago."

B. Wood Wizards, Sutter Creek, Calif.

Roll-Top Desk; quartersawn oak; 60 x 36 x 72, $5,000. Photo by Karen Gottstein.

"We resore antiques (mostly 1860-1910 pieces) and do custom design and woodwork. We have restored many a roll-top desk and decided we could make a bigger and better one. So we started with 400 board feet of rough-cut quartersawn oak, surfaced it and cut it into about 2,000 pieces...."

C. Robert Thomason, Weston, Mass.

Wall-Hung Roll-Top Desk; black walnut; 42 x 20 x 32. Sides are tapered and carved. Writing surface pulls out.

A

B

C

C

D. **George Kuehl,** Cheshire, Ore.

Roll-Top Desk; red oak, walnut; 48 x 28 x 52, $3,550. No nails or screws, pinned together completely with walnut pins.

"The desk will endure beyond the year 2180."

E. **Kingsley C. Brooks,** Medford, Mass.

Stand-Up Writing Desk; maple; 36 x 36 x 52.

"The side of the pigeon-hole unit is staved with each stave itself curved, producing a surface that is curved in two directions."

F. **James Grandbois,** St. Paul, Minn.

Writing Desk; walnut, padauk; 48 x 30 x 34.

"Top is made of ⅜-in. thick padauk, ¾ in. wide. Pieces are glued in individually using go-bars as clamps. Top slides out to expose full pattern. Sides and division pieces made from clear quarter-sawn walnut. One large drawer is under the top, hidden from view."

D

E

F

A. Carter Blocksma, Grass Lake, Mich.

Writing Desk with Chair; padauk, mahogany, cane; desk, $400; chair, $175. Steam-bent chair back, carved seat frame.

"Design was intended for tropical setting with emphasis on light but sturdy construction."

B. Philip d'Entremont, Feasterville, Pa.

Writing Desk; walnut; 40 x 28. Pinned mortise and tenon.

C. Emmett E. Day, Jr., Seattle, Wash.

Desk; Brazilian rosewood, onyx, brass; 56 x 32 x 30.

"Because of the distance between the legs and the non-structural face, angle iron has been placed in the front under the wood for rigidity. The onyx is ¾ in. thick and sits on many sheets of paper. Should the wood perimeter need refinishing, the onyx can be lowered to the new level by removing some sheets of paper. The beveled glass doors are pinned. Finished with Polane."

D. Richard Cohen, Warwick, N.Y.

Desk; angico (Brazil), cherry; 45 x 19⅜ x 33¾. Mitered case, hand-dovetailed drawers, dadoed top and shelf, oil finish.

A

B

C

D

E. **Tom Wessells,** Newport News, Va.

Cantilever Desk; birch, goncalo alvez, walnut; 48 x 30 x 36, $1,500.

F. **Eugene D. Rubin,** Victoria, B.C., Canada

Desk with Overhead Storage; white oak; 66 x 32 x 54, $2,000.

"The desk is constructed so that all lines converge to a single point above the desk. Even the sides and the partitions of the cabinet have been tapered to repeat this element of the design. All parts were chosen and assembled so that the grain reinforces the sense of convergence. The legs and cabinet pieces were tapered by passing them through a thickness planer using a wedge-shaped carrier. The drawer sides are also constructed at an angle, and each drawer runs on a center guide to prevent binding. Each leg is constructed in two pieces: the lower part is mortised through the table; the upper part is blind-mortised into the lower part. The two parts are drawn together using a wedge just below the table top. Each leg is mortised into the cabinet."

G. **Curt Minier,** Seattle, Wash.

Desk; koa; 58 x 28 x 38. End panels are coopered. Large drawer holds Pendaflex file folders.

"I am a full-time designer/craftsman working on my own designs, commissions only, and have been in the Seattle area for 2½ years."

H. **Robert W. Armstrong,** Charlotte, N.C.

Desk; walnut; 41 x 30 x 39, $1,400. Photo by Don Martin.

"Designed with curved back so desk can be located away from a wall—as in center of a room—and offer visual interest even from back."

E   F

G   H

A. **Thomas H. Williams,** Atlanta, Ga.

Desk; red oak; 75 x 30 x 29, $1,900. Carved relief, oak veneer covering.

B. **Alfred Neale Gordon,** Baton Rouge, La.

Prie-Dieu; Honduras mahogany with handmade inlays of avodire, holly, walnut, ebony veneer; 20 x 24 x 30. 100% wood construction, glued mortise and tenon. To avoid discoloring inlays, desk was 'stained' by washing entire piece with lime solution, which reacts with the tannic acid in the mahogany, turning the mahogany reddish-brown, while leaving the various inlay woods unaffected. Desk was then sanded, sealed and given several coats of clear penetrating finish in the usual fashion.

C. **John Kennedy,** Philadelphia, Pa.

Executive Desk; Honduras mahogany; 90 x 36 x 29. Cabinets made with coopered joints and shaped with auto body grinder. Drawers are enclosed in plywood cabinet with coopered sections attached to it. Modesty panel made from ¼-in. mahogany veneers laminated and bent in one piece-mold.

D. **Arno K. Wagenhaus & Ingeborg E.G. Wagenhaus,** Ft. Wayne, Ind.

Bachelor Knee-Hole Desk; walnut, rosewood, maple, walnut burl.

A

B

C

D

E. **Arthur E. Dameron,** Galesburg, Ill.

Knee-Hole Desk; walnut, red oak, maple, birch ply; 50 x 24 x 30. Rope molding made from round stock on a Sears Router-Crafter, one side made flat on the jointer then ripped to ⅜-in. thickness. Joints are mortise-and-tenon and dovetail. Eight 22-gauge sheet-metal corners used to tie the longitudinal members under the top to the panel frames set flush with the wood surface so as not to interfere with the drawers. The only glue used in the desk is in the base corners (splined miter) and the panel frame joints. The major portion of the desk can be disassembled since screws are the principal fasteners.

"After retiring from teaching sheet metal and welding, my long desire to work with wood has become a reality. I built a shop in my back yard, where I really enjoy making the shavings fly."

F. **Lance F. Fredericks,** Great Neck, N.Y.

'Winged Feet' (Executive Desk and Typing Wing); black walnut; 76 x 33 x 29½. Mortise-and-tenon joinery; stacking; hand, ball mill, die grinder; woodburning.

G. **Peter L. Gollup,** Canton, N.C.

Desk; cherry; 68 x 29 x 34. Traditional joinery, steam-bent back. Drawer carcase is a trapezium (no parallel sides), drawers are same shape, dovetailed.

E

F

G

A. **Donald G. Bradley,** Miami, Fla.

Knee-Hole Desk, Chippendale style; cherry, southern maple, red oak; 38½ x 19¼ x 30.

"Features hidden drawer and shelves behind door."

B. **Page Hoeper,** Beverly Hills, Calif.

Portable Secretary; walnut, leather, brass; 16¾ x 4¼ x 10¼. Feathered miter corners, oil and wax finish, solid brass English locks.

"...allows work while traveling."

C. **Maurice Beaulieu,** Anse St.-Jean, Cte. Dubuc, Que., Canada

Desk; pine, cedar; 42 x 18 x 32, $800.

D. **Peter A. Allen,** North Westport, Mass.

Desk & Chair; cherry; 56 x 26 x 29. Photo by Constance Brown.

A

B

C

D

E. **Randel Len Stanley,** Mt. Airy, N.C.

Block-Front Desk; mahogany, poplar; 52 x 32 x 31.

"Every basic technique of fine cabinetmaking went into this piece of furniture, including high relief and round carving, inlay and hand molding and shaping. 500 hours of craftsmanship."

F. **Lynn Sweet,** Frankfort, Ky.

Kentucky Arts Commission Desk; South American mahogany, poplar; 60 x 28 x 30.

"Not until the last few years have I concerned myself with other than the exact copies of 17th and 18th-century English and Colonial New England antiques; of these primarily chairs. It is with this study and practical experience that I approach the construction and to varying degrees the design of original furniture."

G. **Callidrome Design, Inc.,** Cincinnati, Ohio

Desk; bird's-eye maple veneer, particle board, plastic laminate core, brass plate, hand-rubbed lacquer finish; 60 x 30 x 26, $4,500.

H. **Bradford Colt de Wolf,** McLean, Va.

Office Desk; walnut crotch, birch dowels, padauk; 54 x 18 x 28. Drawers open by pivoting on corner hinge turned from pearwood. Right group of dowel legs also can hold phone books and file folder at top of desk.

I. **John R. Harwood,** Cazenovia, N.Y.

Writing Desk for Small Office; red and white oak, cocobolo; 58 x 28 x 29½.

"Mostly traditional joinery used to fabricate a rather untraditional shape. Deep drawers are NK style, stationery drawer is side hung, the rail that supports the drawer slide is dovetailed to the front apron and wedge-mortised to the back, front being the drawer side. The outermost corner of the desk was cut at 45° since it was to point toward the door and not waste precious space used as seating for consultation. Balancing that cut esthetically and structurally led me to the finished piece. The legs, octagonal in cross section, are tapered having a gentle outward sweep and were carved with hand planes and a spokeshave."

E   F

G

H

I

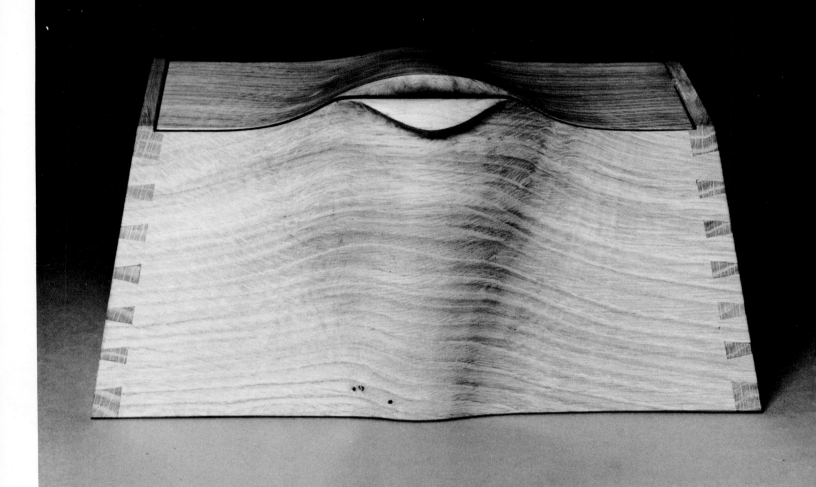

A. **David Hoffman & Deborah Whiter,** Ithaca, N.Y.

Spice Set; red oak, walnut; 24 x 15 x 3, $100. Photo by Robert Barrett.

B. **Todd Lewis Engle,** Columbus, Ohio

Bowl; aromatic cedar; 10 x 6 x 3. Bandsawn and carved.

C. **Claude M. Merrill,** Rome, N.Y.

Bowl; zebrawood; 15 x 10 x 2, $125.

"Decorative/useful is the major theme. . . . This bowl in particular established new direction for me."

D. (and previous page)
Michael C. Fortune, Toronto, Ont., Canada

Desk-Top Container; white oak, brass hinges; 12 x 6 x 6.

E. **David Dickhut,** Durango, Colo.

Jewelry Container; East Indian rosewood, Macassar ebony, Bruneau jasper, sterling silver; 7 x 2½ x 4, $260.

"Made to hold whatever is precious to owner, as a reliquary, or for a ring, a gem, a meditation object."

A

B

C

D

E

F **Barry H. Young,** Columbia, Md.

Weed Pots; padauk, walnut, spalted cherry; 4 to 6 wide x 12.

"When I carve weed pots I usually use wood that I've cut down from the Maryland woods, preferably wood that has fallen down and is spalted to some degree. I have found that both cherry and apple are exceptional for good wood tone. All of the flower arrangements are done by my wife, Gayle."

G. **Martin J. Steinbach,** Downsview, Ont., Canada

Cup; spalted maple; 9 x 5½ x 4.

H. **Ray Kelso,** Skippack, Pa.

Fruit Bowl; cherry burl; 11 x 6. Photo by Joseph Merk.

I. **Tim Atwood,** Orinda, Calif.

Wine Decanter #3; koa; 6½ x 4¼ x 20, $300. Capacity: ⅕ gallon.

"The decanter is constructed from three vertical laminates which are hollowed out before gluing. It is glued with resorcinol resin for high chemical resistance. The finish is tung oil....Sealing the interior posed several problems. The wood could not be left unsealed or the wine would cause the laminates to crack apart. Varnishes or lacquers could not be used because the solvent effects of the wine would in time dissolve them....I solved the problem in the following manner: While the wood is still in the clamps from gluing I pour very hot paraffin wax inside. The hot wax is then driven into the wood with air pressure and the excess wax is poured out. This is hard on the wood but it does a good job of sealing and is the best method I have found so far....The decanter is designed for perfect flow of the wine without any bubbling or gurgling. The airhole is situated so that it can be comfortably covered with one's thumb to control the flow while pouring...no wine will flow back down it and out of the decanter. The decanter is filled through a funnel made of horn."

J. **Mark Lindquist,** Henniker, N.H.

Lapping Wavelet Bowl; elm burl; 8 x 8. Photo by John I. Russell.

"Permanent collection Metropolitan Museum of Art."

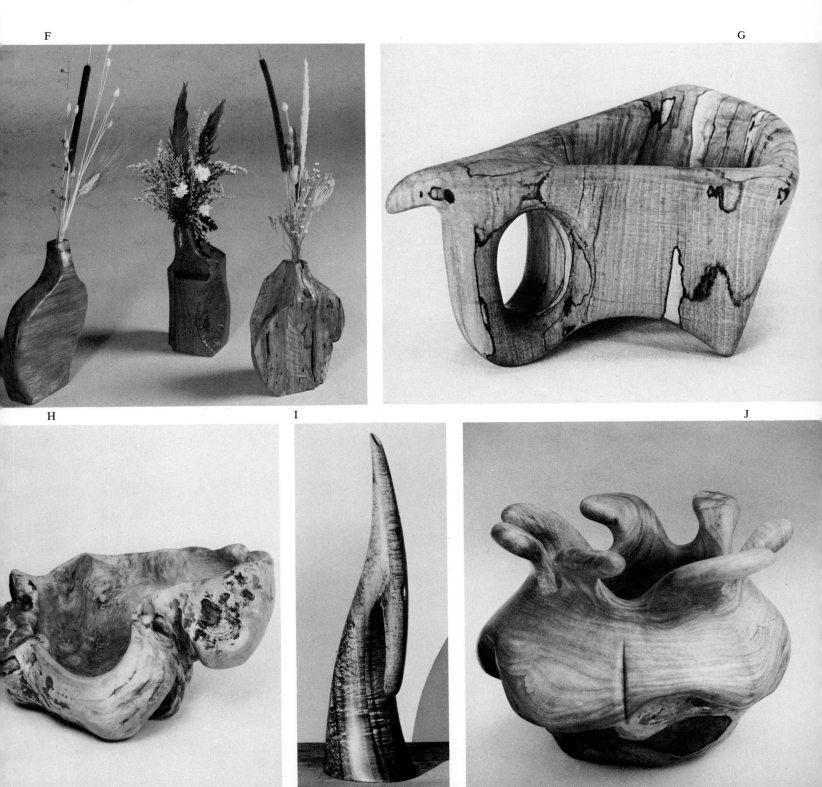

A. **Roger Sloan,** Marcellus, Mich.

Oval-Shaped Box; walnut inlaid with oak roots; 4 dia. x 2¼. Inside turned off center, outside oval shaped on sanding belt. Wooden hinge.

B. **Keith A. Thomas,** Alamo, Calif.

Container; zebrawood, pau-Brazil; 8 dia. x 7. Photo by Robert Hitchman.

"In my attempt to keep the container as light and delicate to the touch as possible, I have turned the inside of the lid. The index marks are brass and were installed to assist one in keeping the grain in the lid and bowl aligned."

C. **Richard Starr,** Thetford Center, Vt.

Wooden Jar with Treaded Top; maple; 3¼ dia. x 5."

"Hand-chased threads; hand-carved flutes on top."

D. **Chris Gutzeit,** Suffern, N.Y.

Small Pedestal Bowl; spalted maple, lacquer, flocking; 4 ½ dia. x 4.

"Lathe-turned, thin sides were obtained through the careful handling of a small turning gouge. The finish is air brush lacquer, eight to ten coats, rubbed to a high gloss. The bottom was sprayed with flocking after the lathe mounting holes were filled."

E. **Thomas Clark,** Bowling Green, Ohio

Wine Chalice, 5½ x 12; Plate, 8 dia.; walnut, silver bands. Split from log, turned green, dried, re-turned and finished. Silver is set in grooves with a little play to allow for movement of the wood. Spiral was carved by hand.

F. **Cary Keegan,** N. Royalton, Ohio

Boxes; osage orange; 5 dia. x 4½ x 3. Faceplate turning. Photo by Dave Hudak.

"I teach woodworking at a home for emotionally disturbed children. . . ."

G. **John H. Franklin,** Larchmont, N.Y.

Mahogany Bowl; African and Philippine mahogany; 8 dia. x 4½.

H. **Francis J. Fortuna,** New York, N.Y.

Bowl; ash; 8½ dia. x 5.

I. **James V. Ryan,** Putnam Valley, N.Y.

Covered Container; applewood; 7 dia. x 5. Turned from green wood. Photo by James O'Gara.

J. **Peter Meure,** Franklin, Tas., Australia

Oblate Spheroidal Box; huon pine; 8½ x 6, $80.

K. **John R. Millen,** New Alexandria, Pa.

Box; cherry; 5 dia. x 3. Relief-carving.

L. **Lucius M. Cline, Jr.,** Greenville, S.C.

Canisters; ash; 6¼ x 10¼, 5¼ x 8¾. Stave construction. Photo by Isabelle Coxe.

A. **Susan Raab,** Germantown, N.Y.

Turned Boxes and Bowls; zebrawood, mahogany, padauk.

B **David L. Erickson,** Milwaukee, Wis.

Container; walnut, maple burl veneer inlay; 7½ dia. x 2¾, $75. Lid has wooden hinge.

"The bowl cover consists of a hinged segment (the larger portion of the cover), a three-segment hinge, and the fixed segment (the smaller portion of the cover, which is attached to the bowl). These three parts of the cover are glued together before turning. Careful gluing and assembly are of critical importance if the hinge is to operate smoothly."

C. **Jim Wallace & Bill Wallace, New Light Woodworks** Wake Forest, N.C.

Container; mahogany; 11½ dia. x 3. Photo by Bob Allen.

D. **Lawrence P. Burbules,** Waterford, Pa.

Containers; spalted maple; 2½ x 8, $22; 6 x 14, $57; 5 x 12, $49. Finished with tung oil and beeswax. Photo by Mary Jo Toles.

E. **Judy Kaufman,** Lagunitas, Calif.

Containers; Oregon maple burl, 5½ dia. x 4½; curly maple, 5 dia. x 4.

A

B

C

D

E

F. **Philip C. Strange,** Woodberry Forest, Va.

Ice Bucket; clear pine, redwood; 8 dia. x 10½, $65. Photo by Bill White.

G. **Stephen Paulsen,** Goleta, Calif.

Bottles; bocote, stoppers of kingwood, ebony, para breadnut. Tallest: 4½ x 2½ x 1, $10 to $200.

"All bottles are hand-shaped, one of a kind, with individual stoppers. I've made about 1,500 of them in two years. Each bottle carries a removable glass vial for contents unsuited to wooden containers."

H. **Gary Edelstein,** Roosevelt, N.J.

Container; cherry, walnut; 5¼ dia. x 7⅜.

I. **Todd Hoyer,** Bisbee, Ariz.

Ring Boxes; walnut, mahogany; 1 dia. x 2. Photo by Richard Byrd.

J. **Bill Long,** St. Augustine, Fla.

Box; East Indian rosewood, padauk, osage orange; 11 dia. x 5, $135. Laminated, turned, sculpted, oiled. Light-colored strips are laminated, not inlaid. Photo by Ken McMillan.

K. **Philip Campbell,** Detroit, Mich.

Containers; padauk, poplar; 6 x 10, 7 x 8, $65. Stave construction.

A. **Dennis C. Walstad,** St. Charles, Ill.

Laminated Bowls; walnut-faced plywood; 5½ x 4. Photo by Creative Images Studio.

"The bowls were constructed by laminating ¼-in. thick pieces of walnut-faced lumber-core plywood into a block, then turning on a lathe. The walnut provides excellent color contrast with the birch and basswood in the core of the plywood. The finish is Watco oil followed by a coat of wax."

B. **Dale Chase,** Chico, Calif.

Bowl; crotch walnut; 3½ x 15.

"This is the finest feather walnut crotch I have ever seen. It is nearly defect-free with rich color, dense wood."

C. **J.D. (Jack) Fenwick,** Montreal, Que., Canada

Bud Vases; balsam poplar, 7 high; wild apple, 4 high; red maple, 5½ high. Faceplate turnings, spalted woods. Interior of vases coated with casting resin. They may be used to hold fresh flowers in water. Photo by Photo Atlas.

D. **John H. Whitehead,** Portland, Ore.

Bowl; spalted red oak crotch; 9 x 4½, $100.

E. **Gordon R. Warren,** Wilmington, Ohio

Vase; spalted maple; 4¾ x 17. Inside coated with melted paraffin.

F. **Felicia Fields,** Felton, Calif.

Bowl; redwood burl; 5½ x 4.

G. **David Zweig,** Westport, Conn.

Mug; sassafras; 7 x 5 x 8½. Turned, then carved. Photo by Camille Stecher.

H. **James W. Rogers,** Bakersfield, Calif.

Compote; black walnut, ash, maple from Oregon; Base, 12 x 9; Top, 6½ x 3, $195.

"This type of turning may seem to some people quite simple to make, but it takes very careful cutting and gluing to have all the points of the dark and white wood intersect the proper way when the piece is turned on the lathe. The time and effort it takes to put all the pieces together is very rewarding when finally the piece is turned to expose the intricate design the contrasting colors of wood produce...."

I. **Thomas J. Duffy,** Ogdensburg, N.Y.

Fluted Vase & Bowl with Bolection Inlay; mahogany, maple; vase, 2 x 8; dish, 2 x 6. Photo by Allen Photography.

"The vase was fluted with a scratch tool while the piece was indexed on the lathe. Both the vase and the bowl have bolection work, a band of maple turned separately and split in half. Both halves were then brought together in a groove cut in the actual bowl or vase. When the glue set, the entire piece was turned to shape and finished."

A. **Dale L. Nish,** Provo, Utah

Decorative Pot, Bowl; black walnut; Small bowl, 5¼ x 4; Tall pot, 4½ x 5½, $130. Tall pot turned in two pieces, surface textured with carving gouge.

B. **John Kemnitzer,** Powell, Ohio

Bowl; ash; 8 x 4¾. Cut from log and turned green; oil finished.

C. **Milo C. Kendall,** Dover, Idaho

Candle Holder & Bowl; staghorn sumac, black walnut; 4¾ x 5½. Sumac stock laminated with walnut.trim top and bottom. Faceplate turned. Polyurethane finish.

"Staghorn sumac rarely gets larger than shrub size. The wood for these two turnings was a giant 6 in. in diameter."

D. **Irving Fischman,** Cambridge, Mass.

Bowl—American Indian Series I-b; teak, zebrawood, walnut; 9 dia. x 7. Laminated, staved construction, lathe-turned.

"Part of a continuing series of bowls interpreting American Indian pottery and basketry into wood."

E. **Don Kelly,** Plainfield, Mass.

Vase; cherry; 8 dia.

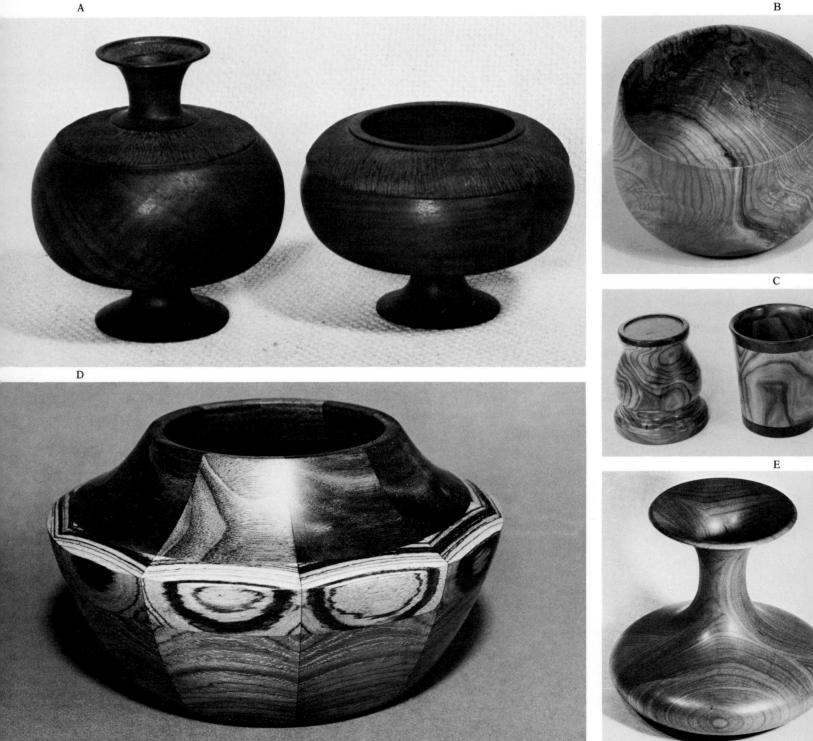

F. **Janice Cole & Warren Kress,** Richmond, Mich.

Weed Vase; bubinga, tropical walnut, afromosia, purpleheart, butternut, padauk; 2 x 3 x 6, $35.

"Vertical laminations were done in a variety of thicknesses, crosscut, then staggered, and laminated again. The shape was roughed with a band saw, at which point a pattern became apparent. We then used a Rockwell 1-in. belt sander/grinder with a 60-grit belt to start refining the shape and to play on the patterns that were developing. We find more freedom here than with a lathe—you can stretch the pattern out into elongated ovals or confine it to perfect circles if you wish. A pattern is always established and gives a pleasing symmetry to the vase."

G. **Henry Schaefer,** Plainsboro, N.J.

Turnings; Plate, red maple, 12 dia.; Bud Vase, plum limbwood, 7½ high; Box, ebony and holly, 6 dia.

H. **John D. Robson,** Vienna, Va.

Bowl; Madagascar ebony; 8½ x 3, $100.

"A piece of ebony with sapwood and heartwood was cut into pieces and the pieces folded to get a repeat of the grain pattern in the laminations. . . . Most of the work was in planning and constructing the laminated blank to achieve the effects I wanted."

I. **David Lory,** Platteville, Wis.

Bowl; hard maple burl; 4 x 9, $140.

"A burl is a grotesque, gnarled malformation on older trees. This bowl is finished with epoxy, which makes it durable and usable for any type of food. It can be washed with soap and water without hurting the finish.

F

G

H

I

A. **Ted A. Poull,** Port Washington, Wis.

Vase; butternut, white ash; 8 dia. x 28½, $300. Cruet; black walnut; 6 tall.

"The vase is completely hollow to the burn mark below the piece of white ash. The thickness of the walls is ¼ in. Each segment is put together with a shoulder or shiplapped joint. This provides three glued surfaces. The work is always done by using two faceplates. The first is put to the bottom of the vase and not removed until the vase is completely finished. A large steady rest is used to hold the walls. This vase weighs only 3½ lb. The cruet is also hollow with a ¼-in. wall."

B. **Dennis F. Ryan,** Rensselaer, N.Y.

Bowl; cocobolo; 7½ x 4. Turned green on faceplate, allowed to dry, then re-turned.

C. **J. Paul Lammers,** Ann Arbor, Mich.

Salad Bowl Set; Serving bowl, Michigan black cherry, 10 x 3½; Individual bowls, amaranth, bubinga, cocobolo, East Indian rosewood, teak, zebrawood, 6½ x 2.

"Each bowl has a different turned shape and separate inlaid banding. All are finished with five coats of clear lacquer. Turnings were made with temporary pine mounting blocks. Each bowl has a branded insignia on the bottom.

D. **Del Stubbs,** Chico, Calif.

Vase; honey locust burl; 5 high, $40. Hollowed out completely; wood is from central California. Photo by David Izzo.

E. **John Matthews,** Westminster, Calif.

Tub; walnut and other dark woods; 16 x 19.

"Every small piece of dark wood in the shop went into this project."

F. **John L. Aebi,** Lafayette, Ind.

Bowl; myrtle; 4½ dia. x 2¾. Turned, inside hollowed with specially made chisels to wall thickness of ⅛ in. Photo by Daniel C. Grayson.

G. **Alan Wilson,** Ringwood, Victoria, Australia

Bowl turned from mallee root, oil finish, tinted polyester filler. Bookends from Murray pine, turned, cut into four and recombined as two, oil finish. Lidded container from Tasmanian horizontal, bark retained, linseed oil and wax finish. Vase of Cyprus pine, pre-soaked in polyethylene glycol.

"Forms determined by the dimensions of the timber and the constraints imposed by the material."

H. **John Gorton Davis,** El Cerrito, Calif.

Tray; curly maple; 17½ x 2, $160. Bottom and rim assembled separately, then fitted together before final turning.

"I started assembling laid-up workpieces for bowls and trays as a way to utilize a cheap supply of black walnut scrap. As the design possibilities and other advantages became more evident, the supply of scrap wood dwindled so that I now cut good lumber into small pieces and glue them together in the size and shape I want. . . . The joinery involved is exacting and time consuming. It takes almost as much time to assemble a workpiece as it does to do the turning and finishing. However, the variations possible provide an enjoyable stimulus and the public acceptance of my work has been most gratifying."

I. **Mark Lindquist,** Schenectady, N.Y.

Vase; spalted sugar maple; 6 x 3. Hollow turning (blind boring), wall is consistent throughout. Photo by Mark Lindquist.

A. **Ronald Gauthier,** Portneuf, Que., Canada

Cook's Kit; wild cherry, leather; 8 to 16, $150. Leather by Jos Binne, St.-Pierre de Broughton, P.Q.

B. **Nicholas Woods,** Douro, Ont., Canada

Liqueur Goblets; padauk, angico; 1⅞ dia. x 6¼. Photo by D. M. Hamilton.

"Freehand-turned on an old Beaver 36-in. lathe, using a ¼-in. gouge ground to an extremely long bevel. Goblet walls average ¹⁄₁₆ in. thick at top, and tend to be too fragile to scrape—very sharp cutting tools are necessary."

C. **David L. Knoblauch,** Kalamazoo, Mich.

Mortar and Pestle; cherry, 3½ dia. x 4¾.

D. **Peter Marshall,** Fairbanks, Alaska

Rolling Pins; bocote, figured maple, copper pipe; 18 x 2.

"I enjoy working with figured maple and rare woods in combination with 'found' materials. One of the rolling pins is turned from a piece of 2-in. copper plumbing pipe with bocote handles carefully fitted and glued on. The other two are made of maple with the figure accentuated with Kentucky rifle stain. All are functional, with the copper preferred by cooks who appreciate that pastry does not stick to a cold metal surface."

A

B

C

D

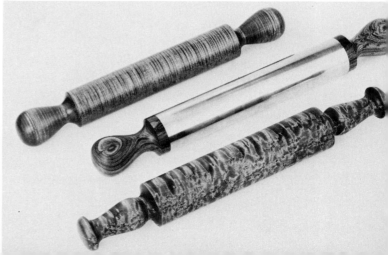

E. **Whit Whitaker,** Boone, N.C.

Double-Ringed Goblet; spalted maple; 1¾ dia. x 5.

"Turned from scrap billet found at a local furniture plant. It was deemed unsuitable for their use."

F. **John S. Wright,** Fairport, N.Y.

Vase; zebrawood; 2½ dia. x 13. Reversed turning.

"The workpiece is made up of four identically sized pieces of zebrawood glued up lengthwise with paper between the segments. The piece is then turned, forming what will become the center of the finished vase. The workpiece is then disassembled and turned inside-out (segments rotated 180°) and permanently reglued. The work is then remounted on the lathe and the outside turned.

G. **Edward S. Nicora,** Wauwatosa, Wis.

Candle Holders; apple wood; 13 x 3¼ (base), $65. The wood was removed from log pile and cured for four months before turning. The lacquer finish resembles marble.

H. **Robert S. Komarow,** Westport, Conn.

Ice Bucket; teak, plastic liner; 10 dia. x 14.

"Wood is excellent insulator, cubes stay quite cold for long time."

I. **Donald W. Brown,** Ft. Pierce, Fla.

Goblets; spalted grapefruit wood; 4½ high. Photo by Richard K. Hightower.

E

F

G

H

I

A. **Dan Warner,** Los Angeles, Calif.

   Rolling Pins; cherry, maple, purpleheart, angico; 16 x 2½.

B. **Gregg Lawrence,** Syracuse, N.Y.

   Mortar and Pestle; maple; 6 tall. Photo by Bergman & Klineberg.

C. **Ronald H. Kerr,** Shippensburg, Pa.

   Candle Holder; walnut; 3½ dia. x 7. Turned, quartered, put turned portion toward center, glued and turned again.

D. **Mark A. Phenicie,** Berwyn, Pa.

   Spiral Candle Holder; Indiana black walnut; 6 dia. x 40.

"Spirals were made with a hand-held router, after which I used drills, chisels, wood rasps and sandpaper to cut out the center section. Spirals are approximately ¾ in. in diameter and approximately 1 in. apart. Therefore, all pieces removed from the center of the spiral section must be small enough to be pulled between the spirals. Approximately 280 hours were spent on this project."

A   B

C   D

E. **J. Steven Cooper,** New Stanton, Pa.

Goblets, 2 x 4; Tray, ¾ x 8; East Indian rosewood.

F. **John A. Leo,** Fairfax, Va.

Knife Block; birch; 7 dia. x 10.

G. **Peter Higbee,** Portland, Ore.

Rolling Pin; maple, black walnut, cherry; 20 x 3. Handles roll on brass pins. Photo by Hal Wood Photography.

E

F

G

A. **Merv Gray,** Bellerive, Tas., Australia

Mobile Sphere; huon pine; 17 x 18 x 3½, sphere 5½ dia.

"Grain pattern in turned sphere is all revealed as sphere rolls on fine edges of base. Sphere will revolve around both inner and outer edges. Because of wedge section of base, sphere pendulums for some time on outer circumference."

B. **Barry Grishman,** Biloxi, Miss.

Kitchen Utensils & Holder; eastern red cedar, teak, maple, ebony, zebrawood, Honduras mahogany, cocobolo, walnut, rosewood; longest utensil, 14½.

C. **Warren Asa,** Glendora, Calif.

Salad Set; Philippine mahogany; 12 x 2½ x 1½.

"I wanted a functional salad set that would hang on the side of the salad bowl. I was pleased with its graceful shape."

D. **Norm Sartorius,** Jewell Ridge, Va.

Ladle; rosewood; 14 x 4, $75.

E. **Donald Craig,** Peru, N.Y.

Soup Taster; cherry; 19 long.

"The spoon's long trough is for rolling the soup back and forth to cool before tasting."

F. **Teodoro Mercado,** Mayaguez, Puerto Rico

Mortar and Pestle; lignum vitae, oysterwood; 4½ high.

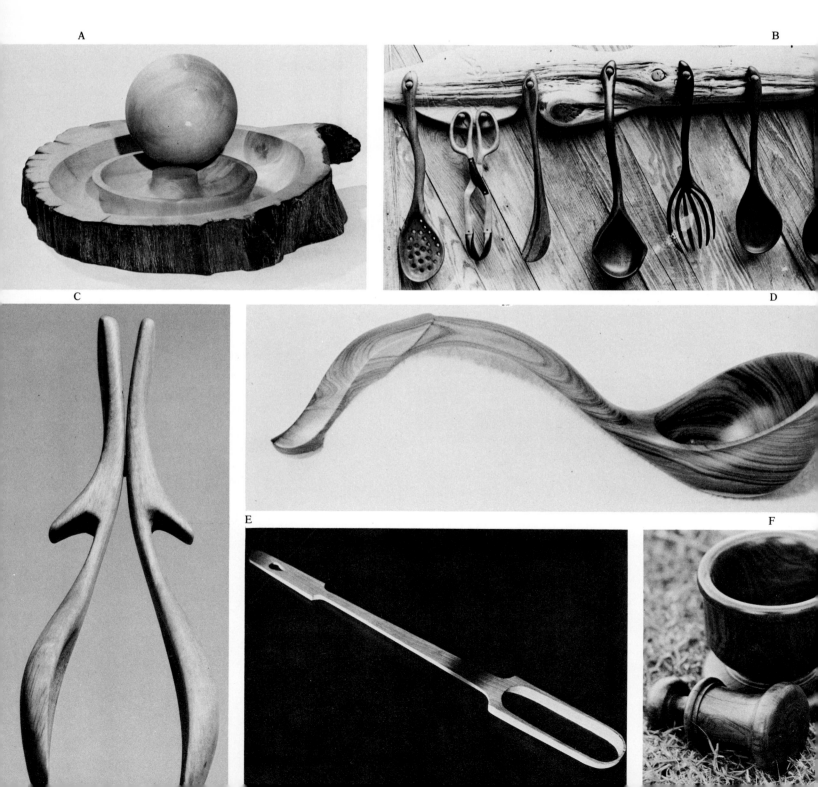

G. **Ray Audet,** Port Moody, B.C., Canada

Spoons; yew; teak; 8 long. Handcarved. Yew cut in woods and hand-milled.

"Teak and yew woods used because of high oil content. Functional item with a sculptural release. I never make the same spoon twice."

H. **George Rutledge,** Albany, N.Y.

Pipe; briar, vulcanite; 6 x 2 x 3. Photo by R. McWaters.

"I wanted a pipe I could set down without spilling ashes on everything."

I. **Norval Humphrey,** Cleves, Ohio

Carved Pipe—Fawn & Doe; briar, $500.

"This pipe won first place at the Toronto show—carving division—at the Canadian National Exhibition."

J. **Thomas Gille,** Madison, Wis.

Honey Dripper; cherry, maple, walnut; 9 long. The head is made of maple, cherry and walnut, glued up and turned on the bias. Finished with linseed oil.

"When held vertically, the rings of the head fill with honey, which stays there until it is turned horizontally, at which point it runs out onto your toast, pancakes or floor. This honey dripper, however, has never been used. We like it so much that it sits in the living room on an end table for people to see and touch and ask 'What is it?' I then reply, 'When held vertically . . .'."

K. **Jerry Richardson,** New York, N.Y.

All Briar Calabash; Grecian plateau briar, English rubber bit; 7½ x 1⅞ x 2⅜, $45.

"Copied from conventional meerschaum shape, with indirect air and tenon holes and well to collect saliva. Bowl precharred, drilling operations very difficult."

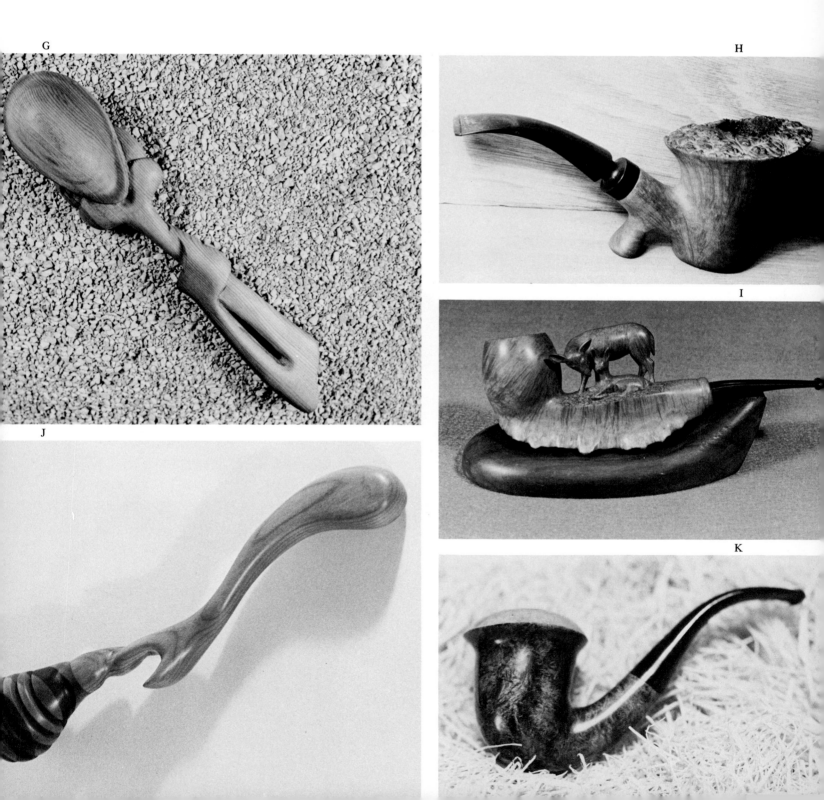

G

H

J

I

K

A. **John Vanderbeek Banta,** San Diego, Calif.

Knife Holder; walnut, birch; German cutlery. Photo by Ryan Roulette.

B. **Bill Kendall,** Nashville, Tenn.

Serving Board; walnut, red oak, white oak; 9 x 10 x 2, $85. Matched end-grain board rubbed with mineral oil, white rubber feet on bottom.

C. **John Vlah,** Gates Mills, Ohio

Bread Serving and Cutting Board; walnut, maple; 20 x 5.

"The relief around the bottom edge of the board gives it a floating effect while in use and adds visual interest when hung on the wall, bottom side out."

D. **Phillip Greer,** Venice, Calif.

Knife Block; teak; 6 x 5 x 10.

"The block was designed to be a functional sculptured piece that possessed an illusion of impossibility. The blades crisscross one another internally by staggering them. The block will accommodate seven knives and one sharpener with blades up to 10 in. long, and a cleaver up to 2¾ in. wide."

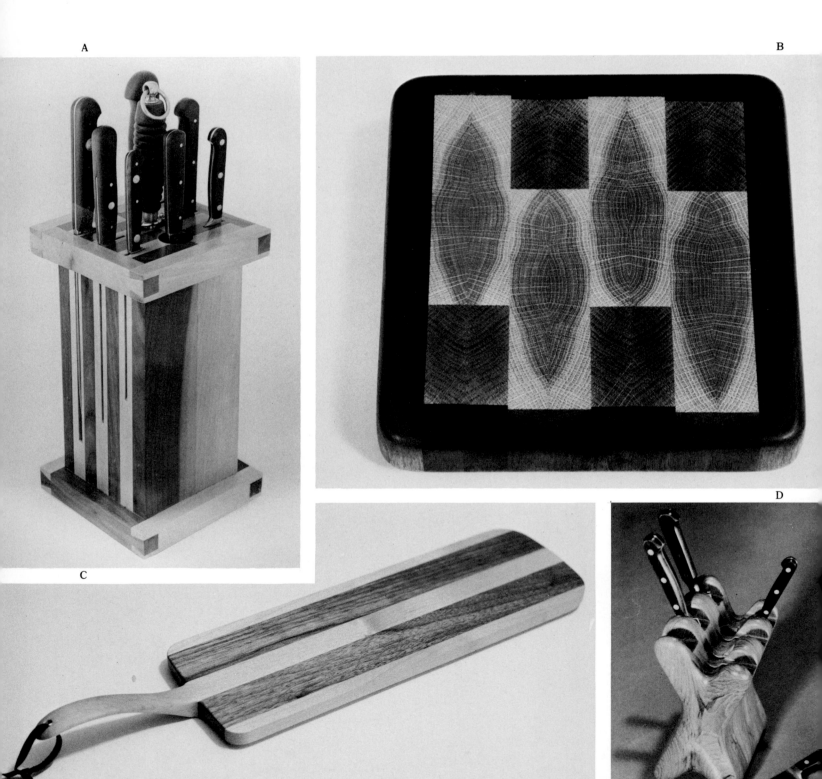

E. **Harry P. Tolles,** Amherst, Mass.

Knife Blocks; maple, walnut; 6¾ x 3¾ x 12.

F. **Wayne Raab,** Waynesville, N.C.

Cutting Boards; maple, cherry, walnut; large, 8 x 24 x 1, $25; small, 8 x 12 x 1, $18 and $12.

G. **Hap Heilman,** Nashville, Tenn.

Butter Dish; walnut; 18 x 8 x 3½.

"The lid is recessed into the base ¼ in., and the surface on which the butter rests is itself recessed ⅛ in. from the top surface. Bread and/or rolls can be sliced and buttered on the larger end, and cheese as well. The larger end has a small, gently curving lip all the way around, which gradually disappears as it reaches the butter dish section."

H. **Daniel Schaffhauser,** Baltimore, Md.

Cutting Block with Storage Drawer; hard maple, white ash, basswood; 20½ x 15½ x 4½. Cutting block is made of 256 pieces of maple; cutting surface is end grain.

I. **John Pomeroy,** Vernonia, Ore.

Tortilla Press; mahogany, ash; 11½ x 8½.

"Produces tortilla quickly and easily. Used with plastic sheets between dough and wood."

E

F

G

H

I

A. **Michael Kucz,** San Francisco, Calif.

Walking Stick; walnut; 36 high.

B. **Eric Sheffield,** Adrian, Mich.

Globe; walnut, brass; 21 x 21 x 30. Globe was made in two hemispheres, each made of laminated octagons and turned separately. Oceans were then carved out by hand and hemispheres glued together. Photo by Denny Short.

"I have been doing woodworking since I was three years old. Two years ago, when I was fifteen, I decided it was time for me to undertake a challenging project, so I created my world."

C. **The Woodworks,** Williamsport, Pa.

Tea Cart; cherry; 30 x 18 x 37.

"The posts receive a ½-in. radius concave cut on the inside corner prior to assembly. All subsequent rounding of edges is done after assembly with a portable router, block plane and file. Rails are doweled to posts."

D. **Jim Kroll,** Waukegan, Ill.

Candle Stand; cherry, brass; 25½ x 14. Photo by Jim Smith.

"This stand holds a 3-in. candle. It has a brass plate cut flush into the top to catch hot wax."

E. **W.E. Wood, Jr.,** Laguna Niguel, Calif.

Pool-Cue Holder; padauk; 37 x 30. Holds eight cues more or less upright. Photo by David Offutt.

F. Dane L. Love, Indianapolis, Ind.

Weaving Combs; walnut; 24 x 8.

G. J. W. Dughi, New Holland, Pa.

Pendant; meerschaum, cypress; 1⅝ sq.

"Some may not consider the wood as the primary material. But the rose was nothing until it was set off by the texture and tones of the weathered cyprus, in perfect complement."

H. Marilyn O'Hara, Richardson, Tex.

Hand Fans; brass, walnut, guinea feathers, 13 x 7 x 2; silver, cherry, peacock feathers, 10 x 5 x 2.

"These fans were made to fit comfortably in your hand. They combine the ideas of something that feels good to hold with functional object."

I. Marvin Kastning & Richard Van Cooten, Darrington, Wash.

Honey Dispenser; white ash, brass; $350/pr.

"The large box, a cooking model (7 x 14 x 11) is designed to hold 25 lb. of honey at a constant temperature. The honey is contained in a polyvinyl bag attached to the valve with 'O' rings. Temperature is maintained by a three-stage heating pad located under the polyvinyl bag. The small box, a table model (4½ x 4½ x 10) is designed to hold 4 lb. of honey and also to support six flower-shaped apportioning spoons. While brass has been used as a unifying material enrichment via lid knobs and inlays, it was chosen primarily for the functional valves, which were designed to cut off the flow of honey cleanly and instantly."

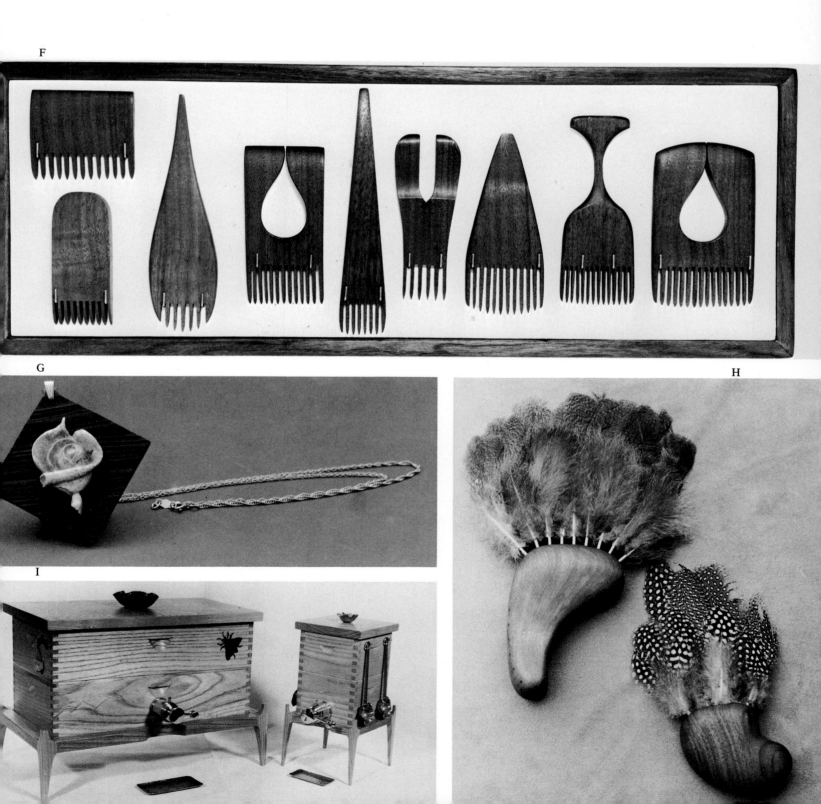

F

G

H

I

A. **Jonathan Wright,** Boston, Mass.

Briefcase; laminated mahogany, leather, laminated leather handle; 45 x 14 x 34 cm., $150.

B. **Elliot Landes,** Winters, Calif.

Chanukah Menorah; rosewood, brass; 12 x 12. Turned.

C. **Carl Gazley, Jr.,** Red Bluff, Calif.

Ancient Egyptian Headrest; walnut; 12 x 4 x 7. Bandsawn and carved from a single block of walnut.

D. **Andrew Cohen,** N. Hollywood, Calif.

Footstool; ash, mahogany; 20 x 10. Photo by Dave Smith.

A

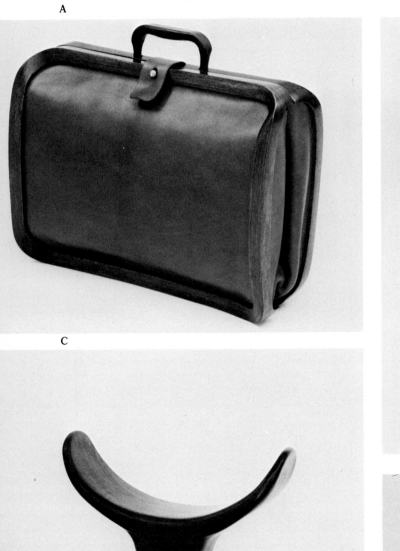

B

C

D

E. **Rick Feldman,** Oakland, Calif.

Chanukah Menorah; rosewood, mahogany; 11 x 8.

F. **Craig Lauterbach,** Monterey, Calif.

Mirror; red oak; 60 x 36 x 8. Stacked lamination, carved with die grinders and sanded with pneumatic drum sanders.

G. **Anthony K. Chickillo,** Philadelphia, Pa.

Bud Vase, Letter Holder, Letter Opener, Ashtray; mahogany, white ash, copper.

H. **Terry L. Evans,** Augusta, Kans.

Hand-Held Mirrors; maple and vermilion with various hardwoods inlaid; 5½ x 11. Sculpted panel involved rounding and finishing each piece individually before setting.

I. **Diedrich Dasenbrock,** Alsea, Ore.

Hand Mirror for Angela; birch with padauk and ebony inlays, beveled oval mirror; 12 x 6 x 2. Made entirely with hand tools.

"This is the second of a series of carved objects made, with love, for special friends."

J. **Karin Healy,** Philadelphia, Pa.

Hand Mirror; maple, walnut; 13¼ x 6 x ⅝. Laminated maple veneer, walnut-veneered plywood back, solid walnut in handle.

"Was designed to be made as a small-scale production item."

A. **Frank E. Cummings III,** Long Beach, Calif.

*Wall Mirror; oak, ivory, 14-karat gold, shells, amber;
21 x 18 x 2. Spline miter joints, traditional sculpture and carving techniques.*

"This wall mirror, like the other works of the artist, establishes an immediate relationship between it and the viewer and thus between the viewer and the artist."

B. **James Cottey,** Clinton, Ark.

Looking Back At Braque; walnut frame, assorted veneers, mirror; 30 x 28 x 72, $1,250. Marquetry; mirror frame strip laminated.

C. **Barbara Wixsom-Harmon,** Long Beach, Calif.

Jewel Box; walnut and padauk; 7½ x 11 x 22.

"The mirror was set in from the front. A groove was made on the inside edge of the wood. A reed was then made to fit in the groove. If the mirror breaks, it can easily be removed."

D. © **Stephen N. Bradshaw,** Indianapolis, Ind.

Cathy's Mirror; walnut, sassafras, hickory; 11 x 11 x 17.

E. **Will Neptune,** Waltham, Mass.

*Wall-Hung Jewelry Chest; mahogany, brass hardware;
13¼ x 8½ x 19½.*

"Sides, mirror frame, drawer fronts are bent laminations . . . used to keep the chest as light and open as possible. The drawer sides were left exposed to add to this effect."

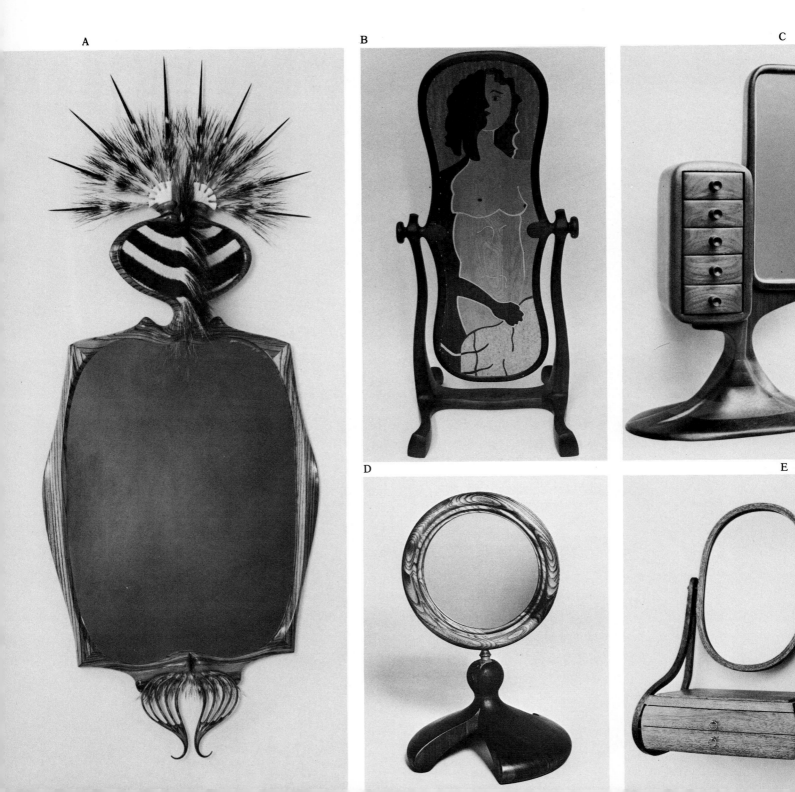

F. **Theodore L. Fisher,** Portland, Ore.

Mahogany Mirror Frame with Foxgloves; 36 x 11, $300.

"This work was done as a challenge to myself to see how far I could push the material. Where the leaves touch the sides of the frame, there is very little wood. Time will tell if this will crack."

G. **Edward Schairer,** Albuquerque, N. Mex.

Three-Way Mirror; vermilion, padauk, mahogany. Tiffany-style (copper foil) stained glass by Sheri Hart.

"Rose pattern is done in amber tones and when light is projected through hole in back of pattern, the rose glows."

H. **Andrew T. Smith,** Bennington, Vt.

Mirror Frame; cherry, oil finish; 15 x 25. Hidden dowel in cross-grain at top provides additional strength; cattails jigsawn to shape and hand-carved. Photo by Wendy Pollock.

I. **John Hughes,** San Jose, Calif.

Bathroom Mirror Cabinet; walnut, teak, cherry, birch, beech; 30 x 2¼ x 48.

A. **Richard Ciupka,** Ville Lorraine, Que., Canada

House Entrance Hidden Mirror; shedua and maple swirl veneer; 38 x 19 x 4. Doweled frame, laminated top and bottom cornice, veneered doors, handcarved door pulls.

B. **Elbert E. Benson,** Oakland, Calif.

Dressing Mirror with Removable Jewelry Box; 24 x 32 x 60. Mirror is beveled and has vacuum-formed back veneered with walnut burl.

C. **Ellen Mason & Dudley Hartung,** Somerville, Mass.

Mirror with Drawer; cherry; 12 x 18 x 36. All handcut joints. Photo by Larry Maglott Photography.

"The open-knot drawer pull is counterpointed visually by the smaller knot on the case top. Subtle rounding softens the piece."

D. **James Bacigalupi,** Los Gatos, Calif.

Vanity Mirror; walnut, padauk, beveled glass; 12 x 3 x 14. Strip lamination; stack lamination for base.

"The design of the mirror succeeds because it says enough without being verbose."

E. **Richard Porst,** Madison, Wis.

Dressing Mirror; walnut; 72 x 24 x 24, $600. Wrought iron by Bob Bergman. Photo by Richard Fulweiler. Mirror slips in through slot at top.

A

B

C

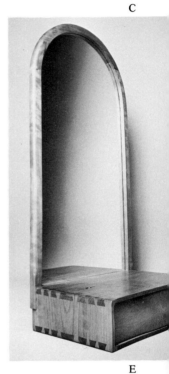

E

D

F. **Bob Bolles,** Hollister, Mo.

Wash Stand; oak (stoneware pitcher and bowl); 30 x 15 x 70; $225.

"The design is based around the oval mirror form, carried to the horizontal plane. The vertical supports are straight on the lower half, but curve up to meet the mirror. The mirror frame back is screwed to the front to ease replacement."

G. **Ruben Guajardo,** LaVerne, Calif.

Standup Mirror; ash; 78 tall.

H. **Girvan Milligan,** Carmel, N.Y.

Clothes Rack; oak; 53 x 36.

I. **Andrew Whelan,** Findlay, Ohio

Down Jacket Coat Hanger; 22 long.

"This piece was all handmade. It started as rough stock; the pads and all the joints were hand-carved.

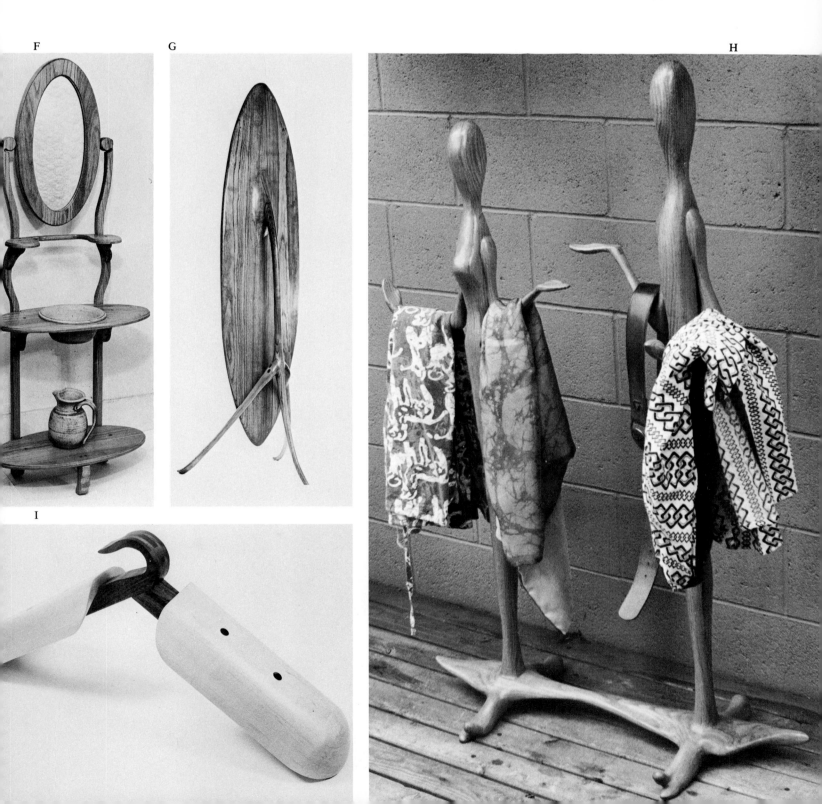

F   G   H

I

A. **Dick Shanley,** Farmingville, N.Y.

Hat-Coat Tree; zebrawood; 19 x 19 x 74. Photo by Ken Spencer.

B. **Denis Collette,** St.-Jean Port Joli, Que., Canada

Coat Tree; red birch; 68 high, $100.

C. **Stephen Laurence Casey,** Sepulveda, Calif.

Hat Rack; red oak; 72 x 30.

"This hat rack was designed as a functional showpiece—I wanted a showpiece that I could use every day....It also had to be easy to transport so I made the top rack removable with a threaded dowel. It fits easily into my car without fear of breaking. All the shapes were carved with a mallet and gouge. Finish is oil."

D. **Michael Ince/Bentwoodesign,** Brookhaven, N.Y.

Lamp; red oak, Manilla line; 36 x 60 x 8. Green wood, hot-water bending.

A   B   C

D

E. **Seth Stem,** Marblehead, Mass.

Floor-Standing Mirror (rear view); black cherry, rosewood; 32 x 36 x 78. Bent lamination. Photo by John Gustavsen.

"Container to the right of mirror holds cosmetics, hairbrush, etc., and arms on the left are used for hanging garments."

F. **Ed Dadey,** Marquette, Nebr.

Coat Rack; maple; 18 x 30 x 69.

G. © **Charles B. Cobb,** Santa Rosa, Calif.

Hall Tree; African zebrawood, ebony dowels; 65 x 15.

"The joints near the top are all lap joints. Many people see them as a unique curved joint—the compound curves throw the viewer off."

H. **Saswathan Quinn,** Emryville, Calif.

Folding Screen; shedua, handwoven fabric; 104 x 73, $1,600.

"The panels are bookmatched and shaped. The fabric was designed and woven by Pacifac Basin Textile Atelier, Berkeley."

I. **Stephen Litchfield,** Chicago, Ill.

Clothing Rack; oak, birch; 48 x 34 x 78. Photo by Stereo Views.

"A simple lever and locating pin are used to support a 4-ft. hanger pole. Each pole assembly is adjustable and can extend from the standard in either direction. The entire unit can be connected to another identical unit by additional pole assemblies, making a modular system.... Hanger assembly is designed to be easily adjusted by one person and to support any number of the heaviest winter garments."

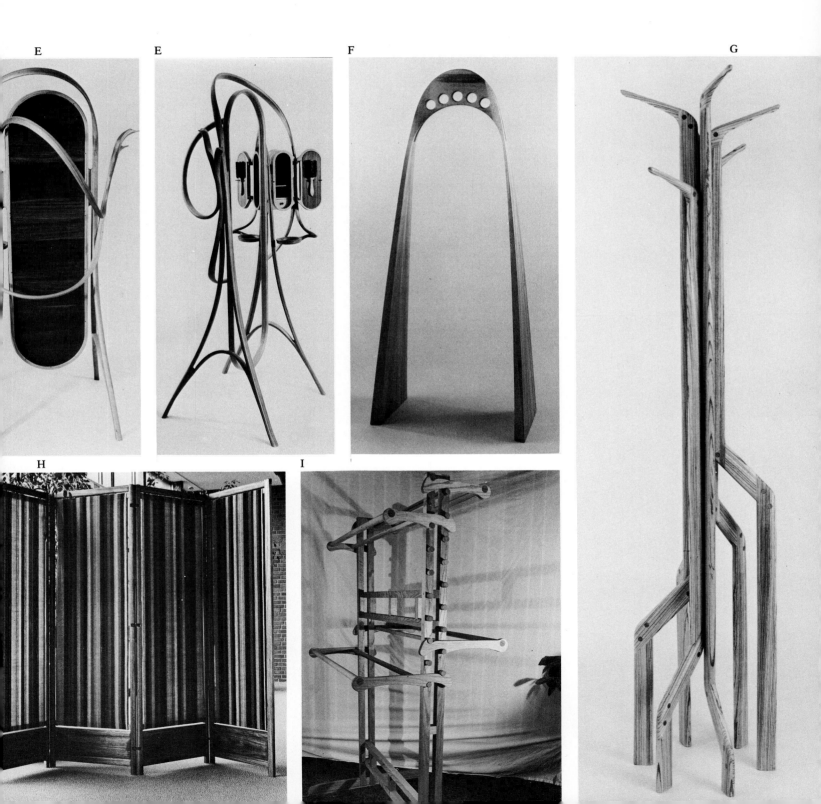

E   E   F   G

H   I

A. **Federico Armijo,** Albuquerque, N. Mex.

Shoe Rack; teak; 20 x 30 x 90. Bandsawn, laminated, turned, formed.

"Designed for a gentleman's dressing room, for his shoe collection."

B. **Ron Curtis,** Bloomfield, Conn.

Screen; cherry, butternut, elm; 68 x 52. Frame is doweled and glued, centers have a tongue top and bottom, frame and center are slotted all around to receive elm panels.

"This piece is a result of years thinking about making screens (and not doing it) and in two weeks of concentration having it fall into place. It took two weeks because each board in the sunburst was fitted by assembling and disassembling each frame for every two boards."

C. **Katherine Svec,** Ames, Iowa

Filigree Divider Screen; cherry; 68 x 56.

"I am intrigued by the challenge of designing the space enclosed by a divider screen. An earlier screen demonstrated pleasing curves but left a disconcerting number of odd-sized scraps. I wanted to see if I could design a screen which maintained a pleasing design but minimized scraps. I was pleased with this one, which completely eliminated scraps by using the cutouts from the first and third panels for the filigree in the second and fourth."

D. **Lewis Korn,** Mamaroneck, N.Y.

Valet; walnut; 18 x 18 x 62. Hand-shaped with spokeshaves and various sanding drums; construction is mainly mortise and tenon. Photo by Bob Zucker.

E. **Neal M. Widett & Susan C. Wilson,** Boston, Mass.

Viking Ship Log Holder; yellow pine, painted red, black, white; 55 x 26 x 36. Photo by Ron Harrod.

"The Revell plastic model kit was the inspiration for this piece."

A   B   C

D

E   E

F. **Judith Clark Bowie,** Madison, Wis.

Interlocking Wine Rack; walnut, cherry, maple; each section 5½ x 8.

"My idea here was to provide the person who owns this wine rack with the opportunity to create his own personal piece. To that end, I provided the pieces, which that person then manipulates as he wishes. The basic module, in which the wine bottle actually sits, has dovetail-type slots on each side. These can be used alone by sliding one module into the other. This creates a staggered, brick-like effect. Additional pieces are also provided which make it possible to stack the modules directly one on top of the other. The dovetail-slide pieces connect the modules. The third type of piece provided gives the owner the option of having solid surfaces on the sides and/or top of the wine rack, thereby making it possible to use the wine rack as a small table. These pieces are one-half of the full connecting dovetail slide and the surfaces line up flush with the outside of the modules, giving a flat outer surface. The dovetail slides may also be screwed under a shelf. The modular pieces then slip on the dovetail slides, thereby hanging the wine rack under a shelf. . . . I build the

parts for this wine rack in three woods, walnut, cherry and maple, because those three woods have similar grain and go well together. By having three colors to work with, the owner may also arrange the colors as he wishes."

G. **Thomas Barnett & Cliff Rugg,** Bowdoinham, Maine

On the Way to the Octave Music Stand; beech, walnut, juneberry; 56 high. Bent lamination, hand shaped; commissioned by a violinist.

H. **Valmore F. Cross,** Sheffield, Mass.

Corner Wine Rack; cherry, oak plywood; 26 x 18 x 45.

"Assemblage from front entirely, with all inserts tenoned on far end and hand-fitted into holes predrilled in triangles at far corners. Near end, mortise and tenon with open top side to allow installation from front, after main assembly. The number of internal pieces, 46, the triangular configuration of the overall design, and the logistics and design problems prior to assembly made this project most interesting."

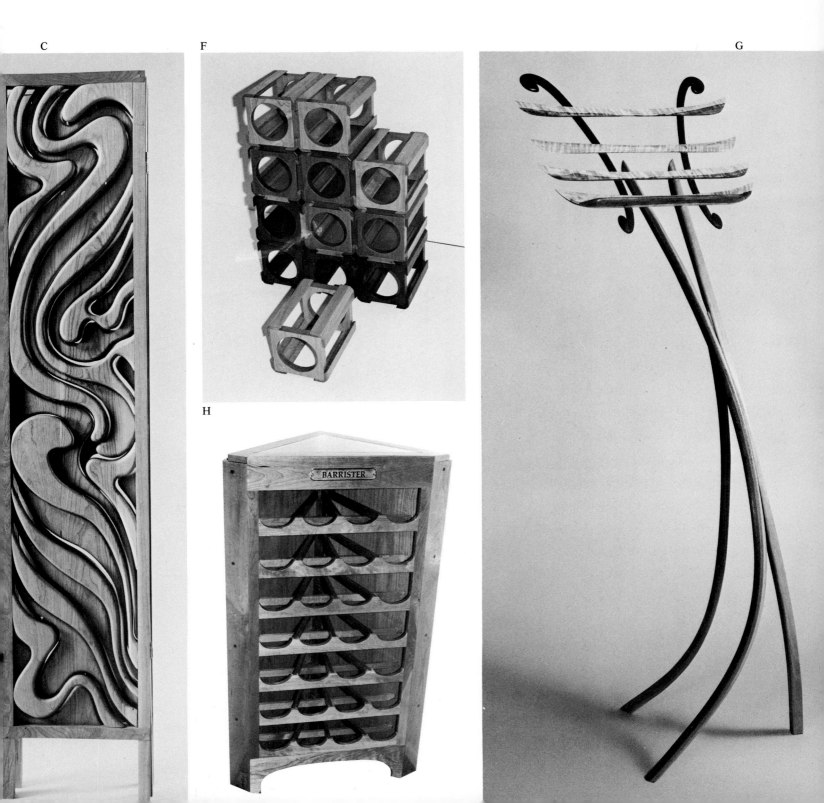

C   F   G

H

A. **Karen N. Hazama,** Canoga Park, Calif.

Music Stand; walnut, rosewood, copper; 16 x 21½ x 50.

"The music stand is adjustable in height and angle of the rack."

B. **Kevin Perkins,** Huonville, Tas., Australia

Music Stand; Tasmanian huon pine; 24 x 31½ x 59. Natural bent shape with split slats.

C. **Richard Porter,** Groton, Mass.

Firescreen; mahogany; 13 x 17 x 50. Chippendale style, crewel embroidery by Mrs. Porter. Photo by Deborah Porter.

D. **John Nyquist,** Long Beach, Calif.

Book Rest With Note Tray; black walnut, ebony, ivory; 40 x 60, $1,100. Turned and carved.

E. **Dick Ryerson,** Crestline, Calif.

Convertible Planters; red oak, black cherry; 36 x 12 x 12.

"May be used horizontally or vertically—one of a set of four modular-sized planters, all of which may be used in two or more positions."

F. **John Slaughter,** La Mesa, Calif.

Music Stand; walnut; 12 x 18 x 38. Laminated ply veneer.

G. **Peter T. Roth,** Livonia, Mich.

Cactus Planter; cherry; 16 dia. x 5½. Wood was obtained from a piece of firewood, split, sawn and then hand-planed. Bottom is plywood, all joints are splined miters. Photo by Foremost Photographic Service Co.

H. **James L. Madigan,** Farmington, Conn.

Omnistand/Dictionary Stand; American birch; 20 x 20 x 44. Hidden steel rods reinforce joints at top and bottom. Book surface is attached with screws.

"The design is influenced by the constructivist movement in modern art, particularly the Belgian sculptor, Georges Vantongerloo, whose work was based on algebraic equations. The neo-plasticism of Piet Mondrian with its straight lines and 90° angles has also had a great deal of influence on my work."

I. **Everett Schwoch,** Dover, Minn.

Lectern; maple, walnut, oak, birch; 22 x 15 x 17, $850. Base sits on turntable.

J. **Newell White,** Rochester, N.Y.

Obelisk Lamp (patent pending); walnut; 43 x 9¼ each face. Louvered reading lamp, dimmer controlled.

K. **Robert L. DeFrances,** Delray Beach, Fla.

Floor Lamp; Appalachian ash, acrylite; 14 x 17 x 65. Photo by Tom McKay.

A. **Timothy J. Zikratch,** Pocatello, Idaho

Floor Lamp; oak, mahogany; 36 x 72. Rheostat control.

B. **Mark Smith,** New Meadows, Idaho

Monkey Lamp; white oak; 7 x 29. Carved from California white oak limb; three-quarters of tail represents natural branching; final curl added with dowel joint; base and top lathe-turned. Oak collected and cured seven years.

C. **Dan Dennison,** Chichester, N.H.

Lamp; black walnut, bubinga, zebrawood, cork; base 12 x 10, $150. Photo by Bruce A. Binning.

D. **Robson Lindsay Splane, Jr.,** Granada Hills, Calif.

Bentwood Floor Lamp; cherry, Brazilian rosewood; 58 x 13 x 52. Laminated, turned and hand-shaped; fiberglass lay-up for lampshade.

"This lamp is part of an eight-piece room setting of furniture, and is designed to cantilever and swivel over a desk, table or chair."

E. **Rion Dudley,** Seattle, Wash.

Desk Fan; white pine; 6½ x 8 x 8. Large pivot is turned, router-made dovetails on base.

"A small, very quiet fan normally used for cooling hi-fi equipment is mounted in the box section. The box can be tilted to any angle."

F. **Joe Hogan,** Peabody, Mass.

Candle Box; elm; 14 x 8 x 5. Photo by Lancer Studio.

G. **W. T. Hibdon,** St. Louis, Mo.

Plant Stands; ash; 7½ x 7½ x 12, 24 and 36.

"Ash boards 1 in. thick were run through a molder to get the sine wave. Edges beveled and boards glued into hollow box plant stands. Top cap is plywood. Designed for mass production."

H. **Ray A. Martin,** Red Lion, Pa.

Advent Wreath Stand; red oak; 30 x 56, ring 15 dia. Laminated of ⅛-in. strips glued together in form, pegged together and glued, then sculpted.

I. **Ralph Z. Neff,** North Canton, Ohio

Lamp Base; butternut, maple burl. Carved and turned.

J. **Joel L. Duncanson,** Mineral Point, Wis.

Dictionary Stand; cherry, hickory, aromatic cedar.

"Beyond reaching the proper dimensions for my 6-ft. 5-in. client and his Oxford English Dictionary, the emphasis for this dictionary stand is on use of wood and clean, exposed joinery. I tried to use wood that had a grain pattern that would accentuate the gentle curves on the top, front rail, leg stretchers. The panel for the top was made from quarter-sawn hickory to bring out those beautiful brown stripes. I got perfect grain match on the four pieces glued up for the panel. The cedar drawer bottom also worked out having good grain match with matching sapwood stripes.

"I tried to soften the whole thing by using gentle curves instead of straight lines. Also, by chamfering with a spoke-shave the edge of a square straight leg, I tried to make the leg appear slightly curved or at least softer looking. Simply put, I tried to make something that wouldn't be distracting in its different parts—which as a whole would be continuous—gentle to the eyes. In trying to do this, the wood itself, its direction of grain, was very important to me."

K. **David Benezra,** Los Angeles, Calif.

Floor Lamp; walnut, glass; 54 x 26, $550. Bent lamination.

L. **Michael Gilmartin,** Atlanta, Ga.

Arc Lamp; mahogany, birch plywood; 80 x 48.

F

G

H

I J

K   L

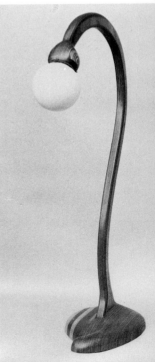

A. **Boris Bowman,** Missoula, Mont.

Swansong Ring Boxes; birch, American black walnut; 4 x 2½ x 1¾. Photo by Light Smith.

"These are cut from single blocks (the waste over the wings provides material for the lids).... The pair are based on a newspaper photo taken near Poitiers, France. I used only oil finish and elbow grease to bring out the natural color and grain of the wood."

B. **Peter Cooke,** Trumansburg, N.Y.

Box; makore, maple; 4 x 8 x 12.

C. **Garo Enjaian,** Van Nuys, Calif.

Jewel Box; black walnut; 8¼ x 3¾ x 1½, $250.

"Wood blank divided for top and bottom, bandsawn to outline of form. Woodcarving chisels used to shape both outer and inner box. Gouge marks left on inside as design feature. Closure shaped by hand with chisels, sandpaper and fine mill file."

D. **Michael P. O'Brien,** Stillwater, Minn.

Jewelry Box; padauk, birch dowel; 7 x 5 x 4. Case joints dovetailed, drawers pivot on birch dowel through entire case.

E. © **Rob Bolson,** Decorah, Iowa

Landscape Box Series II (Jewelry Box); red gum; 14¾ x 3¼ x 1½. Interior routed; shaping done by machine. Hand-sanding, finished with Watco oil.

"All pieces were allowed to adjust to new tensions after all sawing, routing, etc., for a week or more. After replaning, pieces were assembled and finished."

F. **Allen W. Johnson,** N. Augusta, S.C.

Sweetheart Jewelry Box; walnut, felt, brass hinge pins; 11½ x 6¼ x 5¼, $500. Relief-carved top and sides; inverted hearts on sides are handles. Photo by Jim King.

"Hinge pins are blind, holes drilled with dentist's drill. Pins are spring loaded from hinge center."

A

B

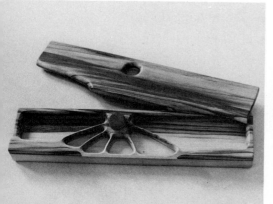

C

D

E

C

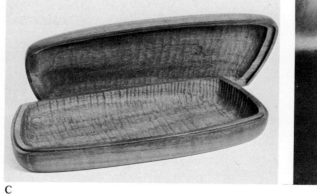

F

G. **Joel W. Gruenberg,** Goleta, Calif.

Jewelry Boxes; 4 x 3¾ x 3¼, lauan, Indian rosewood, Peruvian walnut, Bocote, Honduran mahogany, Brazilwood; 6¼ x 4¾ x 3⅝, walnut burl, wenge, Honduran mahogany, Brazilwood; 7½ x 4¼ x 3⅛, walnut burl, lauan, Peruvian walnut. Sandwich laminations of thick veneer slices, using table saw, band saw and jointer; assembled using rabbet joints and precut dados. Photos by J. Brouws.

H. **Bruce Carlin Byall,** Isla Vista, Calif.

Container; putumuju; 5 x 6 x 9, $160. Bandsawn, sanded, oiled, waxed.

"My work, making containers from whole wood, continues a very old tradition in a contemporary way. Working from the log, I can leave in bark, sapwood, wormholes, etc. Things that would be a defect to some become part of the design. I only enhance what is already there."

I. **John C. Holtslander,** Burton, Mich.

Jewelry Box; teak, padauk; 19 x 9 x 7½.

J. **Bobby R. Falwell,** Murray, Ky.

Tiered Split-Top Box; red oak; 14 x 11. Laminated and hand-carved.

"Each tier is hinged to allow it to slide open in the opposite direction from the next tier."

A. **Jay W. Kratz,** Moab, Utah

Pipe Display Box; walnut, maple; 9 x 8 x 2½. Photo by Perpetual Images.

"The pipes are held in place by pieces of cork, of the same diameter as the pipe bowls, glued to the box.

B. **Allan J. Boardman,** Woodland Hills, Calif.

Small Box; tulip, ebony, silver, suede; 2¼ x 1½ x ⅞. Box features decorative joints—dovetails, finger joints, etc. Silver inlay, suede liner in box and tray.

"This box won first prize in the English *Woodworker* magazine/Lervad competition."

C. **Brad Black,** Denver, Colo.

Box; walnut, pecan, rosewood, coco; 23 x 12.

D. **James E. Blackburn,** Eugene, Ore.

Jewelry Box; primavera, tigerwood, cherry, walnut, pecan, holly, vermilion, bubinga, bird's-eye maple, zebrawood, padauk, orientalwood, Carpathian elm, poplar burl, maple burl, amboyna burl, Brazilian rosewood, benge, lacewood, myrtle, redwood burl, tamo, thuya burl; 20 x 13¾ x 10.

"The only material used on the marquetry section, other than bulk veneer, was ebony and holly in 1/16-in. wide strips. Everything was cut with utility knife and straightedge."

E. **David G. Flatt,** Madison, Wis.

Three-Drawer, Two-Top Opening Container; zebrawood; 5 x 5 x 12. Photo by Skot Weidemann.

"Inside of drawers and spaces are finished as highly as the outside."

A B

C D E

F. **Nils Falk,** Madison, Wis.

Kathy's Box; cherry, walnut; 6½ x 3½ x 8½.

G. **Bob Trumpfheller,** Spring Lake, Mich.

Magazine Display Cabinet; walnut; 20 x 15 x 21.

H. **William N. Koch,** Richmond, Va.

Jewel Cylinder; ash, walnut veneer; 13 x 12 x 12. Vacuum-formed cylinder.

"Very stable container. Velvet-lined drawers display jewelry well. Drawers open easily and provide complete visibility."

I. **Steve Voorheis,** Missoula, Mont.

Ring Box; Honduras mahogany; 10 x 8 x 14. Collection of Barbera Shaiman.

J. **Carl Riggs,** Van Nuys, Calif.

Box; plywood, Masonite; 1⅞ x 3⅜ x 9⅛. Plywood cut on a jig-saw, then laminated. Inside worked on a drum sander, then bottom was attached.

K. **Martha L. Rising,** North Hollywood, Calif.

Box; East Indian rosewood; 16 x 4 x 1¾. Carved with two cast bronze handles, which fit to form press-fit latch. Interior has formed bronze partitions echoing the forms and lines carved on exterior. Photo courtesy of E.B. Crocker Gallery, Sacramento.

L. **Bruce Erdman,** Mt. Horeb, Wis.

Oval Tambour Box; afromosia; 15 x 8 x 4¾, $60. Mortise and tenon construction, template routing, simple tambour construction.

"Principally designed for jewelry storage, using the difficult true oval shape."

F

F

G

H

I

J

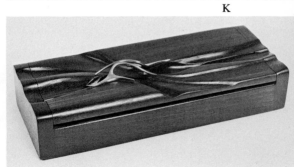

K

L

A. **Ralph E. Karling,** Ketchikan, Alaska

Jewel Box; mahogany, maple, Bakelite; 6 x 4 x 3. ¹/₁₆-in. veneer, linseed oil finish.

B. **Ralph H. Fertig,** Santa Barbara, Calif.

Dual-Compartment Box; Andaman padauk, cherry, suede; 20 x 13 x 9 cm, $120. Laminated wood, routed compartments, ellipses generated to fit lid dimensions.

C. **John E. Stolz,** Fleetwood, Pa.

Laminated Container; mahogany, vermilion; 20 x 13 x 6.

D. **Alan Kooris,** Framingham, Mass.

Jewelry Box; walnut; 18 x 9½ x 4. Mitered edges with feather splines and dovetailed drawer.

E. **Henry H. Armstrong,** Winnipeg, Man., Canada

Jewel Box; bird's-eye maple; 11 x 7 x 2.

"Hand-carved top. Hand-sawn and fitted dovetails. Tung oil finish, hand-rubbed—that is, with fingers, not a rag."

F. **Steve Madsen,** Albuquerque, N. Mex.

Buildings You See on Vacation But Never in Your Own Home Town; zebrawood, tulip, ebony, ivory, silver, Plexiglas; 18 x 6 x 11.

G. **Henry E. Powell,** Northport, N.Y.

Jewelry Box; birch and basswood plywoods, walnut veneer, red velvet lining over fiberglass padding, brass hinges; 10½ x 6¾ x 4, $160. Fretwork.

"The sides of the box and cover are cut out of a single piece. Then the cover is separated. This assures continuity of the grain pattern when the box is closed. The assembly is by tenon joints throughout, and the walnut veneer covers the top tenons. Accurate cutting is a must, otherwise the box does not lie flat when assembled."

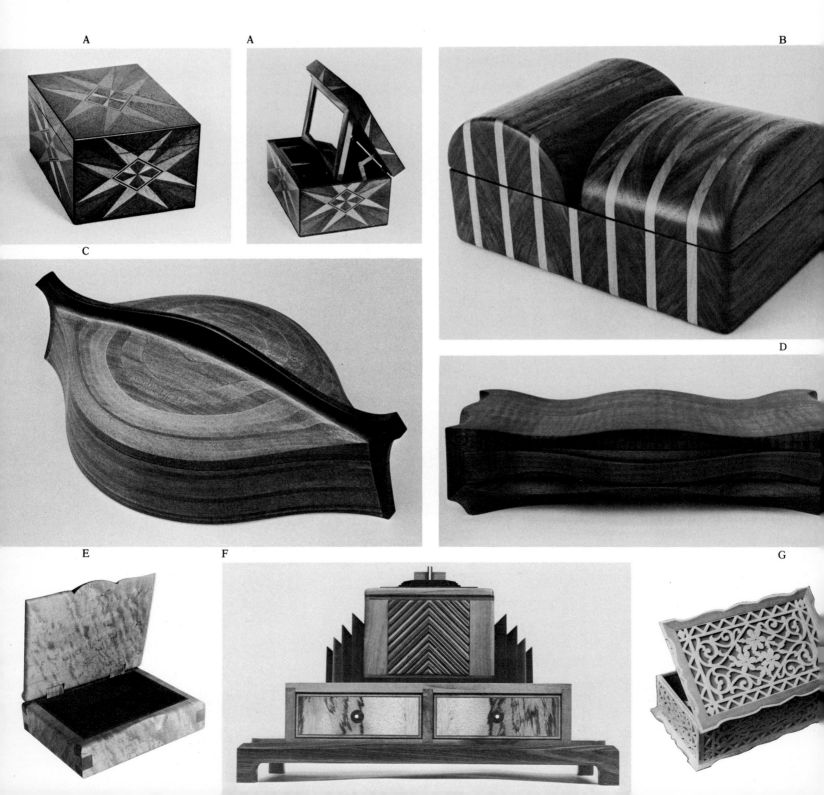

A   A   B   C   D   E   F   G

H. Chas. Rombold, Augusta, Kans.

Box; black walnut; 8¾ x 8 x 3. Photo by Jim Yarnell.

I. Bob Trotman, Casar, N.C.

Six-Face Box; walnut, curly maple; 20 x 6. Stacked lamination, handcarved.

j. Larry M. Litwin, Schenectady, N.Y.

Recipe Box; butternut, walnut, glass; 9 x 12 x 10. Mitered undercut rabbets fit the legs to the sides.

"This was commissioned by a young housewife who wanted a nice recipe box for a newly refinished kitchen done in pecan and teak. She and her husband don't have much time to spend in the outdoors these days, so I tried to bring some of that flavor to them. I made the top into a display case. The bottom of this has a knot dead center, surrounded by burling. The case was filled with an arrangement of butterflies and dried flowers from the wood and fields. Once I had the top I tried several styles for the bottom. It holds two rows of 3x5 index cards."

K. Norbert J. Mikus, Westminster, Calif.

Magic Box; walnut with brass trim; 11 x 9 x 5¼.

"To produce or to cause the disappearance of a given article. Basically it consists of two boxes. An outer box, when unlatched with a thumb or fingernail, opens both top and bottom allowing the conjuror to pass an arm through the box, justifying that the box is empty. A second box, or load compartment, is secured to the underside of the top lid and has a small but visible door and latch.

"When the outer box is swung open, the inner box is hidden behind the top lid, between the operator and the audience. The holes located on four sides are for ventilation in the event that a small animal is to be produced. All the corners of the outer box are reinforced with metal angles placed beneath the moldings to ensure rigidity."

H

I

J

H

I

J

K

K

K

K

A. **Jeff All,** Terre Haute, Ind.

*Armado (Armadillo) Jewelry Box; padauk, zebrawood;
20 x 10 x 9.*

B. **William E. Winter,** Columbia, Md.

*Jewelry Chest; Pennsylvania walnut, commercial inlay;
15 x 9 x 12. Splined joints, dovetails in drawers, velvet linings.*

C. **Joe T. Strother,** Bellaire, Tex.

*Jewelry Box; crotch walnut, rosewood and tamo veneers,
sawn ebony, sawn maple, African walnut; 11 x 7 x 4.*

"Contact cement and white glue were used to assemble a
three-ply top panel. Glue was allowed to age for two years
before sanding and finishing, to eliminate the possibility of
creep and joint opening. The panels were kept under weights
to prevent warping. Resorcinol glue was used to assemble
the main box. The finish is clear gloss Varathane used with
no stains or fillers. The finish was aged over one year to per-
mit full shrinkage before fine sanding and polishing. The
final rubbing was done with jeweler's rouge and water to
produce an extremely high gloss.

"This box and two others that are incomplete are to be
gifts as keepsakes to my wife and two daughters. Every effort was made to create a beautiful and perfect box that
would last several generations."

D. **Richard R. Erickson,** St. Paul, Minn.

*Jewelry Case; teak, black walnut; 11⅛ x 8¼ x 9¾. Photo by
William Erickson.*

E. **Thomas Petry,** Babylon, N.Y.

Box; walnut; 13½ x 9 x 4.

"All wood is from same walnut trunk, air-dried."

A

B

C

D

E

F. **Mark Methner,** Chambersburg, Pa.

Container; rosewood, brass pin to hinge; 4½ x 6 x 2.

"The container and lid are both constructed of laminated pieces of rosewood, each of which was ³⁄₃₂ in. thick. The piece shows the great variety of color and configuration of grain present within a single species of wood. . .The piece has no applied finish."

G. **Hal Boyer,** Saugerties, N.Y.

Jewel Chest; walnut, butternut, pearwood, oak; 14 x 12 x 8.

"Top-opening lids are finger-hinged (⅛-in. alternate slot and finger, mated), anchored to chest wall. Drawer opens by means of sculptured recess on either side. Chest and drawer are lined with black Ultrasuede fabric. My design attempts to portray a somewhat monolithic mass, with sculptured form interrupted only by the recess areas that provide a means to the inside."

H. **John S. Everdell,** Jamaica Plain, Mass.

Jewelry Box; walnut, birch, leather, brass; 13 x 8 x 9.

"This piece was designed to illustrate dovetails. The doors when closed are spring-loaded with walnut springs and catches and can be released when buttons under the front center area are pushed."

I. **Raymond Kowalsky,** Clinton, Conn.

Jewelry Box; walnut, brass, velvet; 12½ x 12 x 3.

"Four pieces of solid walnut are laminated together in the construction of this symmetrical heart-shaped jewelry box. The bottom section is 1¾ in. thick, the inside is 1 in. deep with six compartments. The top lid is ¾ in. thick, the inside is ⁵⁄₁₆ in. deep."

J. **Robert Lovett, Jr.,** Newtown, Pa.

Stationery Box/File; East Indian rosewood, sitka spruce; 11¾ x 9¼ x 4.

"Patent Pending. Holds 300 to 400 sheets of 8½x11 paper. Lid hinges 210°. Hinge made of cast plastic."

F   G   G

H   I

H   J

(and previous page)
Alexander M. Marsh, Holliston, Mass.

Queen Anne Highboy (flat-top); southern cherry exterior, poplar interior; 36½ x 19 x 70⅜, $2,700.

"The chest of drawers is mortise-and-tenon construction, with hand-dovetailing on the drawers and exterior stiles. The upper case separates from behind the molding on the lower case and is guided by four dowels."

A. **Jim Adamson & Steve Badane, Jersey Devil,** Chicago, Ill.

Football House; Douglas fir, redwood; 12 ft. x 28 ft., $9,000 (shell). Photo by Peter O. Whiteley.

"Project was to design and build a studio/office addition to an existing residence (shell only, with owner to complete interior). To save several existing redwoods, the addition is placed 40 ft. from the main house and connected by an elevated walk-through greenhouse.

The structure is two lenticular trusses, grounded with sandwiched 2x6s, sheathed in plywood, cantilevered from concrete piers. The trusses are 12 ft. apart with 2x10 cross-framing forming two levels. The triangular framing provides structural strength, the top arcs carry the roof beams (2x8s), and the spaces between the arcs and triangles are glazed with Plexiglas. A peaked skylight in the center of the cross section gives the roof proper slope at that point and provides filtered light to the interior. Siding is green redwood 2x6 shiplapped on the diagonal (45°)."

B. **Karl Oppen,** Cotati, Calif.

House with Staircase and Railing in Octagonal Tower; exterior: redwood, aluminum-clad wood windows; interior: pine; staircase: vertical-grain fir, mahogany, birch buttons; 64 ft. x 36 ft. x 42 ft. (tower).

"Ideas for the stairs started when I was drawing the house plans; in order to draw the elevations I needed window placement, which of course is dictated by unit rise. It became apparent that to fit scaffolding in the tower I had to start at the top and work down. Because of irregularity in the tower's shape, each tread and riser is individually shaped. Because of changes in rise and run, two flights required four different router jigs. The stringers were notched to accept the 1-in. treads, and the front edge of each tread was dadoed to accept a riser, which made each step in effect a beam,

A

A

B

B

B

eliminating the need for a middle stringer. The railings and pickets were made from 1-in. mahogany, bandsawn, then Surformed and routed. Throughout the construction, I was faced with what seemed an endless number of near duplicate copies to turn out. The 'near' is an important word.

"My experience includes 10 years off and on in woodworking and three and a half years of pure math in college. At age 24 it is obvious that time in trade is not my long suit."

C. Samuel Talarico, Jr., Mohnton, Pa.

Drying Shed; treated posts, green oak, white pine; 20 ft. x 40 ft. Pole construction with open gables for air circulation, 15-ft. to 12-ft. roof pitch and knee wall to economically add second story. Photo by Jim Penta.

"I needed a barn to store lumber and large flitches. I wanted to combine the qualities of easy access, space, strength, and attractiveness. Esthetically, I wanted a building that had its own individual character, yet would harmonize with the existing buildings (which I also built) on the property. The barn has been constructed of the most economical and practical materials available to me. It's almost entirely maintenance free, utilizing materials that can endure years of weathering without upkeep. Treated posts were used to frame the building; the white pine siding will breathe and weather nicely; locust for the stairs; and an aluminum roof, which should last for 30 to 50 years. The entire building cost just $4,000 for materials and was constructed, with the help of a half-dozen Mennonite friends, in just one week from the time the poles were set ready to frame."

D. Robert W. Bailey, Woodleaf, N.C.

House Frame; southern yellow pine; 32 ft. x 24 ft. x 25 ft.

"Frame is fully mortised and tenoned, including horizontal nailers and door and window frames. Layout is on an 8-ft by 12-ft. grid, with 14 continuous 6x6 posts. A central chimney will take the place of one post. All main joints with plates, beams and joists on this grid are drawbolted with ½-in. carriage bolts on threaded rods. Other mortise and tenon joints are pegged. Joists and rafters are spaced 4 ft. O.C. and nailers are spaced to accommodate two batts of 16-in. fiberglass insulation and two of 24 in.

"House is to be solar-tempered, with a large expanse of south-facing glass and a slate-covered concrete slab floor. Back-up heat will be provided by a heat-circulating fireplace."

C

C

D

D

A. **Bruce Lowell Bigelow,** San Francisco, Calif.

*Staircase with Built-In Chest of Drawers and Pull-Out Table;
red oak, ash, birch plywood (interiors); 9 ft. x 3 ft. x 7 ft.
Plywood carcase construction on chest of drawers with oak
web frames between drawers. Drawer construction: NK
design, with dovetail dadoes joining sides to front. Full extension drawer slides. Leg and rail joints are doweled.*

"Designed to allow for maximum utilization and flexibility
within a small space."

B. **David Klatt,** Santa Rosa, Calif.

*Spiral Staircase; Nicaraguan walnut, red oak, $5,000.
Laminated; assisted in construction by Lisa Hemenway.*

A   B

A   B

C. **Robert McKay,** New Denver, B.C., Canada

Spiral Stairs; eastern ash, Douglas fir, spruce. Photo by Bob McKay.

"Construction is mortise and tenon throughout, with lag bolts recessed and left exposed. Its two distinguishing features are the double focus (i.e., the first three treads pivot about the bottom newel post, the next five pivot about the center post and the last three are straight) and the rail, which was laminated in place on tenons at the top of the balusters. I used a piece of string to clamp the strips one at a time, winding it around and around at 1-in. to 1½-in. intervals."

D. **William Davidson,** Santa Fe, N. Mex.

Carved Door; cherry, stained glass; 80 x 36 x 1¾. Panel and frame construction with panel made of face-laminated 8/4 stock bandsawn to rough dimension before gluing. Finished in Danish oil. Photo by Michael Tincher.

"The method of construction allows for a close fit when hanging because floating panel moves within the frame and the only allowance necessary is for expansion of the rails."

C

D

A. **Mel Schockner,** Woodacre, Calif.

'Peacock' Panel Carved on Both Sides: redwood and stained glass; 40 x 18 x 1½.

"Background (side with peacock) carved with router. Design on both sides, including plant-on carved with flex shaft (Foredom), hand finished and oiled. The glass window was designed by Jan Schockner (my wife) and made by David Adams."

B. **Paul Tankel,** College Park, Md.

Entry Door; walnut, glass, rice paper; 80 x 58 x 1¾.

C. **John Bryan,** Yarmouth, Maine

Federal Period Fence; pine, Douglas fir, birch, stainless steel, aluminum; 550 ft. x 66 in., $25,000.

"The finials are eight pieces of 1¹⁄₁₆-in. white pine, glued with Elmers waterproof glue in a veneer press, and turned. The posts are ¼-in. extruded aluminum, built to take a load. After assembly they were sleeved over 6x6 steel I-beams sunk into concrete footings and shimmed with ½-in. plywood for screw-

ing. The rails are Douglas fir, top beveled and fluted on edges. They fasten to the posts with stainless steel hinges, and screws. The alternating-sized spindles are birch. The holes were drilled using a Forstner bit. All wood was soaked in Cuprinol wood preservative twice before being used. Testing assured that the metals would not corrode. It is a fence that is supposed to look over 100 years old, and does, but that will easily stand another 100 years if properly maintained."

D. **Saswathan Quinn,** Emeryville, Calif.

Gate; redwood; 60 x 44. Mortise and tenon joinery, floating panel; all panels and rails shaped.

"This is how it looks after one year outside. The hardware is from around 1910. The doors look the same on the inside as outside."

E. **John E. Schietinger,** Tampa, Fla.

Sunflower Door; poplar; 78 x 32 x 2½. Hand carved; door designed and stained glass done by Victor and Vonnie Verthelsdorf.

A   A   B

C   C

"The door is constructed of four pieces doweled and glued together. It is also reinforced, top and bottom, with a metal bar. The door was hand carved and then the openings were cut and the glass made for the openings."

F. **David Allen,** Blachly, Ore.

Gates to Our Gardens; cedar, fir; 76 x 105. Joinery conceived to enhance the surroundings.

"The garden is a sacred place well worth the energy expended in creating the gates to be used and enjoyed for a lifetime of love and of growing plants."

G. **Tree Woodworkers,** Halifax, N.S., Canada

St. Mary's Bascilica Church Doors; red oak, brass; center front door, 144 x 120 x 3, left & right front doors, 144 x 96 x 3, east & west side doors, 120 x 60 x 3.

"Made using frame and panel construction with through mortise and tenon joints, which were wedged and pegged. The door jambs and frames were laminated from 8/4 red oak using marine glue to a finished thickness of 3 in. The 7-in. deep mortises were chiseled by hand, and all doors were hand-fitted. The initial commitment to the contract called for the reproduction of the original doors using the same dimensions, techniques and processes, whenever possible; therefore, much of the work was done by hand. The doors were finished with two coats of a mixture of boiled linseed oil, turpentine and dryers, followed by two coats of a satin, exterior polyurethane to protect the wood surfaces from the weather. The solid brass hinges are $\frac{3}{16}$ in. thick and measure 6 in. by 8 in. when open. The doors, weighing 400 lb. and 350 lb. respectively, are bolted into solid granite and, like the originals, can easily be opened by any of St. Mary's numerous senior citizen parishioners.

"Tree Woodworkers is a small, independent, worker-owned company, operating out of an historic brewery building on Halifax's waterfront. It was formed in 1973, as a youth-training project and has slowly evolved to its present form. Along the way, many talented, young woodworkers have been afforded a meaningful opportunity to develop their craft. The doors of St. Mary's Bascilica reflect Tree's concern for the maintenance of traditional woodcraft as a viable business and represent a growing expertise in the field."

D   E   F

G

G

A. **Federico Armijo,** Albuquerque, N. Mex.

Doors; Honduras mahogany; 84 x 72 x 3. Laminated and carved.

B. **Rodney & Susan Hill,** College Station, Tex.

Ranch House Door; black walnut; 84 x 54 x 5½. Hand tools.

"The 5½-in. thick walnut door with cantilevered tracery is a commissioned piece for a ranch in central Texas. The door reflects the owners' lifestyle in a most unusual manner....

"The back of the door (shown here) consists of their five favorite erotic Picassos from their large art collection, topped by their Great Dane, terrier and parrot. Supporting the Picassos are two Dr. Peppers (her favorite drink) and a telephone (which is her companion a large part of the day). His camera, car grill, and college emblem finish the lower part of the door. The upper part of the door has a Stradivarius violin, which she bought for her husband when he began violin lessons. On the upper corners of the door are located his favorite stamps in his stamp collection. There are two strings of cacti and succulents and a border of daffodils with an erotic door handle hidden in the daffodil reeds."

C. **Joseph O'Connell,** St. Joseph, Minn.

Door for Petters Fur and Fabric Store; white oak, milled steel; 80 x 40 x 2¼. Carved oak, welded and forged steel. Photo by Lauren O'Connell.

D. **Philip A. Nereo,** Windsor, Calif.

Carved Door, Philippine mahogany; 84 x 36. Hand carved, router used for border and some waste removal.

"One of the things I make is custom carved doors. I do my own design and artwork. I consult with the client on what he has in mind, if anything, as to design and price. Then I draw up sketches of some various possibilities. He picks the one he likes and I bring it into being.

"Solid slab doors obviously have to be made of a stable, straight-grained wood like mahogany or redwood. I usually do a smaller design, echoing the main one, on the inside of the door. This helps to equalize the stresses in the wood, as well as giving the owners something fancy to look at on the inside, which they see much more than the outside. I seal the wood with an exterior satin polyurethane, which I rub down

A

B

C

D

E

F

to give the appearance and feel of an 'in the wood' oil type finish."

E. **Philippus Steven Sollman,** Port Matilda, Pa.

Entry Door; walnut, leaded glass; 80 x 36 x 1¾, $700.

F. **Ron Skidmore & Steve Stenger, Prairie Woodworks,** Bloomington, Ill.

Entry Doors for Restaurant; white oak, walnut; 84 x 72 x 1¾. Splined joints with thread steel rods in top and bottom; finish by Peterson. Photo by Mike Jenkins.

"Original design. A second set was also made with glass instead of walnut panels."

G. **Jim Johnson,** Danville, Calif.

Door; redwood, birch, brass, koa; 80 x 34. Photo by Geri McGlynn.

"This angel is carved on the door of the Francix X. Driscoll home in Walnut Creek, Calif. It is carved in native redwood and secured by hammered-iron hinge straps. The design incorporates an antique gold mosaic halo, birchwood face and limbs, and a koa and brass door pull. The house is a wine barrel 42 ft. in diameter."

H. **James W. Boyd,** Middletown, N.Y.

Victorian Bar; oak, black walnut; 26 ft. x 10 ft. x 8 ft.

I. **William Doub,** Portsmouth, N.H.

Display Cabinets For Art Glass in Salamandra Glass; red oak, black walnut; 16 ft. x 1¼ ft. x 8 ft. Red oak frame with walnut plywood panels. The crest of the casework is carved. The shelves are plate glass with a large mirror in back of center case. After the style of Art Nouveau.

G   H

I   I

A. **Sal Maccarone,** Los Gatos, Calif.

Oak Wet Bar; oak, glass, copper (sink); 91 x 22 x 96, $3,300. Photo by Photo Design.

B. **Griffin W. Okie,** San Rafael, Calif.

Octagonal Jewelry Case; eastern walnut; 84 dia. x 42. Each section glued up independently, then joined together one by one. Lights hidden from all angles. There are seven doors and drawers. Base is covered with material that accentuates the floating look of this case. Photo by Glen Allison.

"Design permits much display in not too large an area. Commissioned by Knight's Ltd., Beverly Hills, Calif."

C. **Neil Homstead,** Florence, Mass.

Display Unit at Don Muller Gallery, Northampton, Mass.; red oak, ¾-in. oak plywood, ⅝-in. A-C plywood, ferro cement, ½-in. Plexiglas, mirror; 16 ft. x 7 ft. x 8 ft. A-C plywood primary vertical support over-laminated with oak and ferro-cement. Oak plywood shelving with ³⁄₁₆-in. oak steam-bent banding, supported by carved oak struts. Designed by Neil Homstead; built by Neil Homstead, Brian Stowe and Robert Walker.

"These units are part of an environment, gallery, and market for well crafted and imaginative work to be enjoyed, displayed and sold."

D. **Michael G. Millner,** Webster, N.Y.

Bar, Elmwood Inn, Rochester, N.Y.; oak, mahogany; 14¼ ft. x 62 in. x 49 in. To be sturdy and also accommodate a large number of accessories (coolers, sinks, ice makers, glasses, etc.), supports must be minimal while retaining structural soundness. Frame of 2x4s and pressboard.

E. **Theodore Mueter,** Santa Fe, N. Mex.

Baking Center for Kitchen; red oak; 15 ft. x 25 in. x 7 ft.

"Rolltop is 7 ft. long, opens 4 in. past top dead center to allow for lighting."

F. **Roger Holmes,** Lincoln, Nebr.

Conference Table; walnut; 75 inside radius x 30 x 30; Witness Table, 42 x 30. Traditional construction techniques in solid bases, tops ¹⁄₁₆-in. walnut veneer on chipboard. Photos by Dan Ladely.

"This is one of a pair of conference tables for the Nebraska State Capitol in Lincoln using natural walnut, air dried. The design is based on furniture and millwork details original to the building."

G. **Don Wallace & Tom Hinz,** Arcata, Calif.

Bar; red oak, Honduras mahogany; 30 ft. x 10 ft. x 11 ft.

"This bar was our first opportunity in eight years of building furniture to make a major statement in a commercial project."

H. **Michael Coffey,** Poultney, Vt.

"Variations" (wall system); Mozambique, white oak. Dovetail cabinet construction; fronts and both sides of both cabinets and shelves are carved.

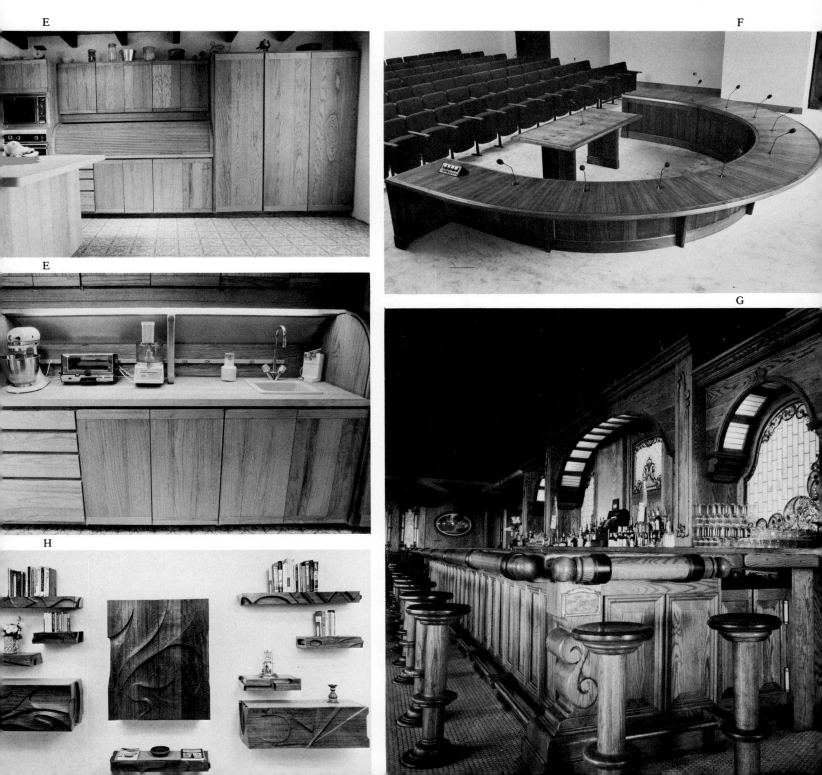

E

E

H

F

G

A. **Tom Simmons,** Soquel, Calif.

Beer/Wine Bar, Cafe Antilles, Arcata, Calif.; madrone, lauan, ash, redwood, fir; 30 ft. x 2⅓ ft. x 4 ft. Milled madrone bar top. Stiles kerfed and bent around facet apex.

"Stiles and panels change in dimension and position as the eye flows around the J-shaped bar."

B. **Jeffrey Rafael Long,** Chicago, Ill.

Bookcase, Cabinets with Couch; koa; 11 ft. x 7 ft., $3,500. Upper cabinet doors resawn and bookmatched; lower cabinets made from single boards cut to yield continuous vertical grain; instrument storage at bottom of cabinets is full-depth to wall; extra storage under cushions. Photo by Joshua Moorehead.

"Made for a concert violinist, this piece is constructed with koa, a wood of great warmth and variety often used by instrument makers. When oiled, its color is extraordinarily close to that of the owner's old viola."

C. **Thomas M. Merida,** Santa Cruz, Calif.

Cedar Bathroom Remodeling: Paneling, Cabinetry and Accessories; aromatic cedar; 9 ft. x 9 ft. x 8 ft., $3,500. Walls first faced with ¼-in. plywood and sheetrock sealed with Thompson's Waterseal. 5/4 cedar, resawn twice and surfaced, applied with neoprene-base waterproof contact cement to ceiling, walls and inside of shower enclosure, grain horizontal. Paneling sealed with both Thompson's and a spray sealer, finished with Synalac waterproof lacquer.

"Although at first the thought of a wooden bathroom might seem somewhat impractical, I feel the finished product proves otherwise. Liberal use of wood in a bathroom offers a warm alternative to high-gloss paint, chrome, tile, porcelain and Formica. After choosing cedar for this job, my biggest fear was that the final result would seem busy to the eye. Accordingly, I kept the design of the cabinetry simple, using soft contours and rounded-over edges to allow the cabinets to blend in with the walls. Of course, the horizontal grain on the finished fronts and ends adds to this effect."

A

B

C

D

D. Robert Whitley, Solebury, Pa.

Demi-Lune Display Cabinet; walnut, curly and bird's-eye maple, ebony, crotch mulberry, white ash; 75 x 18 x 79½.

"Design is a synthesis of the circle or its segments. Notice the circular miters on door frames, which are splined. Behind facing is a mortise-and-tenoned white ash frame. Hinges are hand-sculptured and pegged on doors and cases with a removable ebony hinge pin."

E. J.F. Collins, Hingham, Mass.

Four-Piece Chest-on-Chest Cabinet System; solid walnut, glass; 112 x 17 x 88. Photo by J.D. Sloan.

F. James V. Rutkowski, Columbus, Ohio

Metamorphosis/Bookcase; maple, walnut; 48 x 11 x 72, $800. Photo by Elizabeth Bell Upp.

"Two elements of design, one planned and one unplanned, add to the overall theme. The planned aspect is that the shelves, though all made the same, change. The shelf at eye level may look like a solid, normal board because only its

edge is seen. But as the eyes go downward, a gradual change takes place, till at the bottom, the spaces as well as the woods are clearly evident. To my surprise, when I had finished gluing the shelves to the sides, I noticed that the figures of the sides seem to grow out of the shapes on the ends of each shelf."

G. Steve Clark & Eric Sundstrom, Calgary, Alta., Canada

Wall Cupboard; Swedish pine; 34 x 12 x 42. Material kiln-dried by artist, shaper cutters specially made.

"Piece is seven years old and has never needed catches on the doors, as the fit is just right."

H. Crocker Wood/works, Diane Snow Crocker & Steve Crocker, Walnut Creek, Calif.

Library Installation/Home Office; mahogany, oil rubbed finish; 11 ft. x 2 ft. x 8 ft. Standard cabinet joinery.

"Center section folds down with self-leg to form double-sided work table. Typewriter shelf slides out for use. Drawers range from pencil through file. Unit accommodates electricity for phone, lights, calculators, etc."

A. **Dave LeCount,** Martinez, Calif.

Bureau Dresser; oak, walnut, porcelain, 62 x 38 x 15.

"Design was motivated by customer's request for visible joints and simple finish (Danish oil with no grain filler). All joints are hand-tooled except for drawers. Through tenons are used on the side braces and lap dovetails on the drawer rails and back diagonal braces. The paneling on the sides and back is solid ¼ in., laminated from 2½-in. strips."

B. **Jeffrey M. Hills,** Springhouse, Pa.

Roll-Top Music Cabinet (to hold amplifier, turntable, records); red oak, stained glass; 22 x 41 x 70. Photo by John Tuckerman. Stained glass designed by Jerome Shurr, made by E. Crosby Willet.

C. **Michael S. Chinn,** Long Beach, Calif.

Roll-Top Cabinet; white oak, Brazilian walnut, birch, leather; 24 x 24 x 51. Laminated steam-bending, wedge filling.

D. **Richard Cohen,** Warwick, N.Y.

Chest of Drawers: bubinga, sycamore, cherry, brass; 42½ x 21 x 34¾.

E. **Walter Ambrosch,** Glendale, N.Y.

Cabinet for Clothing or Office Supplies; oak, poplar; 32 x 16 x 28; lacquer finish.

A   B   C

D

E

F. **Forrest Morse,** Henniker, N.H.

Kitchen Cabinets; butternut; 8 x 16 ft. Board fronts are planed using a curved plane blade—no sanding. Photo by Mark Lindquist.

G. **Lowell Holloway, Jr.,** Longview, Tex.

China Cabinet; satinwood veneer, solid core; 57 x 16 x 93. All inlaid with holly, Brazilian rosewood, Indian rosewood, walnut, ebony, amaranth, padauk and dyed veneers. Sheraton-Hepplewhite style.

H. **Vincent Adams,** Goldens Bridge, N.Y.

Bedroom; African mahogany. Photo by James O'Gara.

"Drawer pulls were carved into drawer fronts by using the router with special jigs, gouges and hand planes. Hand-cut dovetails on bed and bookshelves."

I. **Pierre Pelletier,** St. Augustin-Cte. Portneuf, Que., Canada

Stimulation Hall—Battle of the Chateau Guay; white oak.

"The chess game was chosen to symbolize the battle on Oct. 26, 1813, between Canadian troops and the invading American army, 55 miles from Montreal. The showcase cabinets are shaped to represent chess pieces and contain artifacts from the battle; the pawns are benches. Commissioned by Parks Canada-Quebec, fabricated by Boiseries Plessi-Belanger."

A. John G. Steiner Co., Bainbridge Island, Wash.

"These richly oiled, solid teak, floor-standing storage cabinets and solid bookshelves are part of a six-piece installation. They are all built with a variety of self-locking joints. Handcut dovetails, wedged dowels and pinned mortise-and-tenon joints are typical. About $875."

B. Anderson Behling, Santa Rosa, Calif.

Tall Cabinet; walnut, birch burl, smoked glass; 27½ x 17½ x 79, $1,900. Upper door panels of smoked glass and lower panels of birch burl can be removed from door frames by removing a single screw from the inside corners of the top rails, which hold in compression a slip joint. Once unscrewed, the top rail can be pulled off and the panel removed from its frame. The lower rails employ a slip joint that is glued. The panels must be thinner than the tenon on the rail of the slip joint. This technique requires no molding and therefore both the front and back faces of the door frame are alike.

"This cabinet's design is functionally general-purpose, and is being used by its owner for sound equipment, records and tapes."

C. Brian Donnelly, Providence, R.I.

Tool Cabinet; cherry, maple; 30 x 16 x 60. Through-dovetailed carcase, tapered sliding dovetails for shelves.

"Cabinet was designed for maximum tool storage. Sliding drawers and trays allow for efficient organization and accessibility to tools."

D. Ted Ballard, Gold Hill, Ore.

China Hutch; solid oak; 40 x 20 x 78. Frame and panel construction, hand-carved designs.

A   B

C   C   D

E. **Michael Sterling & Tip Wilson,** Portland, Ore.

Hutch; white ash, rosewood, cedar; 27¼ x 13 x 59. Back panel resawn bookmatch; hand-carved door latches; windowpanes can be individually and easily replaced. Photo by Joe Felzman.

"The hutch was inspired by Krenov. We own and are the operators of a small custom furniture shop with 16 years experience between us."

F. **Richard Landergren,** Bloomington, Ind.

Hutch; cherry, leaded glass; 96 x 18 x 76.

G. **Loren Gronewold,** Gothenburg, Nebr.

China Hutch; American elm; 64 x 20 x 70, $2,000.

"I logged my own trees, cut them at a local sawmill, air-dried them two years, then built with power tools and hand tools."

E

F

G

A. **William A. Bush,** Honeydew, Calif.

Armoire; alder, redwood, aromatic cedar; 40 x 24 x 60. Hand-cut joinery, surfaces hand-planed, hand-carved details, wooden latch of navel orange wood.

"Doing my joinery and shaping mostly by hand techniques tends to go against the current trend of machine precision in woodworking, but I feel this approach lends a warmer personal quality to the work."

B. **Steve Kestrel,** Elizabeth, Colo.

Display Cabinet; American walnut, South American walnut, bubinga; 22 x 18 x 78. Bandsawn pieces were stacked and glued one layer at a time with special consideration as to the grain for contraction and expansion. All pieces were precision-cut to within 1/16 in. of finished surface. All joints are precise—some with exposed splines and some with hidden splines. A routed groove between laminations hides the wires to the top of the cabinet. The base is hollow and about 2 in. thick—special clamping jigs were used to laminate the bandsawn pieces.

C. **Jim L. Richey,** Ponca City, Okla.

Chest of Drawers; white pine, maple; 15½ x 22 x 48. Maple drawer guides rabbeted into carcase—slotted screw holes allow sides of carcase to move. Partition mortised (and fox-wedged) to carcase, which is cut from one board. Side-hung drawers.

"Design criteria: simple, direct, 100% function."

D. **Ken Brown,** San Francisco, Calif.

Stereo Cabinet; padauk, Honduras mahogany, kwila; 47½ x 19 x 72. Shades for the lights in the top and bottom shelves and also the showcase bottom are laminated; the bottom is made of eleven 1/8-in. thick strips glued (Titebond) to 3/4-in. birch plywood from Finland (14 plies per 3/4 in.).

E. **Jonathan Hillegas,** Pittsburgh, Pa.

Hutch; oak; 54 x 22 x 72.

"This piece was designed to fit a certain space. . . . The space covered by the tambour door is for a TV set."

F. Paul Don, Ottawa, Ont., Canada

Child's Desk; butternut, rosewood, leather, birch plywood; 46 x 24 x 60, $2,700. Mortise and tenoned, inlaid, top steam-bent with a kettle.

"This child's desk follows loosely an indigenous North-American design (the hutch or 'flat-to-the-wall' cupboard), inasmuch as it consists of a lower half with doors and a separate recessed top half with doors. The design, other than that, is very much my own.

   "The center pulls out and a flap inlaid in leather hinges up and rests on small ratchets. The inlay on the drawers and in the desk top is rosewood, as are the door pulls. Interior shelves and back are birch ply. The curved top is ¼-in. butternut, steam-bent. The remainder of the unit is ⅞-in. butternut. Gnomes are laminated from ⅞-in. stock, then carved. There are doors in the sides of the bottom that open with touch latches. Kids love mystery."

G. Nicholas P. Rumsey, Barrington, R.I.

Tool Cabinet; cherry, walnut, maple; 36 x 16 x 48.

H. David G. Shewell, London, England

Bookcase Cabinet; sweet chestnut, muninga, Japanese oak veneer, ply back; 35 x 9 x 73. Traditional cabinet joints—all stopped double dovetail housings. Extensive carving in doors.

"This piece was commissioned as a wedding gift, and each of the partners' first names began with the letter *M*, hence the double *M* handles. Apart from the two sides, which are curved convexly from reddish muninga, and the ply back, the whole cabinet is made from a single piece of English chestnut that was 2 in. thick. This thickness allowed the concave doors to be carved with integral handles. The design focus of the piece is the double arch of the figure in the chestnut doors, an upward movement echoed in the sides and in the figures of the two principal cross-members. The cabinet lifts from its stand. The shelf consoles are also carved from the same chestnut, and the shelves are discreetly ribbed to add strength. The piece is finished in palest pure beeswax."

I. Amos Galpin, Sun Valley, Idaho

Highboy; maple, pine, fir; 32 x 18 x 68, $2,500. Moldings made with rabbet and round planes. Photo by Dave Alf.

A. **Ann Ross,** Keaau, Hawaii

Hutch; koa, silver oak, birch; 21 x 16 x 76.

B. **Bruce Radomski,** Orange, Calif.

Curio-China Cabinet; red oak, red oak veneer, antique glass; 35¾ x 24¼ x 62.

"My first project to use hardwood, veneer and leaded glass. The cabinet was designed to complement an oak dining set. An interesting project, because I attempted several new media at once—veneering, leaded glass and hardwood."

C. **Charles Zumer,** Bozeman, Mont.

Bookcase; mahogany, maple, walnut, sycamore; 39¾ x 22 x 75½. Solid wood, frame and panel construction throughout, including backs, but excepting lower center section, which is a dovetail box construction.

"This piece was intended to harmonize with a late 18th-century Governor Winthrop slant-top desk. At the same time, I wished it to be clearly of its own time. My client is fond of secret compartments, hence the revolving section in the lower part, which locks in place. The drawers run through, while each door, which opens by means of a pivoting opener from underneath inside the top drawer, reveals only its own half of this section, a false back dividing the two."

A

B

C

A

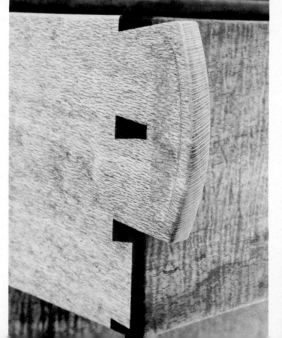

C

D. **William H. Higgins, Jr.,** Richmond, Va.
Highboy; pine; 40 x 21½ x 41½.
"Concealed secret drawer in crown molding."

E. **Cliff Friedlander,** Santa Cruz, Calif.
Yarn and Fabric Cabinet; oak; 37 x 22 x 84.

D

E

E

A. **John Jeffers,** Charleston, S.C.

Liquor Cabinet; ash; 22 x 12 x 78. Photo by F.L. Hiser, Jr.

B. **Jim McEver,** Port Townsend, Wash.

Pipe Cabinet & Stand; cabinet, maple, paldao; 24 x 20 x 32; stand, teak; 16 x 9 x 32, $1,000. Construction is mortise and tenon throughout. All sides of the cabinet are frame and panel. Photo by Earl W. Lawrimore.

"I try in my designs to achieve a certain sense of lightness and simplicity without being plain and uninteresting. The upward sweep of the legs, their inward curve and outward turn at the top, are to create the feeling of the cabinet being suspended in an updraft. The curves in the rails emphasize this upward movement. This flow is carried through in the curves of the vent fins on the side and the bevels on the front of the top, bottom and shelves. The grain on the door frame also emphasizes this upward sweep from the darker heartwood to the lighter wood at the top. The narrow raised panel in the door and back, the differing thickness of the rails and stiles all around, and the set-in position of the door are intended to create an interesting visual (and tactile) texture without creating too much complexity."

A   A   B

C. **W.J. Ripley,** Clayton, Calif.

China Cabinet; walnut, walnut veneer, glass; 82 x 16 x 82. Photo by Tom Wentling.

"The client for this cabinet had two complete sets of fine china and a collection of crystalware, which dictated the basic hutch configuration. The design concept required that drawers and hinges be hidden. The wide lower rails of the hutch doors hide shallow drawers that accommodate cutlery, napkins and tablecloths. The base-unit doors cover storage drawers and shelves spaced for silverware items.... The door pulls are a variation of the crown molding, and the drawer pulls are a variation of the face molding."

D. **Woodworker's Guild, Inc.,** Boulder, Colo.

Block-Front Chest of Drawers; American black walnut, aromatic cedar, birch plywood, brass hardware; 25 x 20 x 62.

"Solid walnut panels and aromatic cedar lining are joined into a single case with dovetail battens, which allow independent movement of the components in response to climatic changes. This item is part of a four-piece bedroom ensemble."

C

D

D

A. **George W. Berry,** Atlanta, Ga.

Armoire; Brazilian rosewood, American walnut, Italian bending poplar; 37 x 23 x 88, $12,000.

B. **Henry Barrow,** Glen Echo, Md.

Standing Bookcase; white oak, grey stained glass; 30 x 13 x 84.

"An experiment of balance between space that is openly visible and accessible and space that is partially visible and not so accessible."

C. **Robert A. Schultz,** Appleton, Wis.

Cabinet on Chest; Honduras mahogany; 40 x 22 x 76.

"This cabinet on chest is designed to contain a woman's apparel and accessories. The right side of the upper cabinet has a sliding rack for slacks, a locking jewelry drawer with trays, two sliding scarf and handkerchief trays and two other drawers. The left side has eight spaces for sweaters plus a shelf for purses. The chest contains three large drawers."

D. **H.L. LeCompte, Jr.,** Towson, Md.

Queen Anne High Chest; walnut, pine, tulipwood, oak; 38 x 22 x 77. Photo by Roy Murrill.

"This reproduction incorporates features that appeared in Maryland-made furniture during the third quarter of the 18th century: an uncarved center drawer in the lower section, and fluted chamfered corners ending in a lamb's tongue. The trifid foot with a shell on the knee was used earlier in Philadelphia during the transition period between Queen Anne and Chippendale styles, but was later taken up by Maryland cabinetmakers."

A

B

C

D

E. **George Frank,** New York, N.Y.

Bookcase; Macassar ebony, sycamore. Photo by Maura McCaw.

F. **W.C. Pellouchoud,** Stoughton, Wis.

Kitchen Hutch; red oak; 30 x 20 x 66.

"Designed for a third-floor apartment with very limited cabinet and work area, this unit fulfills its function admirably."

G. **Holger M. Laubmeier,** Del Mar, Calif.

Armoire; knotty pine; 54 x 28 x 86. Frame-and-panel doors, veiner carving. Photo by Inge Brown.

"By hand-planing, a pleasing texture of the plane added authenticity. There is a satisfaction in using a so-called low-grade wood to create a nice piece of furniture."

H. **Joe Lessor,** Central Valley, Calif.

Entertainment Center; 5/4 walnut frame, teak panels and crown molding; 54 x 21 x 76. Face-frame is half-lap dovetailed, corners of cabinet are splined. Sunburst is made of ¾-in. thick teak triangles. Door pivots out to expose record storage, top shelf rolls out and swivels for color TV, stero shelf rolls out; drawers are for tape storage.

"This cabinet marks the end of the available teak. I took great care in matching the panels for color, grain pattern, etc. Teak has always been my favorite but I suppose it's good the people of Southeast Asia have decided to stop ravaging their forests.

"The cabinet was built to house a customer's electric entertainments. It took approximately 80 hours to complete, and was satisfyingly complex because of the many angle cuts involved. It is a massive piece weighing about 450 lb., but it's solid as a rock and should outlast us all."

E

F

G

E

H

A. **Robert Mussey,** Ann Arbor, Mich.
   China Cabinet; oak, beveled leaded glass; $2,400.
   "First of a series."

B. **Tom Murphy,** Sedgewick, Maine
   Mrs. Vester's Corner Cabinet; red oak, glass; 20 x 14 x 63.

A

B

C. **John Mark Giordano,** Pawtucket, R.I.

Cherry China Cabinet.

"Concept: rigid structure with no glue joints, which too often loosen with time."

D. **Ronald C. Puckett,** Richmond, Va.

China Cabinet; walnut, slumped glass; 30 x 16 x 66.

"The sides of the cabinet were staved, then shaped with a series of tracks and jigs using a router to make the sides concave and convex. The glass for the cabinet was curved in a slumping oven over a plaster form."

E. **John E. Dingle,** Hagerstown, Ind.

Buffet with China Cabinet; white oak; 56 x 20 x 80.

F. **Ben Davies,** Chattanooga, Tenn.

Jewelry Case; cherry, walnut burl; 36 x 8 x 7½.

"Approximate dimensions and drawer arrangement are taken from a Shaker case. This demonstrates, at least in this case, that excellence of form transcends style."

C　　　　　　　　　　　　D　　　　　　　　　　　　　　　　　　　　　　E

F

A. **David F. Zuhlke,** Park Ridge, Ill.

Bachelor Chests; walnut, walnut veneer; 30 x 18 x 30.

B. **R.D. Kalayjian,** Villa Park, Calif.

Curio Cabinet; cherry, cherry-faced plywood; 34 x 16 x 77.

"The cabinet was designed to fit with other pieces in our home, thus the Queen Anne legs combined with a country English cabinet. It is constructed in two separate pieces and is joined by hidden fastenings from inside the lower cabinet. A breadboard-type pull-out leaf is handy and can be used in lieu of a cocktail table or for holding pieces while dusting or cleaning. The top of the cabinet was laminated to shape over a form using four laminates of ⅛-in. plywood. This laminate was then faced with cherry veneer on both sides. The glass in the doors and sides is beveled and polished plate."

C. **Thomas E. Mullally,** Oakland, Calif.

Four-Drawer Ogee Block-Front Chest; walnut, poplar; 35 x 22 x 36. Hand-planing and joinery, frame and panel carcase construction, solid wood drawer construction.

D. **Eric Dewdney,** Cambridge, Ont., Canada

Sideboard; English brown oak; 76 x 20 x 42.

"This is built as three separate units screwed together inside the drawer carcase. Center stretcher is unglued, permitting disassembly. Legs are laminated with end-grain brown oak. Drawer sides are solid oak, through-dovetailed.

"The wood for this project was from a flitch-cut log measuring more than 40 in. in diameter. Estimated age is about 450 years. The wood was dried for about three years."

E. **David H. Jackson,** Portland, Ore.

File Cabinet; walnut, cherry; 28½ x 23 x 43. Photo by Victor Wandtke.

F. **Lee Falkenstern,** San Luis Obispo, Calif.

Dresser; oak; 29 x 22 x 48, $1,000. Laminated sides, top is quartersawn for equal amounts of shrinking and expansion. Photo by Alex Harvey.

G. **Peter Gluklick,** Huntington Woods, Mich.

Stereo Cabinet; American ash; 72 x 20 x 36.

"Designed to accommodate ottomans and a very small apartment. Houses turner/amplifier, turntable and records. Boards are mitered at edges so that grain continues to all adjoining surfaces."

D  E

F   G

A. **James L. Henkle,** Norman, Okla.

File Cabinet; beech; 17 x 17 x 27. Laminating and shaping.

B. **John E. Davison;** Berkeley, Calif.

Cabinet; cherry, bird's-eye maple, birch plywood; 30 x 18 x 29. The maple on drawer faces was resawn and bookmatched.

"The lower drawer is a file drawer and the others are used for writing accessories."

C. **Christopher Murray,** Charlottesville, Va.

Stereo Cabinet; cherry, maple, brass hardware; 61 x 23 x 29. Staved doors. Laminated upper rail in front, staved sides, carved with a router jig.

"Inner dividers for records radiate perpendicular to the front curve."

D. **Neil Wehrlie,** Oakland, Calif.

*Office Credenza; walnut, koa, walnut burl, brass; 70 x 22 x 30,
$1,900. Dovetailed carcase, tambour door right side, file
drawers left side. Photo by Jim La Cunha.*

E. **Carl Zanoni,** Middlefield, Conn.

*Double Chest of Drawers; walnut veneer, Carpathian elm burl
veneer, gumwood veneer, white oak with maple plywood bottoms; 72 x 18 x 30. Photo by James F. Paul.*

"The 1⅛-in. thick drawer faces extend beyond the body of the
chest to provide a distinct focal plane for the boldly figured
walnut on the drawer faces. The extension also serves as a
means for opening the drawers without hardware."

F. **Union Woodworks,** Northfield, Vt.

Bureau; red oak, walnut; 40 x 24 x 40.

"The panels in the frame and panel sides are bandsawn and
splined with walnut. Three sliding trays are contained on the
inside."

D

E   F

A. **Thomas Keller,** Menlo Park, Calif.

Portable Serving Station; teak, brass hinges and latches; 54 x 22 x 33. Doweled case construction; frame-and-panel dividers; handcut lap dovetails; hand-carved handles and sides. Photo by Peter O. Whiteley.

"A base skirt conceals casters with 5-in. wheels, allowing the cart to roll easily over rough floors or shag carpet. All three drawers slide through for access from both sides. A swing-down door beside the upper drawer conceals storage space for a teak carving board and a marble-topped, teak-based warming tray that uses a waterbed heater component as the heat source. The four cabinet doors come free from the case on loose joint hinges, and can be used as trays, each with a lip around the inside edge. The top has a ¼-in. lip around the edge to contain spills. Two adjustable shelves inside augment the cabinet's versatility."

B. **James D. Nash,** Fullerton, Calif.

Credenza; shedua, white oak; 48 x 14 x 36. Finger lap and through mortise-and-tenon joints are used. Slight 'softening' of joint edges provides added textural interest.

C. **Merryll Saylan,** Aptos, Calif.

Collector's Cabinet; alder, clear Plexiglas; 28 x 28 x 45, $2,000. Stacked 12/4, bandsawn, shaped and sanded cabinet. Heat-formed base is 16/4 octagon wedges, turned on lathe. Plexiglas drawers and cantilevered shelves.

"Very handy for collectors of small things—rocks, shells, diamonds, pearls. Plexiglas makes it possible to see everything at once, can't lose anything."

A

B

A

C

D. **James E. Cherry,** San Diego, Calif.

Etagere Stereo and Record Cabinet; oak, cane; 60 x 78, $2,800. Fixed tambour top, felt-lined drawers. Photo by IPC Photography.

"Cane provides background for tree design as well as ventilation for stereo equipment."

E. **Jeff Falk & Phyllis Elana, Seven Circles Woodworks,** Madison, Wis.

Dresser; walnut, mahogany plywood; 48 x 24 x 48, $1,200. Sides are solid wood and dust panels are dovetail-dadoed into sides, glued only at the front. Plywood back and dust panel inserts. Photo by Cynthia Bittenfield.

F. **Thomas Kneeland,** Penn Yan, N.Y.

Wall Cabinet for Telephone; cherry, koa; 20 x 6 x 29.

"The top of the cabinet holds a Slimline phone. Phone books, note pads and pens go in the bin on the bottom door, which provides a writing surface on its top. There is room in the back for a cork board or calendar.

"The curved front doors were built up of three layers of lauan plywood, cross-banded with cherry and cut to size. Some bandings are laminated so they would bend around the compound curves. After banding, the doors were fitted to the case. They are slightly recessed, ⅛ in. at the top and sides, ½ in. at the bottom. After fitting, the doors were held close together and the face veneer glued on all at once. When dry, the face veneer was cut through with an X-acto knife to minimize the gap between each door and maintain the grain pattern.

"I have found designing/fitting hinges for curved doors set into irregular-shaped openings to be most challenging. The bottom door is pinned in place; the back of the writing surface bumps up against a pin on each side for support. The top doors are very light and require only a single double-acting hinge of good quality.

"The case is joined with mortise-and-tenon joints with irregular shoulders to minimize short grain on the inside curve."

D   E

F

A. **Karen Straus,** Barrington, N.J.

Sunburst Buffet; cherry; 40 x 18 x 30.

"Every ray is a separate piece of wood; edges are routed, sanded then splined together into panel. Doors have touch latches; drawer pulls are on underside of each sun. Supports slide out from each side for leaves that flip out from center."

B. **Peter Leaf,** Oakland, Calif.

Machinist's Chest; cherry, Honduras mahogany, maple, oak; $2,250. Mortise and tenon throughout with floating work top end clamps.

"All tools are nestled in rare hardwood blocks and combinations of woods are arranged together to hold tools."

C. **Dave & Anna Weeks,** Scotts Valley, Calif.

Modular Display and Drawer Cases; American black walnut; 24 x 12 x 39, $800. Drawer pulls hand-carved from solid drawer fronts, all panels solid resawn walnut, all joints splined.

"These cases can be used separately or stacked in any number desired. Each case has feet for separate use or to lock into case or stand panel below."

D. **Len Wujcik,** Lexington, Ky.

Chest of Bags; beech, cedar, canvas; 29 x 20 x 66.

"By interpreting material characteristics and limits, the chest of bags is an attempt to deal with the problems of chest construction in the context of mass production and lightweight self-assembly. (Rosan machine-thread inserts allow chest and removable drawer frames to collapse for packing and shipping.) The drawer bags are corded canvas, hung pinched between a double frame. In the bottom of the bag is a slatted cedar frame, which keeps the bag's shape and scents the clothing inside. The outer skin of the chest is canvas pinched between steam-bent beech bands. Feminine in nature and intent, the canvas is laced to form the back."

A   B

C   D   D

E. **Jack Taylor III,** Akron, Ohio

Storage Chest; cherry; 28 x 24 x 27. Wood-hinged doors.

F. **Blaise Gaston,** Charlottesville, Va.

Silverware Chest; doussie; 40 x 18. Laminated and coopered.

G. **Elliott Grey,** Junction City, Ore.

Liquor Cabinet; eastern cherry; 46 x 16 x 29.

"Doors are laminated and handles sculpted out. The center can be used as a rack for wine bottles."

E

F

G

A. **Kathy Cherney,** Cambridge, Ont., Canada

Chest of Drawers; maple, imbuya; 24 x 15 x 48. Bent and laminated uprights; drawer fronts joined to sides with handcut, half-blind dovetails; laminated maple and imbuya sheet back panel; solid imbuya shelves.

"There is not a particular function but linen, material or clothes are best suited for storage."

B. **Jeff Behnke,** Rochester, N.Y.

Chest of Drawers; white oak; 55 x 26 x 38, $1,000. Continuous linear frame houses upside-down U-shaped mitered panel.

"All concave surfaces were cut by putting a diagonal fence across the table of the table saw. By moving the fence and raising the blade, the desired cross section was obtained. The concave surface was then spokeshaved and sanded smooth."

C. **Don Braden,** Oakland, Calif.

Chest; eastern black walnut, Peruvian walnut, oak; 48 x 20 x 28, $1,100. Dovetailed carcase, base has splined miter joints.

A

B

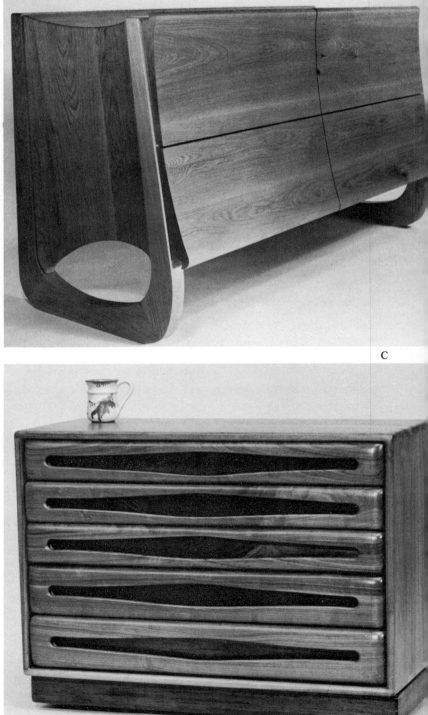

C

D. **Joel Grossman,** San Francisco, Calif.

Silver Chest; koa, rosewood, pine; 30 x 10 x 54. Photo by Doug Winter.

"The drawer faces are double-curved. A convex curve stretches across the length and a concave curve slopes down the face. This was achieved by gluing up about a dozen previously curved strips (averaging 1½ in. wide) into the concave shape. When the face was glued up the whole surface was shaped smooth by hand. The four drawer faces were then cut out of that one piece."

E. **James M. Harris,** Aldie, Va.

Dressing Table; Honduras mahogany; 52 x 18 x 72. Llama sculpture by Malcolm Harlow.

"Left section is a removable jewelry box, which is supported by a slide-out shelf. When the lid on the box is lowered, a plunger is depressed, which lifts the locking bars via the rocking arms at the bottom. Each locking bar catches a hook at the back of each drawer, thus locking the drawer. The lid is locked with a key. The drawers are velvet lined."

F. **Christopher Weiland,** Brush Valley, Pa.

Chest of Drawers; cherry, maple; 24 x 19 x 47. Frame and panel construction; drawer fronts—steam-bent lamination.

D

E

F

D

E

E

A. **Ted Chase**, Concord, Calif.

Standing Chigai Dana; New Guinea walnut, tung oil; 36 x 10 x 48. Photo by Lois Greene.

"'Tana' means shelf in Japanese. 'Chigai Dana' literally translates 'different shelf.' In the traditional Japanese home, the 'Tokonoma' or picture alcove has an adjoining section of built-in shelves, which are usually divided about halfway across the shelf in a step pattern. To the Japanese eye (and mind) these shelves seem to float, and from every viewing angle seem to display a different form. The shelves are most often displayed with nothing on them... as a kind of three-dimensional art object.

"My shelves are an attempt to combine this Eastern flavor with Western function. Because, in a free-standing piece, the shelves cannot be supported by a wall, a different design was used to provide the effect of the floating shelf. It was made with Japanese hand tools and traditional Japanese joinery, such as the 'Kendome' or 'sword stop joint,' which is a single or double mitered joint with a tenon to provide both fluid lines and strength."

B. **Richard Kagan**, Philadelphia, Pa.

Chest of Drawers; walnut; 36 x 20 x 30. Splined miters, mortise-and-tenon joints.

A

B

A

A

C. Tom E. Carnahan, Kemble, Ont., Canada

Undressoir (Chest of Drawers); African padauk, walnut; 21 x 16 x 40. Central pins of drawer fronts extend as handles, French dovetails on carcase bottom and drawer backs.

"Craftsmanship; which should set our pace, but which is, so often, so forcibly, set in ration to our haste.
   "This piece is a consciously-compromised example of expedient craftsmanship; time and quality, matching for reality's share, batched with contradictory care."

D. Mark Leach, Centerville, Mass.

Chest of Drawers; walnut, walnut veneer; 27 x 18 x 48. Veneered bent plywood in solid wood frame, bent plywood drawer fronts.

E. Charles Mark, Alexandria, Va.

Chest; curly ash; 56 x 18 x 20, $650. Frame springs slats on front and back, top and sides steamed; tri-miter showcase joints.

C

D

E

A. **Wendy Maruyama,** Rochester, N.Y.

Sideboard; Swedish pear, curly maple; 60 x 27 x 38. Basic carcase construction, maple interior, side-hung drawers, tambour with canvas backing.

"I have recently taken an interest in Japanese architecture and my work has begun to show an influence of Japanese esthetics, especially this sideboard."

B. **Robert R. Rynell,** Washington, Ill.

Stereo Cabinet; cherry; 60 x 24 x 24.

C. **R. Adin Gilman,** Wendell, Mass.

Sink/Vanity; cypress, epoxy; 36 x 22 x 32.

"I laminated the bowl using epoxy both as glue and as a final coating. The sunburst (each half) is set in a dado in each door frame."

A

B

C

D. **Jeff Butler,** Hubbardston, Mass. (carving) &
Howard Hastings, Barre, Mass. (cabinet)

Gun Cabinet; curly, striped and bird's-eye maple, pine, cherry, walnut; 72 x 24 x 84.

"The cabinet is basically straightforward. The carving is primarily sugar pine, from one 8/4 x 20 x 14 piece. The upper wing and two heads were built up to 4 in. thick; each inner stile and its panel were then carved down to proper thickness. The eyes are solid inlay—maple and cherry irises with black walnut pupils."

E. **Diania J. Smith,** Salt Lake City, Utah

Buffet; oak; 61 x 20 x 36, $2,800.

"The different proportions of the cabinet become a series of connected events. The ribbed base of different colored browns represents the natural earth; from the earth comes the beards of leaves and fruits; these grow into three grotesques reflecting the face of nature; three curved drawers, representing the sun, warm the faces and earth below."

F. **Allan S. May,** Jamesburg, N.J.

Silver Chest; mahogany; 22 x 13 x 24. Photo by F. Van Wetering.

"Two interior drawers are fitted for silver flatware storage. Two bottom drawers and interior shelf are for storage of small silver pieces. Handmade brass fittings from Hong Kong include ingenious lock, which is opened by inserting small bar which releases, for withdrawal, the bolt holding the two doors."

A. **Floyd E. Rank,** Seaview, Wash.

Vanity Chest of Drawers; alder, birch; 44 x 22 x 60. Antiqued blue finish, carved legs and pedestal shelf.

B. **Greg Donovan,** Worthington, Mass.

Stereo Cabinet; butternut, walnut, oak; 27½ x 16½ x 42½.

"I have great respect and appreciation for country living and Shaker designs. I believe these feelings rooted themselves in me at an early age, when my family migrated south from Canada and I spent half a day in the oven of a cookstove my mother had strapped to her back, as she swam the St. John's River.

   "This design is my ideal of a simple dry sink minus towel racks because in fact it was designed to house stereo components. The center shelf holds an amplifier. The back panel is left out for ventilation and to allow wires to pass through to the turntable, which sits in the top tray. Shelves were pressure-fitted into the carcase by means of sliding dovetails with ¹⁄₁₆-in. hardwood pins inserted toward the front to hold the face of the cabinet true. Dividers in the bottom shelf and drawer backs are also French dovetails."

C. **Walter Whiteley,** York, Pa.

Stereo Cabinet; walnut; 23⅝ x 18⅛ x 37⅜, $1,000.

"This piece is inspired from the Louis XV jelly cupboard. Unlike its original use, this has been designed to accommodate a turntable in the top, which lifts up, and records beneath. The drawer is a facade. Except for some of the straight-lined molding, most of the molding and carving were done by hand."

D. **Harris Rubin,** Washington, D.C.

Armoire; white pine, spruce, oak; 35½ x 20 x 72.

"The piece was influenced conceptually by the writings of William Morris and structurally by the furniture of early America. The simple lines and uniformity of dimensions are a response to the designs of craftsmen in the past. Striving for a graceful and yet somewhat naive feeling, I used common woods in the least manipulative fashion. The design utilizes oak in all the mechanical structures, and wood in the stress points (wedged dowels in the back and side panels). It contains no hardware, just wood and glue."

E. **Davis Strider,** Greenville, N.C.

Chest; black walnut; 35 x 24 x 49. Router-inlaid front.

F. **Joe Cunningham,** Aiken, S.C.

Chest of Drawers; wild cherry; 35 x 19 x 43.

"The drawers have a central rail that runs in a grooved piece attached to the frame on which the drawer sits. This prevents fishtailing of the drawers, which run very smoothly."

D

E

F

A. **John E. Carlson**, Haines, Alaska

Bombe Commode; walnut veneer, maple veining; 37 x 20 x 30, $1,800. Photo by Dave Albert.

"The pine for the carcase is bandsawn to the required curvature, then laminated, whereafter the sides and drawer fronts are carved out, using an ax and various hand planes (which I've had to make to match the different curvatures). The parts for the commode are hand-dovetailed together—machine-dovetailing would be improper for this piece and also weaker. The veneer is laid directly on the carcase piece, using the age-old hammer-veneering technique."

B. **Kevin Scott Danell**, Newburyport, Mass.

Mythological Wall Cabinet; Honduras mahogany; 15 x 6¼ x 16½. Cabinet doors are carved in relief, no deeper than ¼ in. at any one point. The unicorn's horn, carved in the round, extends to fit in a hollow on the centaur door and acts as a handle for opening.

"The cabinet itself was made entirely with hand tools and is held together with wooden dowels."

C. **Conor M. Power**, Billerica, Mass.

Jewelry Box; Hawaiian koa; 18 x 11 x 4½.

"One of the interior removable trays contains a music-box system, which engages when the cover is raised."

A

B

C

C

D. **Robin F. Goldstein,** Tempe, Ariz.

Venus Wall-Hung Cabinet; teak, ebony; 26 x 5 x 18. Doors, including hinge, are hand-carved. Sides are bent wood joined to a constructed top and bottom with handcut butterfly tails (ebony). Ebony rim runs completely around back of piece so that cabinet does not sit directly against wall, and also serves to hang piece. Photo by Dana Davis.

"This cabinet is meant to hold small, precious trinkets. . . ."

E. **Nicholas Lester,** Berkeley, Calif.

Persuasive Chest of Drawers; koa, maple, Alaskan cedar; 38½ x 19½ x 57. Drawers have half-blind French dovetails.

"Within the carcase are dust panels of Alaskan cedar. These also act as drawer sides. The dust panels are frame and panel."

F. **Lawrence Bickford,** Berlin, N.H.

Treasure Cabinet; cherry, maple; 8¼ x 5½ x 25¼, $300.

"All front-facing elements are softly curved; sides flare out towards the top. The cabinet was designed around the unusual figure in the door."

G. **James Robertson,** Cambridge, Mass.

Stained-Glass Mirror and Cabinet; mahogany; 48 x 16 x 84. Mortise and tenon frame construction; painted, not mosaic, glass. Glass by Lyn Hovey.

"The side panels slide up for access to the back lighting."

D

E

F

G

F

A. **Gerald C. Nash,** Santa Monica, Calif.

Three Wall-Hung Cabinets; 21 x 13 x 25½; 23 x 13½ x 47; 21 x 13½ x 30. Photo by Erik Nash.

"All are Honduras mahogany except the doors on the left and right cabinets, which are Santa Maria with spalted sapwood. All have spring-loaded bubinga catches and handmade polished solid brass knife hinges. Middle cabinet is dovetailed, left and right units are dowel construction."

B. **Stephen Stokesberry,** Bellingham, Wash.

Cabinet; birch plywood, lauan plywood, mirror, glass; 19½ x 9 x 33½. Doweled butt joints with dowel pin hinges. To open doors, press on outside edge of door.

C. **David Warner, David Warner Assoc.,** New Castle, Del.

Silverware Chest; walnut, mahogany drawers lined with silver cloth; 24 x 12 x 12, $1,244. Drawer fronts cut from one piece of walnut. Drawer pulls hand-carved.

D. **Roger Deatherage,** Houston, Tex.

Display Cabinet; walnut, glass; 13 x 6¾ x 29.

A

A C D

E. **Gerald C. Nash,** Santa Monica, Calif.

Wall-Hung Cabinet; sycamore, black walnut, bubinga, birch, canarywood, caviuna; 13 x 7 x 35. Photo by Erik Nash.

"The doors have two brilliant-red flame streaks. Coved edge detail runs front and side edges of top and bottom and continues down back edges of side pieces."

F. **Patrick J. Robbins,** Papillion, Nebr.

Wall Cabinet; black cherry, glass, mirror; 36 x 9 x 38.

"The piece was designed as a multipurpose functional cabinet. The left-hand corner was cut away to accept light, doing away with shadow-box effect. The door on the right has adjustable shelves. The bottom drawer is for storage."

G. **Craig S. Dascanio,** W. Springfield, Mass.

Wall-Hung Bar; curly maple veneer on ply; 29 x 18 x 42. Veneered bent ply, turned ice bucket, steam-bent splash board, solid laminated drawer front.

"The design was an exercise in total function. The entire lower unit pulls out 8 in. to reveal the mixing surface, which is black lacquered."

E   F

G   G

A. **John Dodd,** Rochester, N.Y.

*Wall-Hung Drawers; figured gum, walnut; 34 x 14 x 11.
Drawers and supports are steam-bent and laminated. Panels
are veneered.*

B. **Filip L. Sokol,** Boulder, Colo.

*Matched Wall Cabinets; Sitka spruce, mesquite; 11 x 6 x 24,
$600. Matched coopered doors of diminishing radius, matched
to sides as well. Adjustable shelves. Soft magnetic catches,
matched backs.*

"To be used with mirror between, perhaps a window."

A

B

B

C. **Robert R. Jorgensen,** Arvada, Colo.

China Cabinets; walnut, glass; 32 x 18 x 72, $1,200. Wooden pivot hinges, solid and veneer ply corners are table-sawn cove cut.

D. **Neal Barkon,** Melrose, Mass.

Wall-Hung Cabinet; cherry; 18 x 7 x 30, $650.

E. **Dennis Fitzgerald,** Elmsford, N.Y.

Wall Cabinet; cherry, cherry veneer, maple, brass; 14 x 10 x 26. Staved door, dovetailed carcase, blind dovetails on drawers.

C

D

E

A. **Thomas Hucker,** Berwyn, Pa.

Wall Cabinet (for spices); French walnut (solid and veneer) over molded ply; 18 x 10 x 40, $800.

B. **Blake Emerson,** Berkeley, Calif.

Cabinet; cherry, steel rods; 22 x 8½ x 14¼. Hand-planed and shaped curved-face doors swing on steel rods in wood. Side edges of doors routed out so 8/4 doors open completely into curved side of cabinet.

A

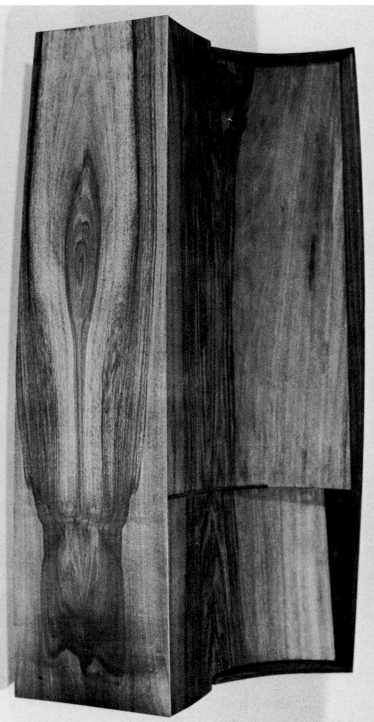

A

B

C. **Ron Callari,** Rochester, N.Y.

Hand-Screw Chest of Drawers; maple, cherry, birch;
83 x 10½ x 59½.

"The threaded sections of the screws were formed with the
use of a jig, first on the table saw, to establish a guide kerf,
and then using a router with a 60° bit. The mitered corners
of the carcase are joined by gluing box-jointed angle sections
into mortises. The drawer construction utilizes through and
half-blind dovetails. The upper three drawers on each side
are hung on wooden runners. The lower drawers pivot on
brass pins within Teflon bushings. The doors are maple
veneer over uniform laminate. The piece was conceived first
as sculpture, then as a functional unit."

D. **Jim Fawcett,** Allston, Mass.

Arrowhead Chest; beefwood, boxwood, elk hide;
14¼ x 7 x 25½.

"Hinges are black ironwood. The trays for the arrowheads
slide out and have soft leather bottoms."

C

C

D

D

A. **Woodpecker Cabinet Shop,** Webster Groves, Mo.

Wall Chest; pecan, oak backing and drawers; 20 x 6 x 31, $250.

"This piece is offered as a limited, signed edition by our shop. It can be purchased with mirror or glass and in a smaller size."

B. **Keith J. DeVore,** S. Hampton, Pa.

Cassette-Tape Cabinet; pahutan, bella-rosa, Philippine mahogany, ebony; 19 x 7¾ x 29. Photo by Bob Fegley.

"Inside the cabinet are five separate units, each holding 24 cassettes. The front two units slide on solid copper rods; the three rear units are portable and come in handy for long trips or visits."

C. **David Kessler,** Boston, Mass.

Cedar-Lined Blanket Chest; red birch, aromatic cedar; 48 x 17 x 19¾, $400. Draw-bored mortise and tenon.

A

B

C

D. **Steve Knopp,** De Land, Fla.

Blanket Chest; black cherry, rosewood, primavera, padauk; 54 x 27 x 27.

"Curved staves that form the top are mitered at the ends on the radius where they meet the end pieces."

E. **Jon E. Peterson,** Brighton, Mass.

Blanket Chest; white oak.

F. **George D. Breck,** S. Sebastopol, Calif.

Jewelry Cabinet; cherry, Honduras mahogany; 14 x 7 x 30, $500. The Honduras mahogany back panel is made of six slices ripped from 8/4 stock and assembled to give a pleasing arch pattern echoed by the top of its frame and the top of the case itself. Photo by Ed Aiona.

B

E

D

F

E

A. **Jay Halverson,** Captiva Island, Fla.

Small Hanging Cabinet; pecan, wormy chestnut; 8 x 12 x 30.
Sliding-dovetail joinery, frame-and-panel door construction.

B. **Thomas W. Tucker,** Portland, Ore.

Blanket Chest; walnut, Tennessee aromatic cedar; 40 x 20 x 20.

"Front, top and back panels are matched. The eye can follow
the grain of a particular board over three surfaces."

C. **Robert E. Larsen,** Olympia, Wash.

Sea Chest; Honduras mahogany; 32 x 18, $1,800.

"This piece was commissioned by Capt. R.B. Jacobs, USN, as
a gift to Admiral Kidd, chief of NATO forces, upon his recent
retirement. All insignia are official and were hand-carved
precisely to scale on all sides. These carvings represent
awards of major importance during his 40 years of naval
service. I'm told that this piece will be presented to the
Naval Museum at Annapolis upon Admiral Kidd's passing.
All carving tools were handmade by me."

A

B

C

D. **Robert Timberlake,** Greenville, N.C.

Tambour-Front Tool Chest; white oak, black walnut, beech; 26 x 12 x 16. Bandsawn, carved and sculpted drawer fronts. Photo by Pete Podeswa.

"Tambour front rolls up into the lid."

E. **Barry L. Lockard,** Belmont, Mass.

Bookcase Cabinet; redwood, birch; 25 x 12½ x 47½. Photo by Eric Neurath.

"This is one of a pair of glass-front bookcases for a study. *L*-shaped wooden battens on the back engage a similar bracket on the wall for hanging the unit. Shelves adjust in height by means of ¼-in. wood dowels, which engage holes on the inside of case walls."

D

E

D

A. **Roland H. Shackford,** Washington, D.C.

Japanese-Type Desk Chest; zebrawood; 7½ x 8¼ x 10. Hand tools only, whittled birch pegs for drawers, handles carved from zebrawood.

B. **Robert Korbonits,** West Chester, Pa.

Tool Box; black walnut, poplar; 32 x 11½ x 18½. Photo by David Korbonits.

"Frame-and-panel doors pivot and slide to store in the sides of the box. The case and all drawers are dovetailed. The drawers have applied cock beading."

C. **Thomasmore Bujak,** Palmyra, N.J.

Hope Chest; red oak, juniper lining; 30 x 18 x 26.

"It is a cedar-lined chest (really *Juniperus virginiana)*, thus on the inside of the lid I carved a quotation from the Song of Songs: 'and the scent of your garments is like the scent of Lebanon.'"

D. **Hal E. Davis,** Memphis, Tenn.

Jewel Box; bird's-eye maple, rosewood; 20 x 13 x 5½. Photo by Brin Baucum.

A

C

B

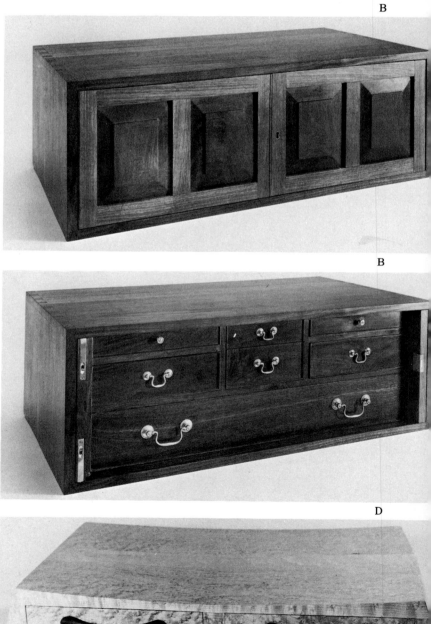

B

D

E. **Stephen Barney,** Seattle, Wash.

Silver or Jewelry Box; teak, western red cedar; 14 x 7½ x 11.

"All surfaces planed with no sanding prior to oil finish."

F. **C. Anderson,** Long Beach, Calif.

Boxes; walnut, oak; 24 x 7 x 15.

G. **Guy Rudisill,** Winston-Salem, N.C.

Silver Chest; walnut, oak; 13 x 14 x 23. Pacific-cloth treatment of drawers; concealed compartment under silver tray; solid wood construction.

H. **Ted Stahly,** Bloomington, Ind.

Hanging Shelves; native cherry, tulip, poplar; 27 x 7 x 32, $165.

"Recessed, circular fingerholds on the drawers won't catch folds of loose clothing as conventional knobs might."

I. **Gerald M. Bellas,** Schofield, Wis.

Loose-Lid Box with Pin Locks; cherry; 13 x 10¼ x 4½. Simple drawer construction using dado joints with floating bottom. Loose lid in mock dovetail joint with pin lock.

"In a series of boxes I tried to take advantage of loose or hinged lids as an integral part of the total design. No hardware was considered and joints were kept very simple, allowing the lids to take on added significance. Carved pins hold loose lids secure. Hinged lids revolve about a dowel where the top and back fit together."

A. **David North,** Franklin Square, N.Y.

Tool Chest; oak, bird's-eye maple; 30 x 12 x 15. Resawn and bookmatched door panels. Photo by Jay Altman.

"Designed to be esthetically pleasing without losing sight of its utilitarian nature."

B. **Harvey Wrightman,** Kerrwood, Ont., Canada

Blanket Chest; butternut, juniper lining; 40 x 20½ x 21.

C. **Kate Joyce,** Bainbridge Island, Wash.

Record Cabinet; American black walnut; 48 x 16 x 18.

"Offers seating as a bench; sliding doors open to reveal dividers for records."

A

B

C

D. **Marsha Vander Heyden,** New York, N.Y.
   Jewelry Box; cherry, whitewood; 21¾ x 7½ x 5½.

E. **David N. Ebner,** Brookhaven, N.Y.
   Blanket Chest; cherry; 40 x 20 x 20, $850.

D

E

E

A. **Robert R. French,** Lakewood, Ohio

Storage Unit for Boots, Gloves, Shoes, etc.; oak, brass; 72 x 14 x 22, $500. Handmade lattice, handle turns into foot for lid.

"Made for some people who own a cottage in Amish country and who have a love for wood. Lattice floor and back allow free flow of air in case items are wet. Adequately treated and removable for cleaning."

B. **Jacques Berger,** Alban, Ont., Canada

Bench Chest; white pine, cedar lining; 36 x 18 x 26. Photo by Mike Thompson.

C. **Jon O. Grondahl,** Staten Island, N.Y.

Toy Chest; pine; 42 x 16 x 30.

"The seat is covered with foam rubber and needlepoint done by my wife. 'DBR' stands for Diana Beth Roggemann, and she is my granddaughter. The painting is Norwegian rose-painting and done with oil colors."

A

B

C

D. **Kevin Chambers,** Boring, Ore.

Tool Box; oak, brass; 31 x 15 x 17. Box-joint corners, solid wood full-extension drawer glides.

"I have been using the box in the shop and on the job for over two years."

E. **Ken Wilke,** San Jose, Calif.

Blanket Chest; 45½ x 18¼ x 22½.

"Hand-carved mahogany panels are of California wildflowers and grapes."

A

D

E

A (and previous page)
Michael Cooper, Santa Clara, Calif.

Turbo; rosewood, maple, poplar, mahogany, ash, birch, walnut, red oak, purpleheart, boxwood, koa, zebrawood, wenge, tulipwood, lacewood, cherry, reeds, vermilion, Baltic birch plywood, aircraft plywood; 136 x 44 x 40.

B. **Daniel Salcedo,** San Francisco, Calif.

Hershey's Chocolate-Syrup Dispenser; walnut; 14 x 19 x 45. Photo by John Kassay.

"Cranking the right-hand wheel in a counterclockwise direction activates the crankshaft connection to the ball weights, moving them in an eccentric upward/downward manner, whilst depressing the suction pump; this dispenses a regulated stream of chocolate syrup into the soda-fountain glass.

"Once the desired amount of syrup is derived through these mechanical transactions, the operator may then affix a new card on the stereoscope provided, settle back and proceed to chug down the acquired syrup in a style best prescribed by discretion."

C. **John Kahn,** Malverne, N.Y.

Compass; padauk, rosewood, bronze; 36 high.

D. **Russell Fowler,** Middlefield, Conn.

1918 Model-T Express Truck; oak, maple.

"In early years Henry Ford would make the basic truck without a body. You could then make your own body or have a carriage shop make one for you. Henry being somewhat conservative, I don't think he would have used raised panels or been quite so fancy with the battery box, nor would he have made the top to come off. I had to make the top four inches removable to get it in and out of my garage. Barns and garages were higher in those days."

E. **Tom Eckert,** Tempe, Ariz.

4:35 A.M. Mountain Standard Time; 12 x 6 x 6.

"Fully functional clock. Photographic Van Dyke print printed directly onto wood."

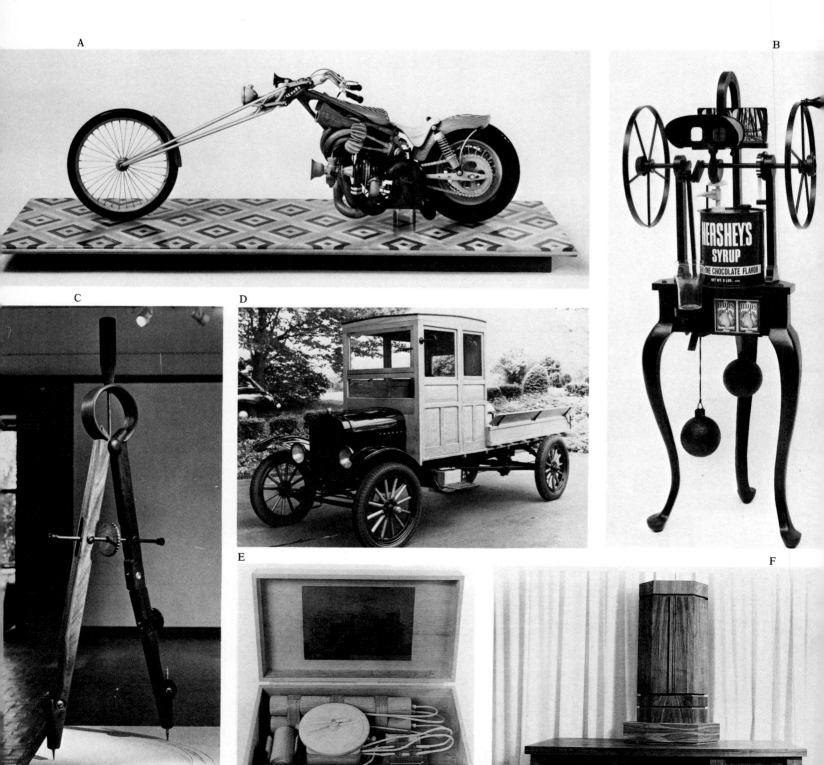

F. **Don Medina,** Stony Brook, N.Y.

Butsudan (Buddhist Altar); walnut, teak; base, 72 x 20 x 18; Butsudan, 22 x 8 x 40.

"This Buddhist altar was designed to house the Gohonzon, which is the object of worship of the Nichiren Shoshu sect. The scroll (Gohonzon) is enshrined in the upper cabinet."

G. **C. Bradford Smith,** Worcester, Pa.

Complicated Simplicity; oak, hickory, beech, birch, maple, ash, poplar, rosewood, Plexiglas, nylon cord, red ribbon, brass, gumballs; 36 x 40 x 66.

"This is a Rube Goldberg inspired gumball dispenser, which, once set up and then triggered by a penny, runs through a calamity of actions and reactions based on simple machine principles aided by gravity, resulting in the delivery of a gumball. Sometimes."

H. **John D. Freeman,** Manhattan Beach, Calif.

Stradivarius Trombone; oak, maple, spring steel; 8-in. bell, 46 long, $800.

I. **William Bellows,** Jamaica Plain, Mass.

Sewing Shears Enlargement; walnut, maple; 36 long.

"Handles are hand-carved with tenons pinning them to blades. Screw is functional, blades move and cut."

J. **Brian Gulick,** White Plains, N.Y.

Dry Sink; red oak, zebrawood, padauk; 17 x 21 x 32.

K. **Eric C. Thiele,** Ayden, N.C.

Fantasy Piece—Covered Bowl #1; ash; 8 x 12 x 12.

L. **Dean L. Wilson,** St. Paul, Minn.

All-Terrain Vehicle/Table; mahogany, Baltic birch plywood; 20 x 20 x 18, $650.

"The table rolls freely. With my machine furniture, I try to make people aware of a delightful interplay of materials and mechanical function not found in commercially produced furniture."

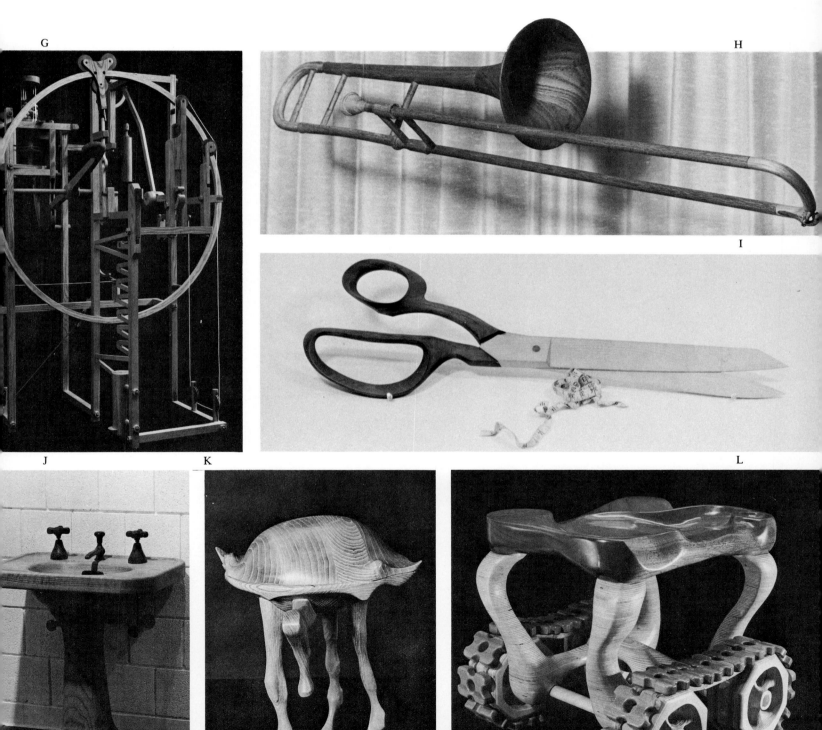

G

H

I

J   K   L

A. **E. James Killy,** Oxford, Ohio

Dexterity In Square; white ash; 66 high.

B. **Mark Maffett,** Lexington, Ky.

Kentucky High Treehouse; balsa, plastic, oil paint; 8 x 7 x 13½. Scale ¼ in. = 1 ft. Photo by Jim Maffett.

"Originally designed to sit on a tree limb fastened to a wall, this piece hasn't been completely finished yet, as it outgrew its intended tree while under construction. . . . Planned mostly in my head; not sketched. Contains approximately 1,700 pieces and took roughly 120 hours to build."

C. **Ray C. Swanson,** Orange, Calif.

Armoire; American black walnut; 1⅝ x 3½ x 6⅜.

"The armoire was copied from a picture in an antique furniture catalog. As I have no armor, shelves were placed in the unit. The small hinges were purchased commercially. All other hardware was handmade from costume jewelry and brass shim stock."

"All the moldings were handmade using jeweler's files and emery cloth. The drawer was made of white pine and faced with walnut veneer and shaped molding. The doors were a challenge. I used three layers of walnut veneer, gluing it sandwich fashion, which allowed me to set the carved panels as well as the stiles and rails. There are 42 pieces in each door, not counting hardware. (The right door lacks a tiny handle, which is still in the photographer's carpet.)

"The finish is clear lacquer directly on the black walnut. No filler or stains were used."

D. **Robert J. Saletzki,** Princeton, Ill.

Toy Wagon; maple; 5 x 3¼ x 3¼. Rods, tires and cleats are metal. Finish is red, green and yellow paint.

E. **David W. Price,** Alexandria, Va.

Rolltop Music Box/Jewelry Box; 10 x 4⅛ x 8³⁄₁₆. Panel construction and tambour carcase. ¹⁄₃₂ walnut veneer laminate forms outer race of carcase tambour track. False drawer hides movement; music operated by opening second drawer.

"I am a cabinetmaker—Smithsonian Institution—and freelance designer."

A

B

C

D

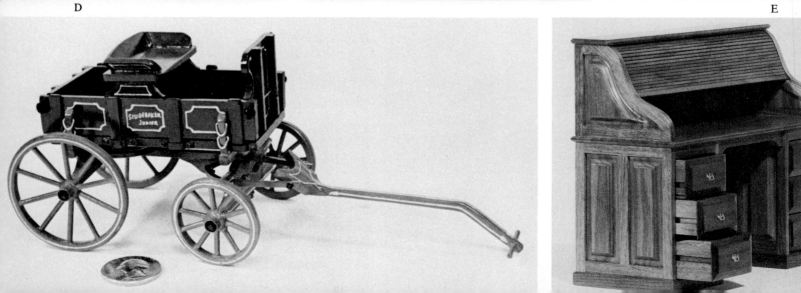

E

F. **Edward F. Davis,** Roseland, Va.

Workbench; cherry, boxwood; 215 x 92 x 70 mm.

"Bench and tools are built to the scale of 1 in. to 1 ft. Tools are made of boxwood, ebony, rosewood, brass and tool steel. All are completely functional. The tools were selected from my collection of 130 miniature carpenter's, cabinetmaker's, cooper's. coachmaker's and woodcarver's tools that I have made."

G. **Edward F. Davis,** Roseland, Va.

Treadle Lathe (Bow Type); cherry, bamboo, brass, steel, leather; 182 x 70 x 186 mm.

H. **Kathy Lewis,** Bridgeport, Conn.

Guild Jr.; mahogany, maple, rosewood, wire, plastic, mother-of-pearl; 1¹¹⁄₁₆ x ⁹⁄₁₆ x ¼. Photo by Noel Giordano.

"Body and neck are one solid piece of mahogany, covered with veneer sanded down to half its thickness. Mahogany sides were moistened and shaped with a warm wood burner. The pick guard was cut from a thinned plastic guitar pick.

The strings are various colored steel-wool fibers. Chips from a mother-of-pearl button were used for fret markers."

I. **Steve Benbow,** Newport News, Va.

Grandpa's Watch; walnut, glass, pocketwatch; 14 x 3 x 2. Photo by Tom Edwards.

"I am a pattern-maker by trade. This was made as a gift for my brother, who inherited Great Grandpa's watch (an 1869 Elgin)."

J. **D.L. Edwards,** Tulsa, Okla.

Pewter Display Cabinet; wormy chestnut, brass pulls; 10½ x 4 x 11½. Mitered box ⁵⁄₁₆ in. thick; carved low cabriole legs with drake (trifid) foot; scroll-saw shaped and pierced frieze on superstructure and skirt; diamond inlay on cupboard doors; lacquer finish.

K. **Silas Kopf,** Northampton, Mass.

Folding Screen; walnut frame and background, poplar, cherry, ebony, wenge, canaletta, elm burl, holly, maple, ash, mahogany; 77 x 74.

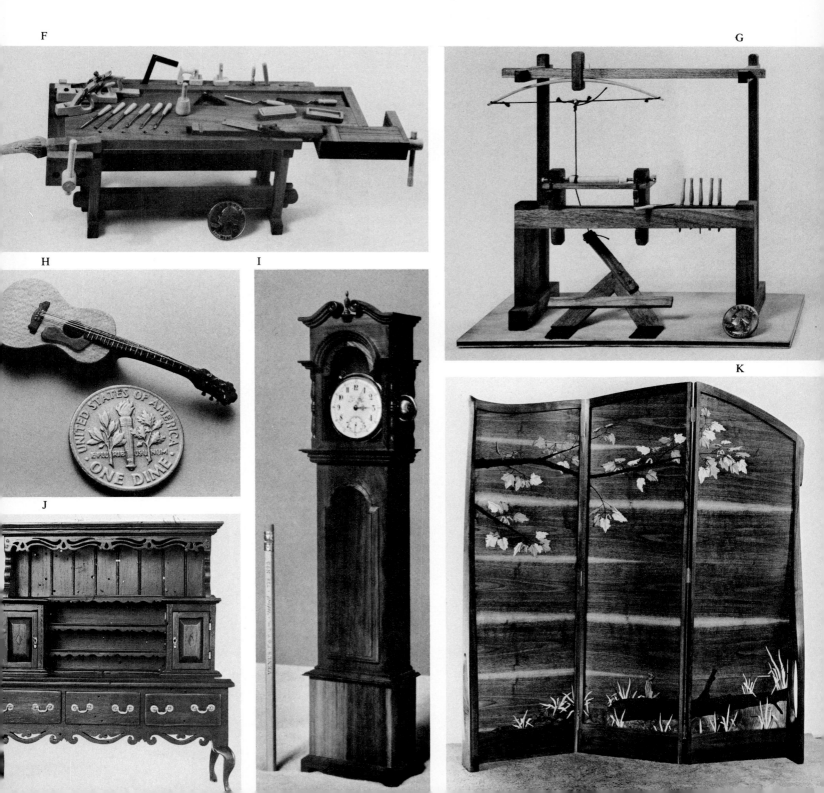

F   G   H   I   J   K

A. Ann Gatto Cimmelli, New York, N.Y.

Victorian Gazebo; pine, bass, padauk, cocobolo, cherry, walnut; 12½ x 12½ x 20, $500.

"Floor is inlaid with hardwoods. This gazebo is part of a series of gazebos I've been working on over the past year. All miniature. If dreams come true, I will sometime have my own space large enough to build a full-size piece."

B. Heinz Norhausen, Laguna Beach, Calif.

Steinbeck's Country Wall Plaque; walnut, holly, cherry, aspen, oak, resin; 45 x 31, $2,500.

"I used hollow-core door panels for greater stability and lightness."

C. Paul L. McClure, Denver, Colo.

The Little Tramp 1899-1977; bird's-eye maple, Brazilian rosewood, Indian rosewood, cherry, walnut, satinwood, poplar; 16 x 23, $450.

"Entirely produced using flexible veneers and knife-cutting."

D. Jeffrey W. Prichard, Strafford, Pa.

Philadelphia Highboy; mahogany, basswood; 8 x 15¼ x 33 (⅓ scale). Hand-dovetailed drawers and case. All carvings accurately reduced from original Affleck highboy. Photo by William J. Pritchard.

"This miniature was made as a wedding gift from an owner of one of the Kittinger Centennial highboys to her daughter. While the bride dearly loved her mother's highboy, apartment life precluded a gift of such large proportions.... The drawers are large enough for jewelry, handkerchiefs, etc. and the scale is such that virtually all of the carving details could be shown."

E. Edwin H. Schadt, Allentown, Pa.

World Map and History of Sailing Ship; 60 veneers; 60 x 38. 3/16-in. square steel rod marks longitudes, time zones, tropics, equator.

"Sixty varieties of veneers, native wood used for state or country wherever possible. Copper wire inlaid for major rivers. Construction time, approximately 1,000 hours."

F. **Poul Middelboe,** Helsingor, Denmark

The Day and the Evening (doors and drawers); Italian pear-wood; 16½ x 23½ x 9, $900.

G. **Bill Woodyear,** Glen Dale, Md.

Still Life for All Seasons; walnut, cedar, plywood, glass; 18 x 12 x 5.

"Shadow-box scene is orthogonal projection attached to ¾-in. plywood shell. All wood subjects, mostly hand-formed, situated in various fixed positions within confines of three walls, floor and roof."

H. **Robin O. Williams,** Oak Ridge, Tenn.

Clock with Swans; holly, walnut, maple, mahogany, benin; 16 x 1½ x 12, $115.

"The basic pattern was adapted from a design by M.C. Escher."

F

G

F

H

A. **William Bader,** Asheville, N.C.

Bobolink; many foreign & domestic woods.

B. **Mary Shelley,** West Danby, N.Y.

Swine Flu 1976; pine, acrylic paint; 15 x 1 x 14.

"This piece was done during the swine-flu scare of 1976, and also because I've always wanted to carve pigs. It is obvious how I felt about the whole swine-flu scare and the shots that were supposed to prevent it."

C. **Roger Rupp,** Knoxville, Tenn.

Coffee Table; solid walnut, 32 veneers; 60 x 24 x 20.

"The scene depicted in marquetry is an interpretation of the painting, 'The Alchemist.'"

D. **Bill Warren,** Middlebourne, W. Va.

Sign; pine; 36 x ¾ x 11½, $75.

A

B

C

D

E. **J. Dennis Klinsky,** Feversham, Ont., Canada

*Launching Day, Collingwood Shipyards; butternut;
17 x 27 x 1½. $1,500.*

F. **Friedolin Kessler,** San Jose, Calif.

*Totem; 2 x 24 x 84, $800. Thin cross-section slices of branches
and crotches, 24 different woods embedded in colored resins.*

G. **Michael Shane Coulter,** Denver, Colo.

The Dragon of Selidor, Orm Embar; redwood; 41½ x 4 x 11¼.

"I now understand what wood is here for . . ., its beauty."

H. **Rita Dunipace,** Jamaica Plain, Mass.

Sculpture; poplar; 15 x 6 x 2.

E

F

G

H

A. **Otto H. Schenck,** Santa Barbara, Calif.

Tool Box; oak; 30 x 9 x 13.

"Tool box is used daily for work: building and installing furniture. Inside is a sliding tray with three compartments for small tools, a special slot for scraper and compartments for planes and a saw. A level is fastened in the fold-down lid."

B. **John Levering,** Glenelg, Md.

Relief Sculpture—Benjamin Banneker Memorial; walnut; 38 x 85. Photo by James Ferry.

C. **Doug Ayers,** Little River, Calif.

Hanging Disc #6-28-78; African wenge; 34 dia., 1½ thick. One board cut and glued with sapwood edges butted together to form white stripe.

"This piece is designed to hang from a single wire so that it is free to turn slowly in the air currents."

D. **Bruce Janssen,** Boyne City, Mich.

Sign; cedar, zebrawood, bubinga, padauk, walnut, gold leaf; 108 x 8 x 60.

"The Arboretum is a restaurant in Harbor Springs, Mich., set in a natural setting on Lake Michigan. The sign is constructed of all natural material in keeping with this concept."

E. **Tom Wolver,** Watsonville, Calif.

Allegory; redwood; 60 x 96, $2,000.

"Alternating convex and concave planes add depth and dimension to hand-carved mural. Site is patio of dentists whose patients can look out of large window and see mural."

F. **Ann S. Vanderbilt,** Vashon, Wash.

Woman of Dreams (Walnut Box); black walnut; 12 x 9 x 8.

G. **Dan Jay Bruiger,** North Vancouver, B.C., Canada

Tristan et Iseult, (Carved Box for Book); black walnut, oiled; 8 x 6 x 2.

E

F

E

G

A. **Frederick Wilbur,** Shipman, Va.

Cooke's Ordinary; redwood; 40 x 30. Photo by Jim Evans.

B. **Scott Wynn,** San Francisco, Calif.

Entrance Gate to the Courtyard of a Restaurant; korina (blonde mahogany); 72 x 84.

C. **Thomas McFarland,** Waynesboro, Pa.

Unicorn of the Wood Headboard; walnut; 93 x 60 x 2.

"The finish consists of three different types. The lightest parts have no finish at all. . .just pure wood. The middle tones are produced with Watco Danish Oil. The dark tones are made with pure black walnut husk juice on the wood."

D. **Joe Falsetti,** Knoxville, Tenn.

City from Above; walnut; 30 x 54.

E. **Chuck Fitzgerald,** Puyallup, Wash.

PHC Trip—Wall Hanging; redwood, pine; 25 x 35 x ½.

A   B   B

C   D   E

F. **Richard J. McCormick,** Ft. Collins, Colo.

Carved Doors; Honduras mahogany; 80 x 78 x 2⅜.

"These doors were my most extensive woodworking endeavor to date, taking nearly one year to complete, working mostly part-time. They are carved on both sides with a separate scene designed to complement the interior of a home in Dallas.

"There are actually four individual panels that form a pair of bi-fold doors closing together in the center. Each pair is hinged together with large cast-steel hinges that are deeply mortised into the sides, and when closed are invisible, permitting an uninterrupted scene. Because of the weight (approximately 280 lb.) three large commercial brass ball-bearing hinges were used on each side of the jamb. The doors open by grasping a carved-out recess behind the foliage of the tree just next to the head of one of the figures.

". . . Even the slightest expansion or contraction of such a large solid door could mean disaster in the form of binding or too large a reveal. It was decided therefore, that each of the four doors would be constructed in layers. . . . The doors have been hanging now for several seasons and there has been no noticeable shrinking or binding."

G. **Herschel E. Westbrook,** Columbus, Ohio

Old Mill; walnut; 12½ x 18, $700.

H. **Harold Nosti,** Brandon, Fla.

On the Wall; oak, pecan, butternut, rosewood, copper, walnut; 48 x 36, $400.

I. **Paul M. Kraemer,** Los Alamos, N. Mex.

Mayan Interior Window Screen; Honduras mahogany; 72 x 48.

"Inspired by a door in the first *Biennial Design Book* by fellow New Mexican, Robert van Arsdale (whom I have never met). Motifs derive from Mayan carving of 900 A.D."

A. **Judi R. Bartholomew,** Milwaukee, Wis.

Pippa (Wall Hanging); black walnut; 14¼ x 30 x 4. Photo by Hans Keerl.

B. **Frank Litto,** New Baltimore, N.Y.

Conestoga Chassis, Wall Sculpture; oak, particle board, basswood, acrylics; 105 x 96 x 2¼, $9,500. Wood inlay, carved particle board, simulated metal parts.

C. **Robert E. Gest,** Livermore, Calif.

Mallard Duck; fir; 13 x 5 x 6.

A

B

C

D. **Vic Wood,** Victoria, Australia

Quatro; blackwood, red gum, silver ash; 30 x 18 x 2. Faceplate turning, lamination.

E. **Don Briddell,** Dallastown, Pa.

Cedar Island Straight Resters; basswood, maple; 12 x 8 x 7, $1,500 each.

"Carved with hand knives from basswood with maple inserted feathers. Feathers deeply undercut and textured with a burning iron. Male bird has flexible polyester cast feet supported by internal steel rods. Hen bird has epoxy putty feet sculpted. Mounted on driftwood and a cast sand base. Painted with acrylics."

F. **Grainger McKoy,** Wadmalaw Island, S.C.

Five Green-Wing Teal; basswood; 36 x 48 x 84 (displayed in Plexiglas).

"Birds are assembled from separate basswood feathers with the basswood bodies hollowed. Support is obtained by the use of steel feathers where necessary. The paint is oil and the birds are life-size."

G. **Robert E. Rice,** Northridge, Calif.

Roadrunner; black walnut; 14 x 2 x 8½, $125. Photo by Michael Karp.

"All carved from one piece—no gluing."

H. **David Longeill,** Red Creek, N.Y.

Green-Haired, Blue-Footed Gooney Bird; basswood, yellow poplar, black walnut, yarn, sneakers. 30 high, $300.

D | E

F | G | H

A. **Clarence L. Thuma,** Kelso, Wash.

Cardinals; Tennessee cedar, driftwood, walnut; 6 x 1½ x 2, $60. Photo by Craig K. Anderson.

"Polishing of raw wood with rubbed smooth 120 garnet sandpaper—sharp corners of sandpaper rubbed smooth by rubbing two sheets together. Penetrating finish wiped off after three minutes. Applied three times. Paste wax applied to enhance shine. The more the raw wood is rubbed with the worn-out sandpaper, the better the shine."

B. **William Koochin,** West Vancouver, B.C., Canada

Bird Bowls: Dove, alder, 18 x 9; Canada Goose, cherry, 20 x 20; Rooster, alder, 24 x 10.

C. **Igor Givotovsky,** Amesbury, Mass.

November's Reindeer; bird's-eye maple, black walnut, teak, padauk, tulipwood, ebony; 13 x 16 x 7½.

"November's Reindeer was inspired by the Scythian totems, golden relics from the tombs of the nomads who inhabited the Soviet steppe. The stylization of detail was taken from the northern west coast. Angular planes in the front legs of the gold Scythian stags suggest that they were probably fashioned after wooden effigies. The vitality and implied motion seen in the stance of this representation is uncharacteristic of the ancient figures, which were cast in a recumbant pose.

"November's Reindeer was a challenge that evolved into what is perhaps the most intricate 'polyglyph' created."

A   B

C   C

D. **Harold H. Hoy,** Eugene, Ore.

Frog Performing Chin-Ups; maple, fiddleback maple and walnut veneers; 24 x 15 x 23.

E. **Stan R. Carney,** Orion, Ill.

Soaring Hawk/Beetle; fir; hawk, 64 x 5 x 21, beetle 21 x 8 x 2½. Designed to hang from the ceiling of an A-frame home.

F. **Robert Rustmann,** East Hampton, N.Y.

Aero III; Philippine birch, masawa; 41 x 19 x 34.

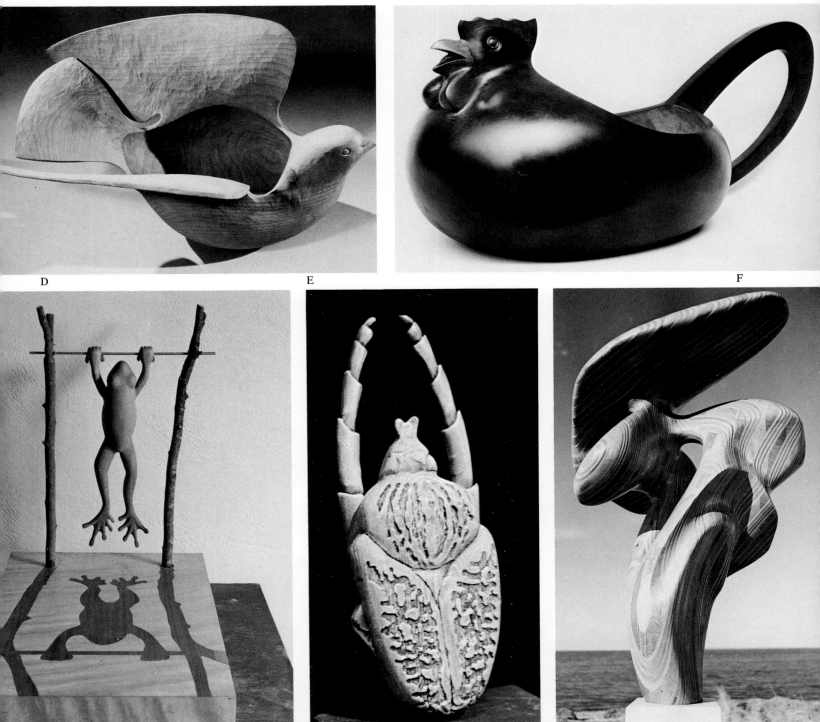

B

B

D

E

F

A. **G. Brad Gray,** Seattle, Wash.

Mantispa; walnut, ebony, maple; 22 x 12 x 26. Puppet has 22 movable joints.

B. **Cliff Long,** Bowling Green, Ohio

Mathematical Surfaces—Peaks, Ridge, Passes, Valley, Pits; maple; 18½ x 1½ x 2.

"This model was constructed using a numerically controlled milling machine to illustrate various shapes for the mathematical surfaces defined by $Z = AX^2 + BY^2$, and to establish numerically controlled milling as a viable tool for constructing teaching aids."

C. **Hap Sakwa,** Goleta, Calif.

Rings; zebrawood, granite, stainless steel; 26 x 26 x 30, $2,500. Turned from one solid piece of zebrawood.

D. **David Ellsworth,** Allenspark, Colo.

Bowl; Brazilian rosewood; 5½ dia.; 0.7 ounces.

"Blind internal turning with bent tools of my own design. Rotted pieces turned at high speed with tiny tipped tools. Thinness of walls is determined by tapping surface while piece is being formed."

E. **Ken Guild,** Mahone Bay, N.S., Canada

Sea Form; mahogany, pine; 14 x 5 x 7, $550. Photo by Knickle's Studio.

"This is a scale model for a sculpture commission and is based on a mathematical formula, which allows precise reproduction in a size five times the model."

A

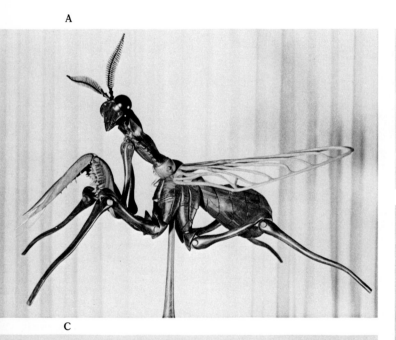

B

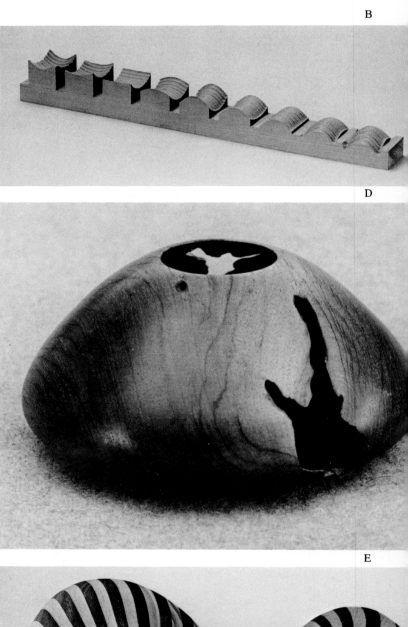

D

C

E

F. **Mark Lindquist,** Henniker, N.H.

Defunctional Sculpture (Forbidden Fruit Tree); elm burl, cherry burl, maple burl, spalted maple, swamp birch, spalted yellow birch burl, curly maple, padauk, ebony, rosewood; 72 X 60.

G. **Jeffrey Vranesh,** Granada Hills, Calif.

Contortion; Philippine mahogany; 5 x 5 x 14.

"The design of the sculpture was acquired from scribbling on scratch paper and a little imagination.... This is my first attempt at woodcarving, but I hope not my last. Woodcarving is a great release from the daily rat race and it rejuvenates all the energy I lose during a long day at the office."

H. **William W. Millenky,** Plainfield, N.J.

Volute; walnut, alabaster base; 25½ x 6 x 8.

"Carved from ¼ section of tree trunk. A spiral of constantly decreasing pitch starts as the concave surface at the base and continues upward within the heavier portion and emerges again at the top."

I. **Richard M. Graham,** Mt. Pleasant, Mich.

Missionary Ridge; ash, maple; 18½ x 8 x 53, $500.

J. **Steve Meder,** Rochester, N.Y.

Chicken; walnut; 8 x 8 x 24.

F

G

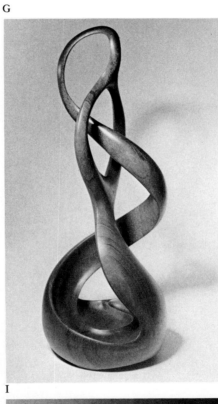

H

I

J

A. **Jon Brooks,** New Boston, N.H.

   Spiral Pillars; oak, ash, beech, birch, maple; 48 ft. x 12 ft. Chain-saw carved, textured with gouge.

B. **Gary Galbraith,** Ellensburg, Wash.

   Woodshaving Storage Spiral, Tambour Cylinder; ash, walnut; 22 x 24 x 47.

C. **Ralph H. Rosenblum, Jr.,** Columbus, Ohio

   Twined Ego Mirror; catalpa, redwood, cedar, walnut, mahogany, purpleheart, basswood, oak, redbud, mirror; 40 x 60 x 1. Each segment hand-shaped and fitted before proceeding to the next. Sanded smooth. Penetrating resin finish.

   "A mirror should present an image greater than yourself. It gives you something to think about all day."

D. **Alan Friedman,** Terre Haute, Ind.

   Positive-Negative #3; fir plywood; 18 ft. x 6 ft. x 4 ft.

A

B

C

D

E. **Andrew Poynter,** N. Cambridge, Ont., Canada

Christening Font; white oak burl, English brown oak, cast bronze; 28 x 36 x 41. Burl carved with pneumatic die grinder, bronze liner sand-cast from plaster mold.

F. **James MacWilliams,** Calgary, Alta., Canada

Platter; willow, Tennessee cedar; 19 x 19 x 1.

"The willow and cedar are in the proportions of three willow to one cedar. The platter was turned outboard on the lathe, and was turned square. This involved very exact cutting."

G. **Herbert Eaton,** Bloomington, Ill.

Untitled Sculpture; white oak, dirt mounds, grass; 40 ft. x 25 ft. x 7 ft. Photo by Kenneth Kashian.

"The timbers were cut and fitted and then allowed to sit for a year before erection. They stayed pretty true and barely creaked when transported by crane to the site. Most of the joining was done with a long-arm adz and a 1½-in. chisel after roughing out with a chain saw. The joints were made to fit the first time or not at all as the size of the timbers pro-

hibited removal for any trimming. The longer tenon is 25 in. long and the shorter one is 17 in. long. Support posts are embedded almost five feet in the ground.

"This piece was designed for a location on the grounds of Illinois State University in Normal, where students could rest, sunbath, climb or study. It is regularly being used for the first three."

E

E

F

G

A. **Trent Williams,** Ft. Bragg, Calif.

Moon Dancer; redwood; 19½ high. Photo by C.M. Rollans.

B. **Scott Hausman,** W. Brattleboro, Vt.

Barney; black walnut, cherry; 30 x 25 x 25. Photo by Henry Babson.

"Staved cone construction, clamping achieved by hinging jointed pieces with masking tape."

C. **Jana Schweitzer, maker;**
Bob Miller, designer; Portland, Ore.

Rosewood Mandala; East Indian rosewood; 12 x 12 x 15, $190. Base and humanlike forms turned on a lathe. Head of human-like form doweled into body, spears shaped with spokeshave.

"The designer was strongly influenced by the Navajo and Hopi Indians, in whose country he was traveling. He dreamt the image, then interpreted it as a mandalic symbol of transition and wholeness, and recognized it as similar to Indian representations of Navajo Yei gods, representing fertility and guardianship."

A

B

C

D. **Ray Fink,** Phoenix, Ariz.

Rainbow Spirit in Red Rock Canyon; ironwood, vermilion, tigerwood, basswood; 36 x 13 x 36, $1,000.

E. **Stephen Hogbin,** Kilsyth, Ont., Canada

Three Sculptures: Fin, Wing, Sacred Leaf; walnut elm, ash; maximum dimension 79 cm.

F. **Charles Zimmerman,** New York, N.Y.

Two-Holed Configuration; maple log; 52 x 10 x 20.

G. **Mark E. Henion,** Waterbury, Conn.

Sculpture; cherry; 84 high.

H. **Bill Horgos,** Larkspur, Calif.

Chess Set; boxwood, brass; 3 x 1⅜.

"So far these guys are pawns."

A. **Peter Mania**, Miramar, Fla.

Ship's Figurehead; laminated pine; 99 x 20 x 30.

"My client wanted an antique-looking ship's figurehead and trailboards in the figure of a viking, to be mounted over the portals of a four-bay boathouse on a lake. The winds prevail north to south, so he requested the hair and beard be blown in that direction. He also wanted the piece to look weathered when first put up and to weather further without total deterioration; so I designed and carved this piece of epoxy-laminated pine, leaving it with a mostly coarse texture to pick up the washes and give the piece a generally encrusted patina.

"Dovetail joints lock the right arm in place at the shoulder and the shield onto the left arm. The broad ax, also a separate piece, slides into the hand. Each trailboard was carved from a 5/4 plank and separately fastened to the body. The entire piece was washed with gesso to raise the grain and then prime the wood, and it was then painted with washes of acrylic paint in muted colors."

B. **Bill Jackman**; Medford, N.J.

Sculpture; oak, paint, copper; 72 high.

C. **Fletcher Cox**, Tougaloo, Miss.

Lamp; pecan; 14 x 14 x 36, $825. Base and stem turned. Arms laminated.

A

B

A

C

D. **R.H. Karol,** Highland Park, N.J.

Kathy; limba; 12 x 6 x 18. Vacation; cherry; 22 x 6 x 11. Posed by live models. Photos by Victor's Photography.

E. **David Hostetler,** Athens, Ohio

Standing Women; elm, 56 high; elm, 77 high. Photos by Jon Webb.

D

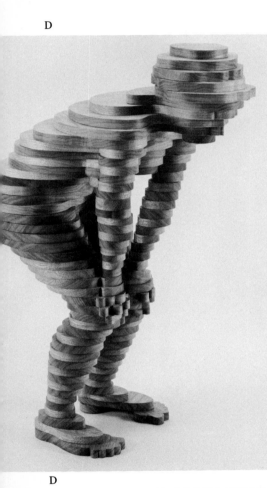

E

E

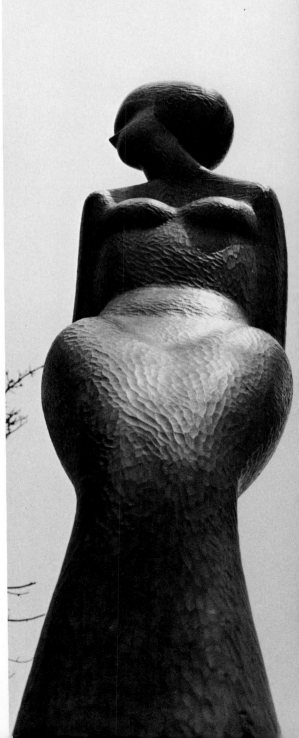

D

A. **Kenneth C. Pacetti,** St. Augustine, Fla.

Marie (Ship's Figurehead); sugar pine; 36 high, $1,200.

B. **Jeffrey Briggs,** Newburyport, Mass.

Beelezubub; mahogany, Appalachian maple, zebrawood; 30 x 32. Photo by John I. Russell.

"The principal source for 'Beelezubub' is *The Dore Illustrations for Dante's Divine Comedy*."

C. **Peter Schmidt,** Freeport, Maine

Abraham Lincoln; maple, birch; 17½ x 12 x 26. Photo by David Smith.

D. **Harry Wunsch,** Westport, Conn.

Helen; mixed woods, acrylic paint; 15 x 15 x 48.

A

B

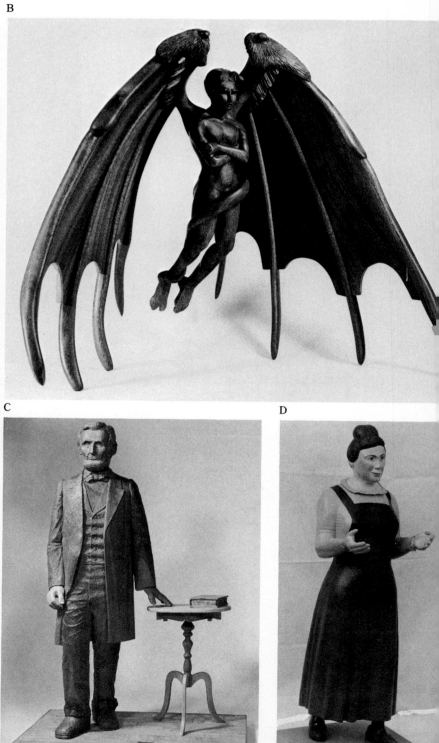

C

D

E. **Richard Carl Urso,** San Francisco, Calif.

Submission; rock maple; 24 x 24 x 36. Photo by Jon Laitin.

"The work was directly carved from a log of rock maple, using only mauls and chisels. The masklike face is neuter, taking on nuances of 'male' or 'female' according to the viewer. The expression is purposely enigmatic, as submission, in any form, may be beneficial or detrimental, depending on the circumstances."

F. **Pier Clout Duntel,** St. Jean Port Joli, Que., Canada

La Louve; white pine; 17 high, $2,500.

G. **Ray F. Githews, Jr.,** Denver, Colo.

Eileen; walnut; $750.

B

E

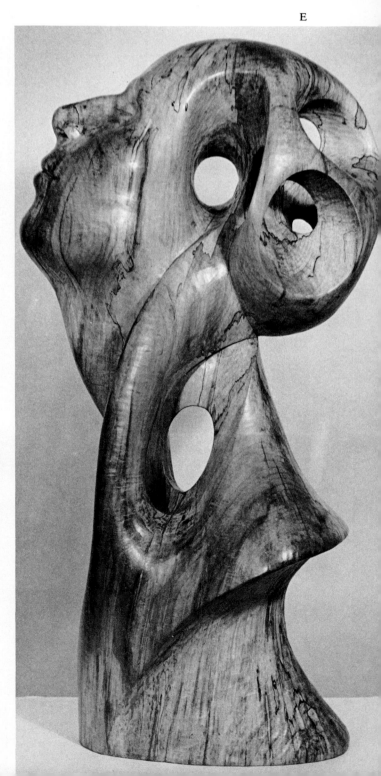

F

G

A. **Gary Campagna,** Corte Madera, Calif.

Wood Carvings; alder; 12 in. to 20 in., $125 to $325.

"All carvings are hand-carved, no power tools. Each piece was carved from a single block of red alder."

B. **Lloyd J. Guillory,** Morgan City, La.

Surprised Cowboy; Louisiana cypress.

"The cowboy and the horse were carved monolithically—only the rifle and the holster are separate items."

C. **Chris Schneider,** Mt. Shasta, Calif.

The Dragon in Water; Port Orford cedar; 30 high.

"Carving directly into the wood—no sketches or models used. As has been said many times before, the only true and lasting form of art is life itself; the only true and lasting form of life is an art."

D. **Bill Amundson,** Denver, Colo.

Ottumwa Rotary Massacre; butternut, basswood, canvas, paint; 72 x 16 x 36.

"The Ottumwa Rotary Massacre is a large wall-supported sculptural diorama depicting a modern-day Indian massacre of Rotarians and tourists around the swimming pool of the Holiday Inn in Ottumwa, Iowa."

A

B

C

D

E. **Joseph Wheelwright**, Cambridge, Mass.
   Cowboys; cherry, walnut, feathers; 82 high.

F. **John Rocus,** Ann Arbor, Mich.
   Harvester; black walnut; 22 high, $1,000.

   "Part of a series of carvings depicting traditional aspects of American life in a contemporary style."

G. **Robert K. Hoffman,** Frederick, Md.
   The Gun Fighter; walnut, cherry; 14 high.

H. **J. Barry Wheaton,** Dartmouth, N.S., Canada
   Mount Saint Vincent University Mace; oak; 37 x 7½ x 7½.

E F G

H

A. **Dorian Stripling**, Ames, Iowa

Standing Figure; gum wood; 48 high.

B. **Ward L. Miller, Jr.**, Sycamore, Ill.

An Old Man; basswood, paint; 8 x 5 x 6, $700.

C. **Norman H. Ridenour**, San Diego, Calif.

Totem and Taboo; Indian rosewood, Elgon olive; 5½ x 5½ x 18. Photo by NKS Ltd.

D. **Charles McDonough**, Glastonbury, Conn.

Satyr; cherry; 23 x 2¾ x 4. Photo by Color Teknika Inc.

"The Satyr is the peghead and neck of a guitar that is now in construction. The entire neck is carved from a single piece of cherry, the fret markers are inlaid walnut and the nut is ivory.... Work on the Satyr instilled a great respect for the third dimension since it was necessary to go into and recarve the head three times before it pleased me. As a graphic/industrial designer and artist, the use and manipulation of two dimensions has been a way of life; that third dimension laid down a challenge."

A

B

C

D

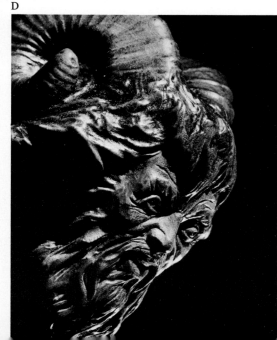

E. **Jamie Maverick,** San Antonio, Tex.

Fly with the Falcon; redwood; 26 long.

"Body designed from authentic falcon. The tires are inscribed Goodyear. Often I make toys. This is more sophisticated."

F. **Albert Weisman,** Peabody, Mass.

Sculpture; elm; 25 high, $600.

G. **Lindley Briggs,** Newburyport, Mass.

Boys and Girls Together; African mahogany, ziracote, zebrawood, poplar, aromatic cedar, wenge, Appalachian maple, oak, Baltic birch laminate; 102 x 72 x 60. Photo by John I. Russell.

H. **William Moore,** Portland, Ore.

Untitled Sculpture; ash; 39 x 26 x 50. Laminated and carved. Photo by Eric Edwards.

E F

G H

Listed below are the names of all the craftsmen who contributed to Design Book Two. For those 80% who make all or part of their living from the craft, we have also included their addresses, telephone numbers and specialties.

Curtis, Ron *170*
Wood Designs
91 Tunxis Ave.
Bloomfield, Conn. 06002 (203) 242-4285
Custom building: structures, decks, kitchens, built-in furniture, interiors, furniture, designing.

Dadey, Ed *169*
The Wood Plant
RR 1
Marquette, Nebr. 68854 (402) 854-3120
One-of-a-kind home furniture, architectural commissions, non-figurative sculpture.

Daigle, Michael *88*

Daley, Mark *93*
Woodsong
2222 S. Sepulveda Blvd.
W. Los Angeles, Calif. 90064
(213) 473-4282
Custom kitchens, bars, hutches, wall units, tables.

Daluisio, Angelo *49*
1447 Kewalo St. #203
Honolulu, Hawaii 96822 (808) 531-5687
Handcrafted, one-of-a-kind, custom-designed, tabletop items made from fine hardwoods.

Dameron, Arthur E. *135*

Danell, Kevin Scott *228*
Logical Myth Woodworking
324 Merrimack St.
Newburyport, Mass. 01950
Hardwood furniture, cabinets & boxes with relief carving done to order.

Danko, Peter *83*
Design & Woodwork
917 King St.
Alexandria, Va. 22314 (703) 836-0774
Limited-edition furniture, chairs, tables, desks, lamps, etc.

Darnell, Paul L. *30*
Wood Works of Mesa
2834 W. Marlett
Phoenix, Ariz. 85017 (602) 246-4262
Custom woodworking, special items & one-of-a-kind; hardwood cabinets.

Dascanio, Craig S. *231*
Windfall Woodworks
16 Banks Ave.
W. Springfield, Mass. 01089
(413) 739-4091
Individually designed furniture.

Dasenbrock, Diedrich *163*
Glass & Woodworking
Rt. 3, Box 91
Alsea, Ore. 97324 (503) 486-4195
One-of-a-kind glass & wooden window hangings, hand mirrors, wall mirrors, wall hangings.

Davidson, William *189*
Wm. Davidson, Furniture Designer, Wood Craftsman
Rt. 3, Box 95 I
Santa Fe, N. Mex. 87501 (505) 983-3049
Contemporary furniture: chairs, couches, tables, cabinets.

Davies, Ben *211*
Muntin Woodworks
606 Barton Ave.
Chattanooga, Tenn. 37405 (615)267-2033
Doors, entryways, furniture.

Davies, Thomas Landon *48*
222 N. Essex Ave.
Narberth, Pa. 19072 (215) 563-6381
Cameras and camerae obscurae. "Functioning original designs adapted from pre-1850 examples."

Davis, Edward F. *251*

Davis, John Gorton *151*
Gort
6807 Stockton Ave.
El Cerrito, Calif. 94530 (415) 524-1506
Woodturning: bowls & trays in laid-up patterns.

Davis, Hal E. *240*
Woodenwork
1293 Tutwiler
Memphis, Tenn. 38107 (901) 274-4627
Functional sculpture & carving; model-making & design.

Davis, Larry *60*
2157 Southeast Blvd.
Salem, Ohio 44460 (216) 337-7729

Davis, Mark *32*
Mark Davis—Toymaker
Sugar Camp, Rt. 2
Rhinelander, Wis. 54501 (715) 272-1249
Toys for people of all ages: painted & unpainted puzzles, push toys, mobiles.

Davison, John E. *214*
Furniture by Davison
2547 8th St.
Berkeley, Calif. 94710 (415) 845-4887
Custom furniture.

Day, Emmett E. *100*

Day, Jr., Emmett E. *132*
Creations in Exotic Materials
7520 57 Pl. N.E.
Seattle, Wash. 98119 (206) 522-9222
Combinations of precious metals, woods, stone, glass on commission. Furniture, jewelry, sculpture.

Deady, Tom *127*
Oak House
26545 235th S.E.
Maple Valley, Wash. 98038
(206) 432-0554
Contemporary, laminated, steam-bent functional & non-functional art pieces.

Deatherage, Roger *230*
Whistlepig Productions
5200 Nett
Houston, Tex. 77007 (713) 864-2556
Custom & limited-production furniture & accessories.

DeFrances, Robert L. *173*
Contemporary Designs in Wood
3202 Karen Dr.
Delray Beach, Fla. 33444 (305) 732-7752
Interior/exterior lighting, decorative pieces, small cabinets, specialty tables.

deGraf, Bradford Rankin *75*
3805 Belle Rive Terrace
Alexandria, Va. 22309
Chairs

Delaney, Daniel J. *26*
Meyer's Woodturning
3118 Broadway
Sacramento, Calif. 95817 (916) 456-2088
Original-design furniture, toys, desks, interiors. Custom wood turning for staircases & columns to 20 in. by 12 ft.

Denninger, George *40*
Box 277
Sugar Loaf, N.Y. 10981 (914) 469-2391
Wood sculpture, pen & ink drawings, sculptured furniture, pianos, architectural & interior design, design seminars.

Dennison, Dan *174*
Dan-D Wood Turnings
Lane Rd.
Chichester, N.H. 03263 (603) 798-5933
Laminated & turned exotic wood lamps, bowls, end tables, clocks.

d'Entremont, Philip *132*
Philip d'Entremont—Woodworker
1451 Bustleton Pk.
Feasterville, Pa. 19047 (215) 357-4712
Custom furniture design.

Dern, Larry *118*
76 W. 4th St.
Eureka, Calif. 95501 (707) 443-5788
Custom wood & stained-glass work.

DeVore, Keith J. *236*
Heartwood Studio
223 County Line Rd.
S. Hampton, Pa. 18966
Furniture.

Dewdney, Eric *213*
22 Blenheim Rd.
Cambridge, Ont., Canada N1S 1E6
(519) 621-2175
Custom cabinets, furniture, accessories.

de Wolf, Bradford Colt *137*

Dick, Edward *42*
Ed's Music Workshop
241 Dublin St.
Peterboro, Ont., Canada K9H 3B9
(705) 743-2641
Repair & restoration of vintage stringed instruments; custom building.

Dickerson, Scott *89*
Scott Dickerson/Woodworker
Box 294
Brooksville, Maine 04617 (207) 326-4778
Custom chairs & other seating.

Dickhut, David *140*
Silver Sawdust Artisans
1015½ Main Ave. #6
Durango, Colo. 81301
Functional sculptures of exotic hardwoods; paraphernalia, lapidary, gold & silver.

Dietrick, David A. *44*
1 Winding La. W.
Westport, Conn. 06880 (203) 226-0686
Banjos, dulcimers, furniture, fine cabinetry; finished work on commission.

Dingle, John E. *211*
Kraft Korner
Rt. #1, 499 N. Sycamore St.
Hagerstown, Ind. 47346 (317) 489-5245
Craft-shop items, plaques, boxes, boards, novelties, home accessories, small furnishings.

Disparti, Nicholas J. *21*
Avocado Clocks & Furniture
635 Howe Pl.
Escondido, Calif. 92025 (714) 746-4484
One-of-a-kind clocks & furniture crafted from avocado wood.

Dodd, John *232*

Dolberg, Stan *25*
761 Boston Post Rd.
Weston, Mass. 02193 (617) 899-7391
Functional sculpture, commission furniture in contemporary mode.

Doll, Michael F. *93*
M.F. Doll Woodworking
3032A Bartlett Ave.
Milwaukee, Wis. 53211 (414) 963-0853
Bentwood personal design, incorporating stained glass, steel, cloth, weaving, macrame: chairs, tables, lamps.

Doll, Norman R. *124*
303 Kettle Moraine Dr.
Slinger, Wis. 53086 (414) 644-5985

Domlesky, Robert *129*
R.R. #1
Shelburne Falls, Mass. 01370
(413) 625-2940
Free-standing furniture.

Don, Paul *203*
Ottawa Woodworker's Co-op
Les Ateliers 157 Nicholas St.
Ottawa, Ont., Canada (807) 233-7510

Donahue, Tim *103*

Donnelly, Brian F. *200*

D'Onofrio, Richard *71*

D'Onofrio, Tom *103*
D'Onofrio
Box 326
Bolinas, Calif. 94924 (415) 868-1070
Sculptural furniture in organic form, carved archetypal themes.

Donovan, Greg *226*
Worthington Woodworks
Old Post Rd.
Worthington, Mass. 01098 (413)238-5936
Traditional designs from wall boxes to timber frames; interior finish (wide pine boards).

Dorogi, Dennis *33*
Dennis Dorogi Dulcimers
Ellicott Rd.
Brocton, N.Y. 14716 (716) 792-9012
Plucked & hammered dulcimers, psalteries, lutes, mandolins.

Doub, William *193*
Wood Works
855 Islington St.
Portsmouth, N.H. 03801 (603) 436-3805
Custom furniture (contemporary & reproduction), residential & commercial interiors, carved signs.

Doyle, Leo G. *28*
Design One
378 W. 53rd St.
San Bernardino, Calif. 92407
(714) 886-2301
One-of-a-kind & limited-edition designs in wood. Consulting, woodturning, sculpture, furniture.

Drenth, Steve *61*
S. Drenth
1491 W. Dowling Rd.
Dowling, Mich. 49050 (616) 623-2090
Hardwood furniture & accessories—"classic & contemporary designs of my own creation."

Dubreuil, Ron *70*
Hoosuck Design & Woodworking
121 Union St.
N. Adams, Mass. 01247 (413) 663-8482
Interior design, one-of-a-kind and limited-edition furniture & woodworking.

Dudley, Rion *174*
Rion Dudley Design
3203 13th Ave. W.
Seattle, Wash. 98119 (206) 282-6653

Duerock, Roy (Dewey) *56*
Design Wood Works
18511 Kenlake Pl. N.E.
Seattle, Wash. 98155 (206) 486-4894
Residential furniture & furnishings, office & commercial furniture & fixtures.

Duffy, Thomas James *147*
Thomas James Duffy—Cabinetmaker
23 Commerce St.
Ogdensburg, N.Y. 13669 (315) 393-1484
Turning, furniture & architectural woodworking.

Dughi, J.W. *161*
11 Union Ave.
New Holland, Pa. 17557 (717) 354-2338
Custom carvings & turnings; carving on turnings.

Duncan, James T. *104*

Duncanson, Joel L. *175*
Chestnut & Clowney
Mineral Point, Wis. 53565 (608) 987-3681
Furniture by commission; traditional frame & panel entrance doors.

Dunipace, R.M. *255*
7 Newsome Park
Jamaica Plain, Mass. 02130
(617) 522-7020
Original designs: handcarved panels, mirror frames, small three-dimensional & relief sculpture.

Dunnigan, Jr., John J. *81*
John Dunnigan Cabinetmaking
R.R. #1, Box 102A
Saunderstown, R.I. 02874 (401)295-8490
Furniture.

Duntel, Pier Clout *273*
533 Rue Bourgault, CP, 311 St.-Jean
Port Joli, Que., Canada G0R 3G0
(418) 598-6020
Bas-relief, busts, statues of realistic and contemporary subjects; "integrated sculpture in wood, stone & brass."

Duszynski, Rick *46*
Buckhorn Mtn. Woodcrafts
465 Buckhorn Mtn. Rd.
Winlock, Wash. 98596
Tropical-rhythm tongue drum (a percussion instrument).

Dwileski, Gerald *127*

Eacker, Geoff *35*
242 Yankee Rd.
Middletown, Ohio 45042 (513) 422-8484
Guitars & dulcimers, traditional & contemporary designs, "emphasis on construction, tone and action;" repair work.

Eaton, Christina N. *14*
Woods End Cabinet Shop
Woods Rd., Box 866
W. Brookfield, Mass. 01585
(617) 867-2220
Custom-made furniture mostly of traditional design, some one-of-a-kind pieces. Commissions.

Eaton, Herbert *267*
Plank & Pin
1302 W. Front St.
Bloomington, Ill. 61701 (309) 828-9542
Sculpture, toys, kitchen accessories.

Eaton III, James B. *106*
The Wood Shop
1841 Wycliffe
Houston, Tex. 77024 (713) 467-5384
Stained pine bookshelves for office libraries.

Ebner, David N. *243*
378 S. Country Rd.
Brookhaven, N.Y. 11719 (516) 286-9340
Solid hardwood music & dictionary stands, coffee & dining tables, stools, benches, chairs, desks.

Eckert, Tom *248*
1019 Bishop Circle
Tempe, Ariz. 85282 (602) 966-6978
One-of-a-kind functional sculptures.

Edelstein, Gary *145*
14 Homestead La.
Roosevelt, N.J. 08355
Furniture, cabinetry, small objects. Commissions considered.

Edwards, D.L. *251*

Edwards, Jack *49*
Red Mountain Loom Works
Box 777
El Rito, N. Mex. 87530 (505) 581-4744
Custom weaving looms, furniture, cabinetry.

Egan, David J. *81*
209 Hayes St.
Kaukauna, Wis. 54130 (414) 766-2001
Interior-exterior doors/entrances, stained glass, custom-made furnishings.

Elana, Phyllis *217*

Ellsworth, David *264*
Coyote Hill
Allenspark, Colo. 80510 (303) 747-2246
One-of-a-kind commissions only.

Emerson, Blake *234*
Open Hand Woodshop
2547 8th St.
Berkeley, Calif. 94707 (415) 848-3722
Custom-made hardwood furniture & cabinets, original designs.

Engle, Todd Lewis *140*
Design Engle
825 S. 5th St.
Columbus, Ohio 43206 (614) 444-3305
"New forms and function, designed conjunction—I fuse the two with screws and glue."

Enjaian, Garo *176*
14155 Hatteras St.
Van Nuys, Calif. 91401 (213) 785-6257
Mirror frames, jewel boxes, small carved trays, bud vases, salt/pepper shakers.

Erdman, Bruce *179*
Sundog Enterprises
300 W. Main St.
Mt. Horeb, Wis. 53572 (608) 437-8790
Oval tambour boxes, tambour silver chests.

Erickson, David L. *144*
David Erickson, Woodworker
3000 N. Murray
Milwaukee, Wis. 53211 (414) 962-9270
Custom woodwork for residential & commercial needs; design service, restoration of wood items.

Erickson, Richard R. *182*
2004 Merriam La.
St. Paul, Minn. 55104
Small turnings: goblets, covered dishes, bowls. Jewelry boxes.

Erpelding, Curtis *120*
Curtis Erpelding—Furniture Designer-Maker
110 Union #504
Seattle, Wash. 98101 (206) 623-8071
Tables, desks & cabinets in a modern idiom, emphasizing joinery and knock-down features.

Evans, Terry L. *163*
Betterwood Buckles
Rt. 2, Box 97
Augusta, Kans. 62010 (316) 775-5909
Inlaid landscape belt buckles, pendants, boxes, accessories.

Everdell, John S. *183*
John S. Everdell—Fine Woodworking
1000 Centre St.
Jamaica Plain, Mass. 02130
(617) 522-6596
Custom contemporary furniture, cabinets, display cases & interiors.

Fabe, Jeffrey B. *74*
JEFFREY FABE/CUSTOM WOODWORKING
3447 Whitfield Ave.
Cincinnati, Ohio 45220 (513) 861-2842
Fader, Lester *49*
Fairly, James *116*
Falk, Jeff *217*
SEVEN CIRCLES WOODWORKS
1203 Williamson St.
Madison, Wis. 53703 (608) 257-2651
Custom furniture, cabinetry, remodeling, carpentry. "A worker-controlled, cooperatively run shop."
Falk, Nils *179*
NILS FALK—DESIGNER/CRAFTSMAN
Hawk School House Rd.
Bloomsbury, N.J. 08804 (201) 993-7789
Furniture, cabinetry, sculpture.
Falkenstern, Lee *213*
LEAF WOODWORKING
165 Graves Ave.
San Luis Obispo, Calif. 93401
(805) 543-6387
Contemporary furniture, cabinets; architectural & boat joinery.
Falsetti, Joseph *258*
927 Volunteer Blvd., University of Tenn.
Knoxville, Tenn. 37916 (615) 974-6732
Large free-standing & relief sculpture, architectural in nature & scope.
Falwell, Bobby R. *177*
FALWELL DESIGNER CRAFTSMAN
Rt. 7, Box 696
Murray, Ky. 42071 (502) 759-1359
One-of-a-kind sculptural wood furniture & accessories for the individual and architectural client.
Fawcett, Jim *235*
Fay, Steve *68*
STEVE FAY, CABINETMAKER
20 Maplewood Way
Pleasantville, N.Y. (914) 769-6663
Fine cabinetry, architectural woodwork.
Fearn, Cabell J. *43*
Rec. Svcs. Crafts Br., Robinson Barracks
APO N.Y. 09154
(Stuttgart W. Germany) (0711) 644640
Musical instruments, instrument repair, woodwork, leather, silver, pearl & silver inlay/engraving, design.
Feldman, Richard *163*
SPLINTER GROUP
2500 Market St.
Oakland, Calif. 94607 (415) 444-1982
Desk accessories, religious ceremonial objects, custom furniture.
Fenwick, J.D. (Jake) *146*
Fenzi, Warren S. *82*
WARREN S. FENZI—DESIGNER/CRAFTSMAN
4127 E. Indian School Rd.
Phoenix, Ariz. 85018 (602) 956-2136
Contemporary furniture, built traditionally.
Ferguson, Jack *113*
HARMONY WOODWORKS
3284 140th St.
Surrey, B.C., Canada V4A 4J7
(604) 536-2267
Free-style design of exposed joinery in hardwood furniture; handrails; custom turning.
Fertig, Ralph H. *180*
RHF ENTERPRISES
1522B Eucalyptus Hill
Santa Barbara, Calif. 93103
(805) 962-1479
Belt buckles, combs, earrings, boxes, cases, cutting boards, clocks, serving trays, plant stands, end tables.
Fields, Felicia *147*
6412 Ashley St.
Felton, Calif. 95018 (408) 335-3036
Turned bowls of redwood burl, manzanita burl, black walnut, acacia, maple & other native woods.
Fink, Ray *269*
FINK'S WOOD JOINT
7036 N. 22nd St.
Phoenix, Ariz. 85020 (602) 943-1310
One-of-a-kind sculpture, imagery furniture, functional sculpture in native & exotic woods.
Fischer, Martin J.V. *62*
Fischman, Irving *148*
262 Harvard St.
Cambridge, Mass. 02139 (617) 868-8953
Lathe-turned bowls, interpreting American Indian designs in exotic woods; custom furniture.
Fisher, Kenneth R. *16*
Fisher, Peter R. *18*
154 Main Entrance Dr.
Pittsburgh, Pa. 15228 (412) 341-3360
Custom woodwork & design. Completed article or design only. Hardwoods, veneers, mixed media.
Fisher, Theodore Lancelot *165*
314 N.W. Glisan
Portland, Ore. 97209
Carving.
Fitzgerald, Chuck *258*
1009 5th Ave. S.W.
Puyallup, Wash. 98371 (206) 848-6576
Turning, designs in wood (laminated).

Fitzgerald, Dennis G. *233*
29 N. Mortimer Ave.
Elmsford, N.Y. 10523 (914) 592-5193
Original designs, one-of-a-kind & limited-production. Interior & architectural woodworking.
Flatt, David G. *178*
DAVID FLATT ASSOCIATES
1245 E. Washington Ave.
Madison, Wis. 53703 (608) 251-2733
Spiral staircases, spiral laminates, dining sets, cocktail tables, seating arrangements, small containers, accessories.
Fleitzer, Mark H. *24*
Flemming, Thomas *79*
Foess, Floyd W. *98*
F.W. FOESS & SON
2134 S.W. 339th St.
Federal Way, Wash. 90883
(206) 927-4251
Handmade furniture, church furnishings.
Foley, Steven A. *86*
Forbes, Joel *64*
Box 125, R.R. #2
New Canaan, Conn. 06840
(914) 533-2041
Limited-production custom chairs & stools.
Forrester, Fred W. *70*
Fortuna, Francis J. *143*
Fortune, Michael C. *139, 140*
MICHAEL FORTUNE DESIGNER/MAKER
86 Nelson St.
Toronto, Ont., Canada (416) 368-3190
"Commissioned residential furnishings. Speculative work is developmental, exploring forms, techniques, details."
Foster, Paul *111*
DIMENSIONAL DESIGN
2016 S. Market
Wichita, Kans. 67211 (316) 264-4833
Custom-designed furniture.
Fowler, Russell *248*
Frank, George *209*
GEORGE FRANK CABINET CORP.
508 E. 117th St.
New York, N.Y. 10035 (212) 534-6810
Cabinet work to customer's specifications.
Franklin, John H. *143*
Fraser, Maurice *72*
MAURICE FRASER WORKSHOP
153 W. 78th St.
New York, N.Y. 10024 (212) 595-3557
Designer-crafted, singly made chairs, chests, small cabinets, coffee tables, classical harpsichords; joinery lessons.
Fredericks, Lance F. *135*
OUVRAGE
46-27 Arcadia La.
Great Neck, N.Y. 11020 (516) 482-0710
Handwrought works in gold, hardwoods, photography, stoneware & textiles.
Freeman, John D. *249*
Freeman, Robert *82*
French, Robert R. *244, 245*
THE FRENCH CONCEPTION
12716 Arliss Dr.
Lakewood, Ohio 44107 (216) 221-2318
Custom-engineered wood products.
Friedlander, Cliff *205*
WOODENWORKS
615 Seabright Ave.
Santa Cruz, Calif. 95062 (408) 427-2650
Residential & commercial custom cabinetry, furniture.
Friedman, Alan *266*
A.F. WORKS, COMPANY & ASSOCIATES
1319 S. Sixth St.
Terre Haute, Ind. 47802 (812) 235-8820
Furniture & sculpture, commissions, one-of-a-kind, using plywood or solid lumber.

Galbraith, Gary *266*
Rt. 5, Box 360
Ellensburg, Wash. 98926 (206) 925-2223
Sculptural furniture for contemporary homes, incorporating bentwood, mixed lamination, joinery & carved form.
Galpin, Amos *203*
AMOS GALPIN CABINETMAKER
Box 503
Sun Valley, Idaho 83353 (208) 726-4747
Replicas of early American furniture made in the manner of the period.
Gaston, Blaise *219*
GASTON, MURRAY & WYATT
1313 Bellview Ave.
Charlottesville, Va. 22901
(804) 293-7357
Custom furniture, entrance doors, cabinetwork.
Gauthier, Ronald *152, 199*
Gazley, Jr., Carl *162*
Gerhardt, Rolfe *37*
UNICORN MANDOLINS
Box 6464
San Antonio, Tex. 78209
Mandolins.
Gershey, James S. *44*
Gest, Robert E. *260*
881 El Rancho Dr.
Livermore, Calif. 94550
Custom-handcrafted carvings, turnings, furniture.

Giachetti, Anthony *54*
ANTHONY GIACHETTI—CABINETMAKER
Box 504
E. Boothbay, Maine 04544 (207) 633-3740
Contemporary casepieces, desks & tables in domestic & exotic hardwoods.
Gille, Thomas *157*
Gilman, R. Adin *224*
INTEGRITY WOOD
Box 225
Wendell, Mass. 01379 (617) 544-7425
Custom-fitted rocking chairs, cabinets, staircases; wood bathtubs, sinks, shower areas & mosaic walls.
Gilmartin, Michael J. *175*
INTERPRETA WOODWORKING
1260 Foster St. N.W.
Atlanta, Ga. 30318 (404) 351-2590
Sculptural & functional furniture through hardwood & stacked plywood laminations. Lighting forms.
Gilson, Giles *123*
GILSON STUDIO
388 Vly Rd.
Schenectady, N.Y. 12309 (518) 785-8649
Experimental design, sculpture. Other materials besides wood.
Giordano, John Mark *211*
176 Newport Ave.
Pawtucket, R.I. 02861 (401) 726-3596
Furniture design, stringed-instrument design, specialty woodworking.
Gissen, David *13*
50 Rollingwood La.
Concord, Mass. 01742
Wooden hand tools, custom furniture.
Githews, Jr., Ray F. *273*
Givotovsky, Igor *262*
THE ARTWORKS
Rt. 110
Amesbury, Mass. (617) 388-5090
Polyglyphs: sculpture composed of interlocking units of domestic & exotic woods, abstract & representational.
Gluklick, Peter *213*
PURITAN RESTORATIONS
10035 Borgman
Huntington Woods, Mich. 48070
(313) 873-1390
Design, fabrication, restoration, installation of furniture, cabinets, architectural millwork. Wood, plastic, metals.
Goldfrank, Janice *122*
Box 52
Austerlitz, N.Y. 12017
Furniture, custom woodworking, short-run production.
Goldstein, Robin F. *229*
297 S. Wilson Ave.
Tempe, Ariz. 85281 (602) 968-4636
Carving, bending & shaping.
Gollup, Peter L. *135*
52 Old Clyde Rd.
Canton, N.C. 28716 (704) 648-3723
Limited edition & one-of-a-kind furniture.
Gonczar, John *115*
THE WOODWORKS
96-1219 Waihona St.
Pearl City, Hawaii 96782 (808) 455-4257
Custom furniture.
Gordon, Alfred Neale *134*
Gordon, Glenn *65*
GLENN GORDON/WOODWORKER
514 W. Webster
Chicago, Ill. 60614 (312) 929-9736
Furniture, commissioned & speculative, "designed to reveal the structural elegance within the plank."
Graham, Richard M. *265*
RICHARD M. GRAHAM SCULPTURE
Art Dept., Central Michigan University
Mount Pleasant, Mich. 48859
(517) 774-3025
One-of-a-kind expressionistic sculptures.
Grandbois, James P. *131*
GRANDBOIS WOODWORKS
253 E. 4th St.
St. Paul, Minn. 55101
Inlaid dining & game tables; chairs.
Gray, G. Brad *264*
GRAY DESIGN
115 S. Jackson St.
Seattle, Wash. 98104 (206) 623-6107
Custom architectural & marine woodwork.
Gray, Merv. *156*
46 High St.
Bellerive, Tasmania, Australia 7018
002-441970
Found-wood turning & spherical forms.
Greenberg, Alan & Denise Eagleson *87*
Greenwood, Peter L. *77*
GREENWOOD'S EXOTIC WOODWORKS
1 Parish Rd.
Farmington, Conn. 06032 (203) 677-7020
Exotics only, rosewood specialty. Old-world furniture designed; no veneers.
Greer, Phillip *158*
Grew-Sheridan, John & Carolyn *83*
GREW-SHERIDAN WOODWORKING
3 Columbia Square
San Francisco, Calif. 94103
(415) 431-8476
Custom & limited production household & commercial furniture, store fixtures; small woodworking classes.

Grey, Elliott *219*
ELLIOTT GREY—FURNITURE MAKER
25494 Hall Rd.
Junction City, Ore. 97448 (503) 998-8271
Tables, chairs, rockers, sideboards, spiral stairways—original design & shipped anywhere.
Grishman, Barry *156*
BARRY GRISHMAN—
DESIGNER/MAKER IN WOOD
15824 Belmont Dr.
Biloxi, Miss. 39532 (601) 374-2135
Accessory pieces in exotic woods—cigarette cases, jewelry chests. Furniture commissions.
Grondahl, Jon O. *244*
83 Champlain Ave.
Staten Island, N.Y. 10306 (212) 351-4032
Custom-made furniture, Norwegian rose-painting.
Gronewald, Loren *201*
Grossman, Joel *221*
GOOD WOOD
223 Mississippi St.
San Francisco, Calif. 94107
(415) 863-5022
Custom furniture & design.
Gruenberg, Joel W. *177*
PAULSEN-GRUENBERG WOODWORKS
7333-B Lowell Way
Goleta, Calif. 93017 (805) 968-6743
Miniature jewelry presentation boxes to medium-large jewelry boxes in walnut, manzanita & ceanothus burl figure.
Grun, Robert L. *110*
Guajardo, Ruben *167*
2383 6th St.
LaVerne, Calif. 91750 (714) 593-4891
Tall-back, bentwood rockers, custom mirrors, custom roll-top desks, pieces on request.
Guild, Ken *264*
GUILD ENTERPRISES
217 Main St.
Mahone Bay, N.S., Canada B0J 2E0
(902) 624-8572
Sculpture, furniture, small toys.
Guillory, Lloyd J. *274*
Gulick, Brian *249*
29 Harwood Ave.
White Plains, N.Y. 10603 (914) 949-5977
Gundry, Hugh *22*
WHIMSICAL WOODCRAFTS
203 S. Fair Oaks Ave.
Pasadena, Calif. 91105 (213) 795-0145
Hardwood toys & boxes, custom sculptural work, prototype design & development, small production runs.
Gutzeit, Chris *142*
TURNED STYLES
63 N. Airmont Rd.
Suffern, N.Y. 10901 (914) 357-3277
Decorative & functional accessories turned in plain & exotic woods.

Habicht, Mark R. *68*
213 Dunkirk Rd.
Baltimore, Md. 21212 (301) 377-7075
Sculpture & wood design.
Hale, Douglas *109*
DOUGLAS HALE ASSOCIATES
59R Trenton St. #2B
Providence, R.I. 02906 (401) 351-0856
Halverson, Jay *238*
Hampson, Nick *123*
NICHOLAS HAMPSON DESIGNS
101 Brannan St.
San Francisco, Calif. 94107
(415) 957-1042
Sculpture.
Harbertson, Nile W. *113*
WOOD CREATIONS
1265 22nd St.
Ogden, Utah 84401 (801) 392-9338
Custom furniture, special creations.
Hare, Russ & Carol Gable *59*
EMPORIUM FURNITURE WORKSHOPS
36461 Green St.
New Baltimore, Mich. 48047
(313) 725-2911
"We build original furniture designs, using traditional tools, techniques & hand-rubbed finishes."
Harris, James M. *221*
EBENEZER BROS.
Rt. 1, Box 42AA
Aldie, Va. 22001 (703) 327-4684
Free-standing & built-in wall storage units, architectural paneling, furniture.
Harris, Jeffrey *105*
JEFFREY HARRIS FURNITURE
1663 11th St.
Sarasota, Fla. 33577 (813) 365-3669
Contemporary hardwood furniture, specializing in large-format inlays of oak, black walnut & padauk.
Hart, Peter E. *109*
Hartung, Dudley *166*
Harwood, John R. *137*
GRASSY LANE STUDIOS
Box 448
Cazenovia, N.Y. 13035 (315) 655-8254
Gift items, one-of-a-kind furniture; mixed media with enamels & metalsmithing by partner.
Hass, Ivan *97*

Editor: John Kelsey
Copy editors: Laura Cehanowicz, Richard Mastelli
Designer: Roger Barnes
Layout and pasteup: Barbara Marks
Typesetting: Nancy Knapp
Editorial assistant: Mary Pringle Blaylock
Production coordinator: JoAnn Muir

. . . With special thanks to these members of the Taunton Press staff and friends, who all pitched in: Carole Ando, Irene Arfaras, Bob Bruschi, Gloria Carson, Ruth Dobsevage, Dorothy Dreher, Emma Frid, John Grudzien, Marie Johnson, Cathy Kach, Cindy Lee, Betsy Mastelli, Viney Merrill, Janice Roman, Melinda Roman, Nancy Schoch, Kathy Springer.

Typeface: Compugraphic Aster, 8 pt. text & 24 pt. display
Paper: Mead Offset Enamel, 70 lb.
Printer: Connecticut Printers, Bloomfield, Conn.
Binder: Sendor Bindery Inc., New York City.